DISRUPTION BY DESIGN

HOW TO CREATE PRODUCTS THAT DISRUPT AND THEN DOMINATE MARKETS

Paul Paetz

Apress®

Disruption by Design: How to Create Products that Disrupt and then Dominate Markets

ISBN-13 (pbk): 978-1-4302-4632-9

ISBN-13 (electronic): 978-1-4302-4633-6

Managing Director: Welmoed Spahr
Acquisitions Editor: Jeff Olson
Editorial Board: Steve Anglin, Mark Beckner, Gary Cornell, Louise Corrigan, James DeWolf,
    Jonathan Gennick, Robert Hutchinson, Michelle Lowman, James Markham,
    Matthew Moodie, Jeff Olson, Jeffrey Pepper, Douglas Pundick, Ben Renow-Clarke,
    Gwenan Spearing, Matt Wade, Steve Weiss
Coordinating Editor: Rita Fernando
Copy Editor: Kezia Endsley
Compositor: SPi Global
Indexer: SPi Global

Distributed to the book trade worldwide by Springer Science+Business Media New York, 233 Spring Street, 6th Floor, New York, NY 10013. Phone 1-800-SPRINGER, fax (201) 348-4505, e-mail orders-ny@springer-sbm.com, or visit www.springeronline.com. Apress Media, LLC is a California LLC and the sole member (owner) is Springer Science + Business Media Finance Inc (SSBM Finance Inc). SSBM Finance Inc is a Delaware corporation.

For information on translations, please e-mail rights@apress.com, or visit www.apress.com.

Apress and friends of ED books may be purchased in bulk for academic, corporate, or promotional use. eBook versions and licenses are also available for most titles. For more information, reference our Special Bulk Sales–eBook Licensing web page at www.apress.com/bulk-sales.

Any source code or other supplementary materials referenced by the author in this text is available to readers at www.apress.com. For detailed information about how to locate your book's source code, go to www.apress.com/source-code/.

Apress Business: The Unbiased Source of Business Information

Apress business books provide essential information and practical advice, each written for practitioners by recognized experts. Busy managers and professionals in all areas of the business world—and at all levels of technical sophistication—look to our books for the actionable ideas and tools they need to solve problems, update and enhance their professional skills, make their work lives easier, and capitalize on opportunity.

Whatever the topic on the business spectrum—entrepreneurship, finance, sales, marketing, management, regulation, information technology, among others—Apress has been praised for providing the objective information and unbiased advice you need to excel in your daily work life. Our authors have no axes to grind; they understand they have one job only—to deliver up-to-date, accurate information simply, concisely, and with deep insight that addresses the real needs of our readers.

It is increasingly hard to find information—whether in the news media, on the Internet, and now all too often in books—that is even-handed and has your best interests at heart. We therefore hope that you enjoy this book, which has been carefully crafted to meet our standards of quality and unbiased coverage.

We are always interested in your feedback or ideas for new titles. Perhaps you'd even like to write a book yourself. Whatever the case, reach out to us at editorial@apress.com and an editor will respond swiftly. Incidentally, at the back of this book, you will find a list of useful related titles. Please visit us at www.apress.com to sign up for newsletters and discounts on future purchases.

The Apress Business Team

*Dedicated to the entrepreneurs
and disruptors who change the world*

Contents

About the Author

Paul Paetz is the CEO of Innovative Disruption, a boutique consultancy that works with innovators to bring disruptive products to fruition and market success. His deep knowledge of the patterns of disruptive innovation was first acquired through the school of hard knocks way back in the 1980s, when he began his career with a highly innovative software company that could have disrupted the market, but didn't. Over the years, he remained curious about, and continued trying to discern why, some companies with superior technology never had breakout success, while others with unlikely products scored big. Clay Christensen's *Innovator's Dilemma* resonated strongly with Paetz's earlier experiences, and he found his true calling when he joined The Disruption Group, a consultancy that specialized in providing advisory services concerning market disruption. In 2008, he founded Innovative Disruption to advise and assist startups with disruptive potential, and also to provide analysis and advisory services for larger companies whose markets were being disrupted. Paetz is the creator of the Disruption Report Card, a tool that scores disruptive potential, and he is the author of the popular blog *Disrupt This*.

Acknowledgments

This book project ended up being much bigger than I originally thought it would be, and there were definitely times when I thought I might not finish. I owe a debt of gratitude to many people who encouraged me along through the long process from first outline to finished manuscript.

Several people shared thoughts with me on the ideas and writing and helped me clarify my thinking and create a better book—some may not even realize that's what they were doing when we talked about how disruption works or what I was writing, but if you are one of those, know that I am grateful for your listening skills, questions, and insights I gained along the way.

I want to specifically acknowledge Hubert Palan, Brian Dowling, and Alex Cristescu for their suggestions, reviews, and feedback. I want to thank Andre Edelbrock, Darryl Green, and my friends at Ethoca for allowing me to tell part of their story. I want to thank Fred Wilson for allowing me to use some of his thoughts, Carla Thompson for being so incessantly positive and excited about disruptive innovation, and Heather Wied and Dougal Cameron for considering becoming guinea pigs.

I want to call out Mike Urlocker, especially, who made me realize I could make a career out of being disruptive, and for asking me to join him at The Disruption Group. Mike has remained an occasional sounding board, and we had many animated discussions about the rise and fall of Blackberry, and why I thought Apple would disrupt the company in 2007 before it was obvious to most of the world. He was also the person who told me I absolutely should write this book after I was first approached by Apress about the possibility.

I also want to thank Alex Kisin and Paul Bassett for getting me into the technology business and for the many crazy, late-night discussions and arguments that started me down this path. Also a shout out to Andy Staniewski, whose backhanded compliments always showed respect but left you wondering what he really thought.

Thanks also to my editors at Apress, especially Jeff Olson and Rita Fernando, who were more patient with me through this long process than I had a right to expect. I hope this final product justifies their confidence in me.

Finally, my wife Chris and boys Nicolas and Conrad deserve a big thanks for tolerating my many nights in the basement banging on the keyboard. They could be reasonably forgiven if they thought I'd never be done.

Introduction

Entrepreneurs are simply those who understand that there is little difference between obstacle and opportunity, and are able to turn both to their advantage.

—Victor Kiam

There are four necessary and sufficient conditions that must be present for disruptive innovation to occur:

- An addressable market scarcity (see Chapter 1)

- A unique solution to key jobs customers need to be done that mitigates the scarcity (Chapter 4)

- When compared to possible alternatives for accomplishing the job, the price-to-value ratio is significantly lower than any other solution, often by a factor of two or more (Chapter 7)

- Execution (Chapters 4 through 10)

The causal connection of these four levers to the pattern of disruptive innovation is one of the key insights in this book that I learned through years of working as a disruption consultant and by dissecting my prior experiences with software companies that had disruptive potential but failed to achieve it.

I have come to think of disruption theory, and the market pattern by which disruptive innovation is recognized (Chapters 1-3), as being like the ripple pattern of waves in a pond after a stone is thrown in the water. The ripple is evidence that a stone was thrown, an artifact of the event that created it, but if you don't know that a stone was tossed to create that pattern, you can't reverse-engineer it by studying the pattern and trying to recreate it by other means. That's the reason I wrote this book.

The patterns observed and documented by Clayton Christensen in *The Innovator's Dilemma* are indicators that disruption happened (or possibly is happening), but they are the visible manifestations of disruption, not the causes (the ripple, not the rock). These four necessary and sufficient conditions are the stones that create the ripple patterns, and as simple as they are, their impact in terms of creating change and economic growth is truly stunning.

Understanding how these factors interrelate gives disruption theory true predictive value, and gives you the ability to create market disruption by design. I hope that this book succeeds in conveying how that happens, and that it becomes one of the key tools used by innovators for planning their product and market strategies and business models.

My path to studying and applying disruption theory was driven by early frustrations I had in my career. What struck me as a software marketer, product manager, and sales executive was how unpredictable success seemed in our business. You could do everything the way business schools said product marketing was supposed to work, yet fail. Conversely, you could come to market with a poor-quality product and so-so marketing, but be there at the right place and time and, with a bit of luck, succeed spectacularly. I saw waves of technology products come and go, and the more I knew about them, the less predictable success seemed.

I first came upon the work of Clayton Christensen in *The Innovator's Dilemma* about 15 years ago. It was interesting, but I wasn't ready to absorb its meaning. I was too busy trying to change the world marketing innovative software products to pay attention. It was an interesting time in the history of technology, and especially software, because at the end of the 1990s, we had just experienced the biggest decade of capital expenditures for technology infrastructure that we may ever see, largely driven by Y2K spending.

Many have misattributed this spending boom to the first wave of excitement over the Internet and dotcom companies. The Internet was not the reason for the boom—just one of the principal beneficiaries. No doubt, the release of Netscape Navigator created a big stir and got everyone excited about the internet, so there was a wave riding a wave. However, the less exciting reason the capital budgets were there and needed to be spent was Y2K remediation.

If you were in the middle of it, it was a heady time. A rising tide lifted all boats, and if you were in the tech business, you were making (or raising) a lot of money, no matter how good or how bad the idea. Notwithstanding the Pets.com sock puppet and the colossal amount of money flushed down the toilet on Webvan and Herman Miller's iconic Aeron chairs, we all thought we were changing the world.

Of course, the evidence that it was all because of fear of what would happen to the systems when the clock turned over on the new millennium came, when suddenly with about three months to go in 1999, almost all spending suddenly stopped. No one was really sure whether the power grid would shut down, satellites would fall from the sky, and that we'd instantly revert to the stone age without heat or water, all because programmers in the 1950s had recorded the year with two digits instead of four in order to save a couple bytes of precious memory.

The reason so much spending happened on new technology in the last few years of the 1990s was that companies figured if they needed to spend $10 million to fix 30-year-old mainframe systems, maybe it would make more sense to spend just a little bit more and replace them instead. So, in a period of about five to six years, we either fixed or replaced all the systems technology that had been put in place in the previous three decades. Enterprise software and hardware spending was the first bubble to burst. The dotcom bubble took a little longer to fully deflate—it wasn't until 9/11 that all the air was let out—but by early 2000, it was apparent that the party was over and the carnage was beginning.

My career in the software business had begun almost 20 years before that, when dinosaur mainframes still roamed the earth, but minicomputers were rapidly asserting their place in the evolutionary timeline. Tech was mostly the domain of business (B2B) in those days, although accountants were starting to use this strange new software called a VisiCalc spreadsheet on Apple II PCs, and some people even started buying personal computers for home use.

I worked for a company that it's almost guaranteed you've never heard of. We had this really cool technology for automating reuse of software building blocks to accelerate assembly of COBOL software. (I know; that really dates me.) It could perform some pretty nifty tricks, like assembling native code for multiple platforms from a common specification.

I could recount lots of war stories, but suffice it to say that we thought that absolutely every company would need our product once they saw how powerful it was. One programmer could do the work of 5 to 50 people, depending how much customization was required to generate an application.

The software reuse engine and "frame technology" that enabled this was pretty advanced stuff. The tools built on top of that core technology allowed us to do things like generate modules in different languages in a single pass, bind graphical interfaces to COBOL systems running on a mainframe or minicomputer, and offload mainframe code development to PCs. There were alternatives in the market, to be sure, but there was truly nothing that could do some of the things we could. We often had customers come to us after failing with more popular competitive tools, and unlike the others, we could always make it work because our architecture was almost infinitely elastic and malleable.

We took a great deal of pride in the performance characteristics of what we did. Our code was more efficient. We could tailor the system to the most complex of hardware and software environments. We were the first to be able to do some important things technically, in some cases as much as

18 months ahead of the market. Other companies eventually added some of these features, implementing them poorly (technically speaking), but with much greater success selling them. Whatever happened to the "better mousetrap theory"?

We were moderately successful. We were always profitable. However, we had competitors we thought had crap products that sold 10 times what we did. That led to lots of navel-gazing. Would we sell more if we just added this one feature that a rival had? Were our salespeople just plain bad? Did we not know how to market? Did we have the wrong partners? Were we not investing enough in product development and marketing? Did our management suck? Being mediocre or moderately successful is far worse than failing, because you keep thinking maybe if you just tweak this one thing, everything can be fixed. Endless arguments ensued.

The one thing nobody believed was a problem was the quality of our people. Hands down, I have never worked with a group of people so eclectic and so brilliant. Every single person was above average—even our receptionist and admin staff were smarter and more interesting than people you'd meet when you left our office and ventured into the "real world." It sounds much like being at Google or Apple or Facebook today.

Why is all this relevant to a book about how to disrupt markets by design? The one thing I always wondered was how such an excellent team of people who designed such fantastic quality tools ended up with competitors dancing circles around them. Why did they get big, and often cash out with handsome paydays, while we toiled away and never seemed to break through? Sure, we made a profit and we got paid okay—but were we deluding ourselves? Were the people we knew at other companies smarter or better than us? What were we doing wrong?

Those doubts and questions were stuffed in my back pocket, especially during the late years of the 1990s, when business was just that good for everyone. Then came the crash. New sales were truly excruciatingly difficult to come by, no matter what you were selling. Customers were deferring purchases and upgrades as long as they possibly could. The boom-to-bust transition was almost overnight, and made us long for the merely lousy business climates of the 1990–91 and 1980–82 recessions.

I had never stopped being curious about the earlier questions about why great people plus great product equaled mediocre results. It was a puzzle for me to solve, and I was going to figure it out. In the early 2000s, I started a marketing services company, and finally had some distance and time to read and reflect, so I set about on a personal mission to try to dissect the good, bad, and ugly from my earlier experiences.

When I re-read *The Innovator's Dilemma*, a light went on. The pattern fit, and although technically we weren't disrupted, I also began to understand why we had not been disruptive. In 2003, *The Innovator's Solution* was published, and my copy is still full of stickies with notes and pages with highlighted passages throughout.

Coincidentally, I got talking with an old friend who was stepping away from his research director position at UBS Securities (where he had made the original BUY call on Research in Motion based on applying disruption theory before the Blackberry became an explosive hit) to start a small boutique consultancy (The Disruption Group), which would offer services and education around disruptive innovation. Then he said something like, "hey, you grok this disruption stuff—do you want to join me at The Disruption Group?"

I did that and it gave me even more time to puzzle over, dissect, and try to explain what had happened in my prior life. I realized that while powerful, our software was overly complex and best used by rocket scientists and nuclear physicists. We had never approached the product, segmentation, or positioning from the perspective of jobs our customers needed to do.

Our pricing made sense to us, but not at all to the customers. We had things we could and should have made freely available that would have helped immensely in building out an ecosystem, but instead we tried to keep them secret and extract high rents. Everything we could have done to make our product disruptive, we had done the opposite. Our competitors weren't hugely better than us at any of these things, but they only had to be good enough in comparison and stay simple (our honest assessment would have been "inferior") to sell lots.

It's 10 years later, and I've counseled disruptors and wannabe disruptors, and I've learned from first principles how to be disruptive on purpose. This book shares the lessons that I had to learn the hard way.

Along the way, I realized that the essence of disruptive innovation is much simpler than even Clay's books lay out. In fact, the pattern that Christensen has discerned (and that I summarize in the first chapter) is an indicator of disruption, but it is not causal, as I expressed in the opening to this introduction.

In other words, if you have an inferior product at a low price that targets an undesirable market that incumbents will run from rather than fight for, it bears the fingerprint of disruption. However, it could also just be that you've built a crappy product that no one wants.

That's the challenge that potential disruptors face: how can you tell the difference between disruptive and crappy with no potential to disrupt? How can you predict reliably where disruptive opportunities exist? How do you create and implement a strategy that maximizes your probability of being disruptive? How can you be disruptive over and over again, even disrupting yourself when necessary? How do you do these things deliberately, rather than by accident or in an ad hoc way? How do you avoid being distracted by ill-informed media and pundits who label every new technology-based product as disruptive? Why does being disruptive even matter?

I ambitiously set out to answer these questions in this book, and to provide a guidebook to designing and executing a disruptive business strategy.

The Fundamentals

Disruptive Innovation

The Greatest Theory of Business Growth and Value Creation, Ever

---

Most controversies would soon be ended, if those engaged in them would first accurately define their terms, and then adhere to their definitions.

—Tryon Edwards

Disruptive Innovation is the single-most talked about business concept today, especially in the technology business. It permeates boardrooms, both as a strategy for innovators to follow and as a threat to existing businesses. Technology startups around the world, with Silicon Valley as ground zero, virtually all fancy themselves as disruptors.

Why the buzz about disruption? Quite simply, it's about growth and creation of shareholder and economic value. Extraordinary growth and value creation. Disruptors typically enjoy market cap growth rates 20x or more the index averages, and they can in a matter of years make old business models and industry norms obsolete, going from nothing to becoming the new incumbent market leader.

We know the big stories. Facebook started in a dorm room as a way for college kids to share personal details with others on campus; in short order it became the dominant social networking metaphor, with over one billion members and an IPO valuing the company initially at over $100B. Then there's Google, providing a better, simpler search engine, growing to dominate online advertising, and going on to create the only real alternative to Apple's iOS (iPhone) platform with Android. And of course, there's Apple, the quintessential serial disruptor that was only months from bankruptcy in 1997, yet became the most valuable company on the planet less than 15 years after Steve Jobs returned to the helm with a string of hit products that changed music, telecom, online digital good sales, and mobile computing industries (which are in the midst of finally dethroning the PC).

And even as more and more retail moves online, Apple revolutionized offline retail as well, with stores that are not only unique, but generate more revenue per square foot than any other retailer. That doesn't even include the unparalleled success of Jobs's other venture, Pixar, which holds the highest average gross receipts of any studio in history and the highest grossing animated movie of all time (*Toy Story 3*).[1]

The list of current and recent past disruptive innovators are a who's who of the modern world, including names like Twitter, Whole Foods, Netflix, Amazon, Microsoft, Oracle, Starbucks, LinkedIn, and many more. But there is also a dark side—a long list of disruptors who were one-trick ponies, who failed to stay on top of the changing market needs and failed to respond to a newer generation of disruptive innovators. Perhaps you remember how innovative and important companies like Yahoo, Nintendo, RIM, Best Buy, Myspace, Nokia, and Blockbuster were just a few years ago?

So, we can, without much trouble, identify the big names that have defined categories and dominated them, but not all disruptors are so huge. How well can we identify the disruptors that serve smaller or less-visible markets? Can we apply the theory to identify niche companies, still small but approaching the rapid growth phase, that have the potential to disrupt their markets, or that are in the process of doing so right now? Can we reliably predict who will be a disruptive innovator? Better yet, can markets be disrupted on purpose, and not by accident?

The answer to these questions is *yes*, for the most powerful thing about disruption theory is that it describes a repeating pattern that offers high predictive value. But only when we understand how it works below a skin-deep level.

---

[1] In March of 2014, Disney's *Frozen* surpassed *Toy Story 3*'s gross box office receipts to become the top-grossing animated film of all time. It is notable that since Pixar merged with Disney, the Pixar brain trust is running Disney's animated division, with John Lassiter acting in the executive producer role for *Frozen*, just as he did for *Toy Story 3*. In fact, Pixar's biggest accomplishment may well be the revitalization of Disney's moribund animation studios, which went nearly 20 years without a certifiable hit after *The Lion King*.

For all the talk, disruption theory is remarkably poorly understood. It's not hard to find ad agencies and designers calling themselves disruptive. Companies that have not yet created a product and have no customers call themselves disruptive. VCs describe their investment strategy as disruptive. Even arts festivals celebrate Justin Bieber as a disruptor! Easily 90% of those claiming to be disruptive have no chance of ever disrupting a market, and have not even read the original books by Clayton Christensen, the Harvard professor who first identified the phenomenon and articulated the theory of disruptive innovation. It's hard to tell whether the misunderstanding is because of the misuse of the term, or the misuse is because of the misunderstanding.

We can't fix all that, but as the goal of this book is to be a guide to creating disruption by design, it's important that we agree on some definitions and review the key things we're trying to embed in products, services, and business models that aim to be disruptive. This first chapter provides a condensed working version of the theory that I will refer back to through the rest of the book.

Key Definitions

For clarity, I will not attempt to redefine what disruptive innovation means, as others seem to want to do. Christensen's theories have been proven in the real world, and it doesn't help to improperly label things as disruptive that aren't.

On the other hand, disruptive innovation has become, in a few short years, the most talked about innovation theory possibly in history. But unfortunately, it is inevitable that as terminology passes into common usage, it is applied as a metaphor or explanation for virtually every business success or failure. Particularly in the media, we find it increasingly misused. For that reason, I have extended my discussion of the theory to assert what disruptive innovation *isn't*. (Later in this chapter, I also extend Christensen's work to provide an explanation of why disruption theory works, grounded in economic theory, which should also help clarify what makes an innovation disruptive or not.)[2]

I have attempted to provide short, succinct definitions to refer back to, and in a few cases, I have refined or narrowed the definition for the purpose of either greater understanding, or to qualify and restrict the discussion to things we can actually control. (Often there are regulatory constraints, currency

---

[2]For a complete understanding of the theory and the observations it was drawn from, I encourage you to refer to Christensen's original works, in particular *The Innovator's Dilemma* (Boston, MA: Harvard Business School Press, 1997) and *The Innovator's Solution* (Boston, MA: Harvard Business School Press, 2003) co-authored with Michael Raynor. However, for practical application, you shouldn't need more than is presented in the first section of this book.

imbalances, international labor force differences, and socio-political forces that may contribute to or inhibit disruptive innovation. It pays to be aware of these, but they aren't the kind of disruption that you can design for.)

Disruptive Innovation

Disruptive innovations are innovations that are inferior to, or which underperform, available market solutions. When I say "inferior" or "underperform," I don't literally mean lower quality (although that may be the way in which the disruptor is inferior) or performance as it is often thought of in terms of "power" (for example, engine *a* has greater horsepower and torque than engine *b*). Instead, these terms are relative to attributes that customers value in the existing product alternatives.

So, for example, streaming audio services are inferior in several ways when compared with CDs. Lower-quality sound, lack of ownership, lack of permanence/persistence, access to music depends on availability of a live internet connection—all characteristics that consumers were thought to value highly.

What makes such innovations disruptive is that they create new dimensions of value that the old product category or business model is unable to address by satisfying unmet or underserved needs. In other words, they compete based on a different set of benefits that the new approach or technology enables. These benefits typically include simplicity, convenience, accessibility, significantly lower price, or ease of use, but can occasionally include breakout innovations[3] that redefine the product category while still appearing "inferior" to the existing class of users.

Disruptive products generally appeal to new or less demanding users when introduced (they "compete against non-consumption") but get better over time until they are able to satisfy mainstream consumers, and usually at a lower price than the old class of "better" alternatives. (In this book, I will generally refer to disruptive innovations as products to keep it simple, but they can also be services or business models, or some combination thereof.)

---

[3]The iPhone is an example of such a breakout innovation. It was positioned in the market as a phone (or as a smartphone). But in reality, it was the first handheld computer that was simple enough—and with elegance of design integration—for the consumer market versus the business market, where products such as the RIM Blackberry already had a stronghold. The iPhone was inferior to the Blackberry in two major ways at its introduction (from the perspective of incumbent "business users"). It lacked the security that made the Blackberry a favorite of IT departments, and it was initially offered through a single carrier—AT&T—exclusively. RIM also attacked the iPhone for not having a keyboard, but consumers did not see that as a compelling disadvantage. As a superior internet appliance, it competed against non-consumption in the consumer markets, eventually disrupting the Blackberry's business user market as well.

There are two sub-types of disruptive innovations: low-end disruptions and new-market disruptions.

Low-End Disruption

Low-end disruptions are typically products that are inferior quality, often missing key features expected by existing users, but that can be offered at a substantially lower price due to different production methods or some patentable advantage. This appeals to customers who can't afford the existing products or who don't need the quality or full set of features offered by incumbents, enabling capture of segments that are undesirable to the current market leaders.

New-Market Disruption

New-market disruptions are targeted at segments that are not served at all by incumbent products, and/or they accomplish a different set of desired results so differently from the incumbents that they create new categories of use cases. Often, when such products are introduced, it isn't even clear what they are for or how they will be used.

Twitter, for example, has dramatically changed (and improved) how many companies do customer service and track emerging issues, as well as giving voice to popular movements such as the Arab Spring. In the process, it has emerged as the first place many people turn for breaking news, disrupting functions previously performed by television and radio, and in turn becoming an information source for traditional media. Of course, it is being applied in many other ways—as a promotional tool for marketers, a replacement for "water cooler gossip," a global open conversation tool, a personal broadcast tool for celebrities to stoke their fan clubs and for fanatics to follow their favorite celebrities, and more.[4]

New-market disruptive innovations tend to be economical enough to be used in distributed (versus centralized) locations, or their affordability enables uses that were impractical before, or they are radically easier to use, eliminating the need for specialized skills.

---

[4]While Twitter is a powerful example of a new-market disruptor, it is also a special case, since it was never purpose-built or marketed for any of these applications. Much of the general applicability of Twitter comes from its constraints (limited number of characters to type a message, transience of messages, lowest common denominator nature of text-only messages initially) together with the fact that it is a free service. Most of the things it is used for would likely not have emerged if users had to pay for them. It is also a low-end disruptor for many of the markets it disrupts, both because its price is "free," and because of its limited function when compared with broadcast media, for example. Often, the most successful disruptors have properties of both new-market and low-end disruption, as Twitter does.

Sustaining Innovation

In disruption theory, a sustaining innovation is the opposite of a disruptive innovation. The purpose of a sustaining innovation is to better serve existing customers or to enable higher-end uses. This usually means additional features, upward compatibility with older products, better quality and reliability, and so on.

They can be incremental and small innovations or breakthroughs—it doesn't matter which—so long as they are targeted at offering more capability to existing customers or addressing competitive upgrades. The vast majority of all innovation—well over 99%—is sustaining (including much technological innovation that is incorrectly labeled as disruptive by its creators and marketers, simply because it has a technology component to it).

For example, adding fluoride to toothpaste, creating new flavors and packaging and dispensing options, offering new colors and sizes, adding whiteners—all of these are sustaining innovations. To disrupt the toothpaste market, you would almost need to eliminate the need to brush teeth—perhaps with a food additive, or with something you could drink that would clean your teeth, if that were possible. Similarly, new car models and enhanced engine technologies—hybrids and electrics and other alternative-fuel vehicles—all these are sustaining, as are major updates to software, such as the upgrade from Windows 3.1 to Windows 95.

The difference between sustaining and disruptive innovation can be confusing, especially since they are relative terms, and it is possible for an innovation by a market incumbent to be sustaining, which if introduced by an outsider to the industry, might be disruptive. When in doubt, an easy way to think about the difference is to ask yourself the question, "What market is being disrupted and why?"

If the industry incumbents aren't being unseated or losing market power or being pushed out of the category altogether, then the innovation is likely sustaining. If incumbents adopt the innovation or introduce it themselves as a next-generation product, it is almost certainly sustaining.

We will come back in the next chapter to the difference between sustaining and disruptive innovations, and how your frame of reference can make an innovation simultaneously disruptive and sustaining (and why this is in your control). Understanding this is often the key to creating disruption by design.

Disruptive Innovation Model

Disruption due to innovation occurs because market incumbents do what comes natural and what they believe the "market" wants. That's because they often define the market as existing customers for a category of product, and what competitors offer, as their frame of reference for improvement. This is illustrated in Figure 1-1.

Disruptive Innovation Model

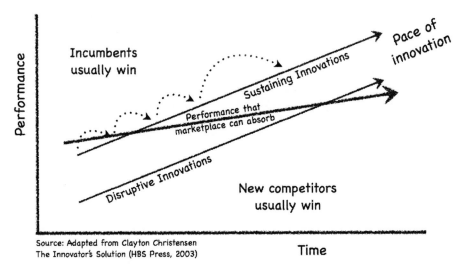

Figure 1-1. The disruptive innovation model illustrates how challengers with innovations that are "inferior" to incumbents gain a market foothold by competing against non-consumption while simultaneously changing what the market values, and then improve over time until they are "good enough" to become the new market incumbent. This is possible because in most mature markets, incumbent products exceed the true performance needs of most of their customers, saddling themselves with a higher cost structure that the market isn't willing to pay for if there is a significantly lower-priced alternative.

The market as it exists today lives on the line labeled "Sustaining Innovations" in Figure 1-1. Its slope represents the path and rate of improvement in product performance due to innovation. At the beginning, performance of new products almost always begins below what mainstream customers want and are able to use, but rapidly improves until it crosses the line labeled "Performance that marketplace can absorb."

What's critical to the phenomenon of disruption is that after a product is introduced and gains traction in the market, the pace of innovation, both due to competitive pressures and what market research says customers want, almost always proceeds faster than customers are able to absorb and use the changes. The result is that very quickly, these two lines intersect and, after this point, further innovation exceeds the requirements of most customers.

For simplicity, the model shows one line of "Performance that marketplace can absorb," but in reality there are many lines depending on how different customers use products. The most demanding customers will have a performance line that is higher and steeper, which moves the intersection further to the right, but eventually even those customers will be "over-served" by all products in the category.

We see this manifested in new features making no competitive difference to winning or losing sales, buying decisions being made almost entirely on price, and falling margins as the new features increase cost while customers demand lower prices. In other words, the market has become "commoditized." It is at this point that incumbents start to become vulnerable to disruption.

Disruption occurs when a new and usually inferior product enters the market at a significantly lower cost, targeting customers whose needs are over-served by incumbents. In Figure 1-1, this is represented by the third line labeled "Disruptive Innovations."

Often, but not always, new technology enables a greater efficiency/lower cost product, but it hasn't matured enough to match the quality of what's already in the market. For example, transistors where not as good for hi-fi sound production as vacuum tubes, although they had a significant advantage in smaller size and heat production, which made them ideal for cheap, crappy-sounding miniature transistor radios that kids could afford to take with them everywhere in the 1950s.

Incumbents often see disruptive innovations as "toys" when compared to their advanced products, and they either can't or choose not to compete against what they consider low-margin junk, and don't wish to undermine their brand position by aiming down-market. But, because these products are inexpensive and "good enough" when compared with the alternative of doing nothing, a low-end niche uses them.

After introduction, disruptors get on a path of upward improvement just like the incumbents (relative to their own product development path, these are "Sustaining Innovations," even though they are represented by the slope of the disruptor line), which makes the new product suitable for an increasing number of over-served, existing-market customers who are happy to trade lower quality or fewer features for much lower cost.

Eventually, the disruptive innovation reaches the point where it is able to satisfy the needs of the majority of the market, and the incumbent's customers begin to abandon it en masse in favor of less expensive, easier to use, more convenient products. At this point, the incumbent is displaced from market leadership, or "disrupted."

Christensen describes how "asymmetries of motivation" are one cause of disruption, since incumbents can see the changes happening but are not motivated to fight for low-margin, undesirable niches. To the disruptor, on the other hand, the low end represents the easiest sales to make and the market welcomes their product, even if low quality, since the alternative is to do things manually, or not solve the problem at all.

Just as on the battlefield, it's much easier to win when your competition is not motivated and chooses to lay down arms or to flee rather than fight.[5] With low-end disruption, it is almost never in the incumbents' interest to fight for low profit or even money-losing niches (at least by traditional measures), which is why the model illustrated in Figure 1-1 almost always results in the disruptor winning when the battle is from the bottom. On the other hand, if wishful market entrants try to attack on the incumbents' turf, targeting the high-end customers with "better" products, the incumbents will almost always win, as they are both motivated and better resourced for the fight.

There is a different asymmetry of motivation for new-market disruption, because creating a new-market innovation usually represents a large investment risk for an incumbent, while the innovator is already committed to taking risks and has nothing to lose.

Disruption Fingerprint (How to Know If an Innovation Is Disruptive)

Disruptive innovations are identifiable because they follow a common pattern (described in the model above) and exhibit recognizable attributes. The degree to which these attributes exist determines the probability of market disruption. I have labeled that set of attributes a *Disruption Fingerprint*. They include:

- Inferior when compared with available alternatives

- Addresses needs that are unmet or underserved in the initial target segments

- Initially targets a small market niche

---

[5]One of the greatest battles never fought occurred during the American Civil War when, after Atlanta was defeated and burned to the ground, Sherman's army marched on Savannah. In a matter of days, Sherman was able to blockade Savannah and put it under siege. Though the Confederate army under General William Hardee had 10,000 men stationed in good positions to fight for Savannah, after the demoralizing devastation of Atlanta, Hardee decided to decamp and fled Savannah with his troops during the night on hastily built pontoon bridges across the Savannah river. With no soldiers left to defend the city, the mayor of Savannah rode out to meet Sherman the next day to formally surrender, based on a promise that his city would not suffer the same fate as Atlanta. This is the reason why Savannah, to this day, has one of the best-preserved antebellum historic districts in the country.

- Customers are unattractive to incumbents (low-margin, can't afford existing products, often low-income, unskilled)

- Designed for moderate-to-low-growth segments

- Created by outsiders (startups, companies not thought of as competitors)

- Employs different channels, or disintermediates traditional channels altogether (goes direct to consumer, for example, bypassing distributors and retailers)

- Enjoys a sustainable cost-of-production advantage enabled by (patentable) technology or new business process

- Has one or more advantages to the new user—ease-of-use, flexibility, simplicity, convenience (often advantages that are less valued by existing users, and certainly less critical)

- Competes against non-consumption

These are the most significant identifiers that are usually plain to see. There are other qualities as well, but if you see an innovation that has all of these attributes, it's a good bet that you're looking at a potential disruptor.

Of course, to be disruptive, an innovator has to actually disrupt a market, which also implies that they have an economically viable business model and the ability to execute on their vision. Since we can't know those things without knowing more about the resources (financial and otherwise), skills, and organizational capabilities of the innovator, I leave that aside for now. It's critical though, if you're going to design for disruption, that you know whether or not the market opportunity has disruptive potential.

In Chapter 3, I spend more time discussing how to predict disruption.

Anti-Disruption Fingerprint (How You Can Be Sure That an Innovation Isn't Disruptive)

Already by these definitions and identifying attributes, it should be clear that not all innovation is disruptive or has disruptive potential. As I noted earlier, too many entrepreneurs throw around the term "disruptive innovation" as if it means "high tech," or they believe that all innovation is disruptive. While we can dismiss that as hype, for our purposes it matters a great deal since our objective is to disrupt a market, which means we have to also know when innovation isn't disruptive.

It becomes even more difficult and important to do when you recognize that the term "disruptive" is a relative concept. The same product can be disruptive if produced by one vendor, while from another, it can be sustaining. Depending on the nature of the alternatives it's being compared to, it can be either disruptive or sustaining, and sometimes both at the same time. The anti-disruption fingerprint looks like this:

- Directly targets a crowded marketplace with a "better" product

- Attacks the bread-and-butter segment of the market leader

- Depends on the same channels, partners, and suppliers as the incumbent

- Targets the low-price segment of the market, but does not have an inherent cost advantage over competitors

- Is more difficult to use, less convenient to access, needs specialized expertise to operate, or is more complex than alternatives already in the market

- Addresses needs that are well-served by low-cost, affordable alternatives

- Represents a performance breakthrough

- Is a more cost-effective solution introduced by the market leader to attract cost-conscious consumers

Any one of these can be a disqualifier for success in disrupting a market. Two or more is certain to fail.

An example? Nokia Lumia phones, based on Windows Phone technology, are different and destined to occupy a small niche, not to disrupt a market. Why are they disqualified? They:

- Don't offer any substantially different use case or application from either iOS or Android devices that could drive mass adoption

- Target a crowded marketplace that has already decided Android is the open standard and iOS the higher-end integrated and closed option

- Target bread-and-butter segments of the leaders

- Use the same channels as incumbents

- Target a mid-market price (the worst possible position for a disruptor)

- Have no cost-of-production or volume advantage that would enable lower prices than Android-based phones

- Aim to be "better" at specific features (recent promotions focus on camera superiority)

Now, I don't believe that either Microsoft or Nokia were targeting disruption, but rather to occupy a niche where consumers prefer a consistent interface metaphor from their PC to their mobile devices. I am using this strictly as an example to show that being based on a different technology, even on a platform available for others to build on, neither certifies nor guarantees a disruptive innovation.

However, it is a useful example, because many people confuse niche products (which have no chance to dominate markets) and disruptive innovations (which displace leaders). Niche products can be quite profitable if they stick to the advantages that they offer and don't try to be all things to all people, but they aren't and can't be disruptive.

What Creates the Opportunity for Disruption?

One area that Christensen has not explored much in his research is the identification of indicators that help predict markets that can be disrupted, or which are in fact, ripe for disruption.

Based on the previous sections, you might surmise that creating an inferior product and selling it for a lower price than alternatives would pretty much guarantee that you'll have a disruptive innovation. Unfortunately, it's not quite that simple. While disruptions often are cheaper and lower quality than what came before, just being cheaper and lower quality might mean that you've created something that no one wants.

There are three principal factors that create the opportunity for disruption:

- Scarcity

- Default corporate management behavior

- Human nature

Scarcity

Scarcity is a shortage of anything that people desire or need. It is the economic impact of scarcity that creates the potential for disruption. To understand that, let's consider the opposite of scarcity—abundance.

Take air, for example. We assume that supply is limitless: it is an abundant commodity that we can freely consume as needed. When you think about it, this is actually quite remarkable—air is one of the most critical things needed for survival other than food and water, it is extraordinarily valuable, but because it is abundant, it is free to consume.

Scarcity creates the opposite condition. Consider a good whose supply is severely restricted but whose need is extreme. For example, what would happen to the price of a life-saving drug whose worldwide supply has dwindled to just 100 pills, and new production has ceased because it depends on a mineral that is only available from a single, politically hostile country? What if 100 people globally are dying from the disease, and it requires 30 pills to be cured. In this scenario, only three people can be cured, but 33 times that number are in competition for the available supply.

The elasticity of demand approaches zero for such a good—if you want to live, you would be willing to pay whatever you have to get access to the remaining pills. Competition and desperate need ensures that someone else will take them if you don't, which theoretically means if the wealthiest sick person is a billionaire, the supplier could ask $1 billion for 30 pills and get it.

Economic theory assumes that the supply for most goods and services is finite, and that price is the factor that balances the supply and demand curves, effectively providing the mechanism by which society rations scarce resources. So, as illustrated in the classic graph, Figure 1-2:

- If demand increases, the price will increase and supply will increase to meet the new demand

- If demand decreases, the price will fall and less supply will be produced

- If supply increases, the price will fall and more quantity will be demanded

- If supply decreases, the price will rise and less will be demanded

Supply and Demand Curve

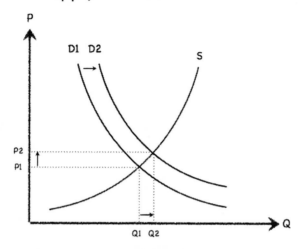

Figure 1-2. The supply and demand curve illustrates how price is the balancing factor that establishes equilibrium between the two. As demand shifts from D1 to D2, the price rises from P1 to P2, and the quantity made to supply the demand rises from Q1 to Q2, as suppliers are willing to make more in exchange for making more profit, all things being equal. There tends to be an assumption that supply is constrained (either due to an artificial or real shortage of the good), so only demand and price are truly variable. Disruptive innovation dramatically alters constraints on supply, causing massive deformation of this graph.

At least this is what happens in a free market with perfect competition. The concept of scarcity underlies this graph, with an embedded assumption that there is latent demand that will surface for any good if the price is lower.

Scarcity can be thought of as an artificial or temporary condition, generally caused by:

- Lack of alternatives
- Monopoly or limited (oligopoly) control of supply
- Cost to produce the good in question

Every disruptive innovation does one or more of these three things:

- Causes a major shift in the supply curve through increased productivity
- Creates alternatives that are good enough to address unmet needs of a larger percentage of the population
- Significantly lowers the price, making goods more affordable to low-end consumers

A significantly lower price also shifts the demand curve because it makes it possible to serve low-end consumers who can't afford the existing market solutions, or it attacks monopoly control of supply by creating new sources and new substitution alternatives for products in different categories. Thus, the result of disruption is always to create abundance from scarcity.

To illustrate this effect, let's look at a few examples to appreciate that this idea of creating abundance from scarcity is a universal property of disruptive innovation.

Henry Ford's Assembly Line for Manufacturing Cars

In North America, Henry Ford is widely thought to have been the inventor of the automobile, although he wasn't even the first U.S. carmaker. In fact, Karl Benz in Germany was the first to create a commercially viable car, followed by others in Germany, France, Austria, and England. There were even carmakers in the United States before Ford.

Yet, popular belief is that it was Ford who started it all. In fact, Ford's contribution was mass production via the mechanized assembly line and the division of labor into small repetitive tasks (making people part of the "machine"), combined with offering twice the prevailing day's wages to keep skilled labor from leaving.

These innovations made Ford Motor Company far and away the most efficient and most productive car manufacturer, able to produce eight times the output of other factories in the same amount of time. The Model T was also a far simpler and more modular design than the better-quality cars already being made in Germany and elsewhere, specifically targeting the "working man" as the customer.

Ford was proud that at the wages he paid and his cost to produce cars, all of his laborers could afford to buy a car, for an average of four months' pay. They were also simple to maintain—an important consideration given that in the early days, the car owner did most of their own repairs, especially when the car broke down in the middle of a trip.

The impact of Ford's assembly line and philosophy of producing cars as cheaply as possible was that car production exploded, with sales approximately doubling each year (a nearly 100% annual compounded growth rate) for most of the first 15 years Ford was in business. By 1918, 50% of all the cars sold in the United States were Model Ts.

By the 1920s, other manufacturers were forced to copy Ford's assembly line techniques, and Ford's market advantage began to dissipate, particularly when Alfred Sloan (General Motors) introduced his own innovation of multiple car brands that appealed to customers with different aspirational values, as well as a car model from low-end to high-end in each brand so that consumers could trade up and remain loyal to the brand as their means grew. Henry refused to respond, insisting that Ford make only one type of car in one color (black), until it was almost too late (a pattern of the disruptor missing the next opportunity and themselves being disrupted, something I'll come back to).

When they finally did copy GM's brand approach, GM had become the largest carmaker, and it held that position for more than 70 years. However, Ford remained the number two supplier of cars for most of the 20th Century, and when the Model T was finally discontinued after 20 years of production, more than 15 million of them had been produced. It's because Ford so dominated car production in the early years and was the first to make cars affordable for the everyday consumer, that so many believe that Ford invented the car.

The first Model T, considered cheap in 1908, was priced at $825. By 1916, it had fallen to just $360. The net is that Ford's innovation addressed scarcity both through the scale of productivity enabled by his assembly line and by his low-price focus. He created abundance from scarcity.

Cultured Pearls

Luxury goods are a special economic category where demand increases more than proportionally as income increases. Many luxury products exhibit the property of "Veblen goods," where pushing the price up increases demand, as a higher price acts as signal that the product is more desirable or better quality. We see this effect with diamonds today, for example, and much of this is due to the perception of rarity (extreme scarcity), which is as much because of near monopoly control of diamond supply by one company (De Beers) as it is "true" scarcity.

Through most of human history, pearls were not only a luxury good, but their rarity also made them even more desirable, and consequently they were also Veblen goods. They were so scarce that the higher the price, the more they were desired, and the easier they were to sell to wealthy consumers.

The rarity of pearls was attributable to the difficulty of harvesting them, and the low probability that the oyster would both produce a perfectly round iridescent pearl and that it would be of a reasonable size. Literally hundreds of oysters had to be opened to find a single pearl naturally, and many, many more than that to find any quantity of quality pearls to make jewelry from.

Until the early 1900s, natural pearls were found and harvested by divers spending hundreds of hours scavenging the bottom of sea beds, and in the process killing the oysters, whether they had produced a pearl or not. It was not only a time-consuming and often-fruitless search, but many divers died seeking a day's pay.

In 1916, a method of inducing an oyster to create a pearl by implanting a very small piece of mantle tissue from a donor shell into another oyster was devised. Cultured pearls look nearly identical to natural pearls, though at the core they have a different structure because of how they are started. Though still labor- and time-intensive—after implantation, it takes one to three years for a cultured pearl to develop, and the longer it takes, the lower the yield as many of the oysters die—the process is still hundreds of times more productive than the accident that a natural pearl is.

Thus, cultured pearls created a radical increase in supply that caused a drastic drop in the price. Though still a luxury good, pearls are no longer a symbol of great wealth, and only natural pearls are considered Veblen goods today. Ironically, the only way to tell the difference is to put the pearl under an x-ray to determine how it was formed.

It's hard today to even imagine how valuable pearls were before the cultured pearl process was invented and became common. A single pearl would be mounted as a centerpiece in a unique pendant, pin, or other piece of jewelry, and a large one of high quality would have been a collector's item. A string of matched pearls was almost unheard of before cultured pearls were introduced, and the few that were made carried extraordinary price tags. In 1917, for example, Cartier purchased with a single double-strand of natural pearls, valued in 1917 dollars at $1 million, the 5th Avenue mansion in New York that became the Cartier store.

The combination of cultured pearls flooding the market and the onset of the Depression caused the price bubble for pearls to pop, and by the 1950s, every middle class woman could afford a string of pearls. Today, a fine cultured pearl is still an expensive gem, and you can spend several thousand dollars for a necklace of the best. They can't be mass-produced. But in comparison, a string of natural South Sea pearls can easily run into several hundreds of thousands of dollars.

The disruption of cultured pearls created relative abundance where there was once extreme scarcity, and in a matter of a few years, the price fell by several orders of magnitude. Again, we see that disruptive innovation transforms scarcity into abundance, with the result being radical deformation of the supply and demand curve.

Information and the Coming Era of Big Data

A current example and forward-looking prediction will hopefully drive home the relationship between scarcity, abundance, and disruptive innovation.

As recently as a couple of decades ago, it was extremely costly to gather and create databases of information. Any company that wanted to do so had to first purchase extraordinarily expensive mainframes or supercomputers, invest in very expensive storage, conduct labor-intensive research to gather and format data, and then hire teams of highly paid programmers to write custom applications to process and analyze it—all to create usable information.

Today, we are awash in free information that can be readily searched for and downloaded from the "cloud." Want competitive research? Visit your competitor's website, check out LinkedIn, or download their SEC filings from the Edgar database, and in 20 minutes you will know more than was possible with months of intense digging and research 20 years ago.

In a few clicks, Wikipedia can tell you almost anything you want to know about any subject with a higher degree of accuracy than used to be possible with the infinitesimally smaller *Encyclopedia Britannica*. And if something new related to that knowledge happened this morning, it's probably already been updated.

When you attend a weekly sales meeting today, the level of insight about customers, prospects, competitors, trends, market opportunities, and changes since last week that is expected was impossible to provide in the 1990s. The pervasive connectivity of the internet, nearly universal broadband connections, and mobile devices that can access this data anywhere and anytime have made business intelligence—that was impossibly expensive and nearly impossible to do by an organization as large as the U.S. government—nearly free and accessible to anyone with an iPad.

Beyond this new status quo, we have fire hoses of data being generated daily by sources such as Twitter, Facebook, internet searches, blog postings, RFID information, cookie data captured from websites, real-time sensor data captured from the explosion of "smart" devices from phones to cars, and many other sources.

One of the current buzzwords that has many excited is so-called "big data." Big data is a catch-all term that describes datasets that are so large, they are beyond the ability of our software tools to capture, process, and make sense of in any reasonable amount of time. Examples are datasets being generated by Twitter, Facebook, and others.

In that data, we believe there are opportunities to understand how customers perceive us and what exactly they want out of product development. That data provides predictive modeling of global trends and enables sentiment analysis. Ultimately, it's nearly impossible to predict which products and services will create disruption. But we know there will be many, because big data is creating abundance where there was once scarcity.

How Does Scarcity Direct Us to Disruptive Opportunity?

My conclusion is that there will always be disruptive opportunities where something is in short supply or when customers feel like they are being screwed. As a general observation, scarcity manifests in the market in a few different ways:

- There are few suppliers of a good that feels like it is priced artificially high. (In the U.S. market, broadband internet access and mobile data plans come to mind).

- Lack of supply, or lack of choice, manifests as really bad customer service—companies feel that consumers have no where else to go, and no one else does service any better, so why should they invest in it? (Think of the airline industry or of utility businesses).

- High demand exists regardless of price, but regulatory red tape and acceptable profits may be difficult to make because of the production quantities needed to be a viable business. (Think about the impediments in bringing life-saving drugs to market or keeping supplies in stock for drugs that are low-demand yet critical for certain treatments. Think too of how abuse of the patent system by pharmaceutical companies keeps prices high, and how the risk of hit-and-run lawsuits prevents many drugs from being produced at a reasonable cost).

In other words, the lesson to take from understanding the relationship of scarcity and abundance to creating disruptive opportunities is to look for markets where customers are angry and dissatisfied with available products or services, or where nothing has changed for a long time or everyone agrees that prices are too high and customers are treated like crap. If there is a lot of complaining, there's probably an opportunity for disruption. The list of industries that meet that criterion isn't hard to compile:

- Insurance
- Financial services
- Air travel
- Healthcare
- Energy
- Telecom
- Internet access

- Retail service
- Housing creation
- Real estate services

And, those are just some of the big ones. If you see a solution to one of those, and you aren't currently a market participant but can see opportunity to create a commercially viable product, you probably have a disruption waiting to happen.

Default Corporate Management Behavior

While scarcity in some form needs to exist to create the economic opportunity for disruption, it's not the only condition that is needed for disruption to occur. After all, if an incumbent saw disruption coming, the rational thing would be to do it yourself or block it before a competitor attacked and won your market.

In many markets, we do see incumbents vigorously trying to protect dated business models to preserve their market position. For example, the music and movie production industries would prefer to stop all progress in their domain completely, and routinely lobby governments to extend copyright protection far beyond what it was ever intended to do, creating abusive anti-consumer rules that block people from using what they've already paid for. We saw this aggressive anti-competitive behavior in the debate over the ultimately scuttled SOPA (the Stop Online Piracy Act) of 2012.

The second enabler of disruption in a sleepy industry is default corporate behaviors. These behaviors are so ingrained and assumed, that they are actively taught and encouraged as part of the discipline of professional management in traditional MBA programs. Central among them is the notion that the role of the corporation is to maximize profits and shareholder value. It isn't that this is a completely wrong idea, but it is at best only half the picture.

The crippling effects of these behaviors on a business facing the prospect of disruption in their industry is not obvious and, in fact, is a bit counterintuitive. Let's take a closer look at each.

Maximizing Profit and Shareholder Value

These two ideas are so core to our belief in what a company's purpose is that it is practically sacrilege to suggest they are part of the disease that undermines a company's ability to respond to disruption. Corporate management is there to execute the wishes of the owners after all, so if the owners want more profits and increased value of their corporation, how could it be a bad thing for managers to focus on it?

It turns out that the problem is really how managers go about trying to maximize profits and shareholder value, by focusing on numbers rather than on what creates the numbers.

There are three behaviors that profit maximization drives, particularly in large public companies today.

- Focus on operational efficiency
- How innovative projects are funded and return on investment is calculated
- Focus on the short term

Let's explore the corrosive effect each of these behaviors has on the ability to fend off looming disruption.

Operational Efficiency

Operational efficiency seems like a logical behavior and on the surface, it certainly is. Once a business model has been proven as a way to satisfy customer needs and to be profitable, the following are all commendable things to do: optimizing processes by cutting unnecessary costs, automating production for higher productivity, eliminating unnecessary steps, sourcing from suppliers who offer the least total cost, and designing repeatable and measurable human processes so that performance can be tracked and improved over time.

In fact, outside of finance, this is the majority of the quantitative education offered by MBA programs. And, to some degree, this makes sense for educators as well—it's easier to teach mechanics and to assess how well it's been learned than teach students how to innovate or how to think about a business strategically, for example. So these skills, and the philosophy of ever-increasing efficiency, are drilled into MBA candidates as a mantra with almost religious fervor.

The problem is that operational efficiency has nothing to do with the reasons that customers choose your product. In the short term, it's great because it can extract more profit from the same resources and pass on savings to the consumer at the same time. In the long term, it causes companies to lose sight of the imperative to delight the customer, to understand what customers are trying to accomplish with their products, and to evolve to solve customer problems better.

In other words, when operational efficiency becomes the main goal of the business, it tends to squeeze out investment in future health. In fact, disruptive innovation is antithetical to operational efficiency—it necessarily involves experimentation, uncertainty, going down paths that will not yield results, and unpredictable returns even on successful projects. New products that can grow to replace current revenue streams and the high margins from previously disruptive products can only come from new disruptive products.

The paradox is that unless it is explicitly part of the company's purpose, and some percentage of resource is allocated to experimentation and discovery of unmet needs, the company will behave as though disruptive innovation is a virus and attack it with cultural antibodies. Moreover, as an organization focuses more and more on efficiency, it loses the ability to innovate new business models and disrupt itself before others do. Most large companies reached this evolutionary state years, or even generations, ago.

How Return on Investment Is Calculated

The approval process for virtually all projects that require investment includes a projection of future cash flows and calculation of an internal rate of return (IRR). This works fine if the success of the project is predictable, and if future cash flows and the associated risks can be accurately projected.

IRR is the discount rate that results in the NPV (net present value) of all future cash flows totaling zero. The reason companies use IRR is that it allows easy comparison both against the return of other projects and against the opportunity cost of using capital some other way (for example, putting it into bonds, buying a company, and so on).

In theory, a project with an IRR of 60% is better than a project with IRR of 25%, which is better than a project with IRR of 10%. And, if the cost of capital is 9%, then each of these projects could be approved. If insufficient resources are available to complete each of these, then IRR can provide direction to prioritize which projects to invest in.

There are many documented problems with IRR, such as the possibility of having two different IRRs for the same project, small projects with small returns being valued above big projects with large returns but lower IRRs, and so on. The purpose here is not to debate structural flaws with IRR, but to focus on how it mitigates against disruptive innovation.

The issue with disruption is that it has a great deal more uncertainty associated with it than sustaining innovation. By definition, sustaining innovations are projects that can be managed to a budget and have a predictable cost and return. I can estimate pretty closely how many additional units I can sell if my next product model includes a big red "off button," and if it delivers more power to brighten my screen together with a longer lasting battery. (At least I can in theory. In practice, however, everything isn't equal, and I can't predict competitive behavior or preference for their enhancements over mine, when a recession or major political upheaval will happen, or whether a disruptor is on the horizon and about to eat my lunch.)

Disruptive innovations, on the other hand, target new niches of unknown size with lower-margin products, hard-to-predict growth rates, and higher risk of failure. In fact, part of the risk is that we may not exactly hit the customer's "job to be done" in the first release, even if we have a pretty good idea what it is, or that technologically meeting that requirement may be harder than thought or even impossible. By the time the risk and uncertainty for any individual opportunity is factored in, the IRR for a disruptive product (which has the potential to undermine existing products with higher margins) can look awfully bad in comparison to projects that focus on sustaining innovation.

In fact, imagine that you positioned a potentially disruptive innovation to upper management as a project that:

- Targets a smallish niche
- Proposes a lower-margin, inferior product
- Projects low to moderate growth
- Targets "undesirable" users
- May make existing distribution channels unhappy
- Has the worst-looking IRR of any of the potential projects the company could undertake

In most companies, you'd be committing career suicide and writing yourself a ticket to nowhere. Yet, that's what disruption often looks like, and those are the projects that create new markets and delight customers.

As a result, IRR as a measure almost institutionalizes the bias against potentially disruptive projects ever getting off the ground (unless, by some miracle, they gain visibility with the CEO who sees the strategic potential and "greenlights" them).

Short-Term Focus

There is little to explain here. Clearly, most public companies today are focused on quarterly earnings. Executive management is rewarded with healthy stock options and grants, theoretically to align their interest with the shareholders. And, because the incentives are often tied to quarterly earnings and to stock price, directly or indirectly, this reinforces the plumping of numbers now at the expense of investment for the future.

Sustaining innovations are those targeted at the needs of current users of current products. There is a known mainstream (mass) market, generally of considerable size. In this environment, a new product targeted at the needs of new users with unknown market size or growth rates that is likely to take two to three years to show its potential is beyond the horizon of any short-term quarterly or even annual planning exercise. If significant research and development is required, it may be two or three years longer than that.

Few in corporate America are willing to place a bet that will involve significant cost, may disruptively undermine the market for the current bread-and-butter product, and that won't show up as meaningful revenue and earnings within the average expected tenure of the current CEO.

Human Nature

In *How the Mighty Fall,* Jim Collins outlines how success can lead to failure. He outlines five steps:

- Hubris born of past success
- Undisciplined pursuit of more
- Denial of risk and peril
- Grasping for salvation
- Capitulation to irrelevance

Although I believe there is weakness in his analysis, particularly in the diagnosis of the second step (this is only one of many possible missteps that can be born of hubris, and I see lots of evidence of alternative paths to doom), the overall observation that success can create failure, and that it starts with hubris, or over-confidence, is very apropos.

We see this every day—successful organizations are full of overconfident people taking credit for the success. Hubris permeates the culture, with even the most neutral of participants attributing their good fortune to their own wisdom, strategy, foresight, and brilliance. The roles of luck, timing, competitive missteps, partner contributions, and simply being in the right place at the right time are often unseen or dismissed.

This doesn't just happen in big, long-established *Fortune* 500 companies. Often among the most over-confident are disruptive innovators who enjoyed a meteoric rise, growing to industry dominance from nowhere in just a few years. Critically, the arrogance of success blinds the organization to the possibility of failure, as well as to seeing signs of weakness that are obvious to everyone but those on the inside.

This does, of course, lead to denial of risk, but not just risk of over-reaching from the inside and belief in your own engineering brilliance, but also ignoring external risk. Hubris-afflicted organizations believe they are immune from attack, that outsiders could never understand the market as well as they do, and that the "cheap toy" that's being sold as a low-end alternative at the bottom of the market could never be a threat to their dominance.

So, the most frequent response is to do nothing, because to take those risks seriously would be an acknowledgement of fallibility. Kodak. RIM. Yahoo. Circuit City. Motorola. We know where that path leads.

If market disruption seems inevitable, it's often because the examples we see in the news frequently exhibit all three of these conditions in spades:

- There's a controlled market of scarcity, with buyers desperate for supply, lower prices, and choice

- Markets are controlled by large corporations that have overshot the needs of most customers, are focused on short-term results, and have ceased to do meaningful innovation

- Managers are over-confident and boastful

What Market Disruption Looks Like

Disruptive innovation is fun. Its result—market disruption—is not. Regardless, it's useful to have a reference story to remind us what can happen, and how it is both surprisingly slow to take root, yet amazingly fast to conclude.

Here's the story of Kodak, from the beginning to the end, from the perspective of disruptive innovation.

The End of the Kodak Moment

Much has been written of the failure of Kodak. Most of it misses the point and fails to correctly diagnose what exactly disrupted Kodak's business and whether it was inevitable.

In the beginning, Kodak was a disruptive innovator. In fact, it was a serial disruptor under the founding leadership of George Eastman (this pattern will sound familiar as you proceed through the book). Not that Eastman was trying to disrupt anything—it was simply that his vision for the company made disruption almost inevitable.

Let's start the story at the beginning, when photography emerged from science labs to become a business. It unfolds about 40 years before George Eastman and the history of Kodak.

Daguerreotypes: The first commercial photographic process was invented by Louis Daguerre in 1835, and was offered "free to the world" by the French government in 1839 after Daguerre was awarded a lifetime pension for his work. The daguerreotype was a positive image (which meant one of a kind), created by fuming iodine gas onto a piece of Sheffield plate (silver foil on a copper plate), and then exposing it to light. Its chief advantage was that it was cheaper than commissioning a painting. For the first time, average people could get their portraits done. Disadvantages: expensive, slow exposure, fragile image (that could be wiped off the plate with a finger, so were generally framed behind glass for protection), one of a kind, and required a high level of expertise to produce. You could say that daguerreotypes were a disruptive innovation for portraiture, but I don't want to go back any further than this.

Wet plate (collodion) photography: The next great advance in photography was the creation of a negative image on a glass plate by coating it with a carrier emulsion (collodion) into which bromide, iodide, or chloride was dissolved just prior to creating the plate. After allowing the plate to dry a little (to a moist gel), it was immersed in silver nitrate, and then put into the camera wet, exposed, and then immediately developed. Advantages: the negative image was "permanent" and could be used to create many (positive) copies of an image, and it was much cheaper than the daguerreotype. Disadvantages: the image had to be recorded wet and exposed within about 15 minutes of creating a plate, since the plate quickly lost sensitivity as it dried. Photography outside of a sitting room was very inconvenient, as you essentially had to have a mobile darkroom to mix chemicals and do all the processing one image at a time. It quickly disrupted daguerreotypes though, because the lower cost and ability to make copies were significant advantages that made photography start to spread quickly.

Dry plate photography: The next evolution was to create a pre-coated plate that did not require a travelling chemistry lab in order to capture pictures. A gelatin emulsion with chemistry that was stable enough to dry was used to cover glass plates that were sealed in black frames, and the photographer could then snap the frame into his camera in seconds, pull the covering black metal out of the frame, and then open his lens to expose the plate. When the exposure was complete, the plate could be re-covered and a new one inserted into the camera immediately to take another picture. Processing needed to be done quickly, but not instantly, which meant it could be done in a clean, controlled environment. This process was invented in 1871, and it became popular quickly as it was immensely more convenient, enabled plates to be pre-prepared (enabling multiple pictures to be taken in a short time), and allowed shorter exposure times (which made portraiture much easier). It also enabled a division of labor—the photographer could employ an expert to make his plates and simply worry about the picture taking, opening the field to a broader range of people. The chief disadvantage was that it was more expensive than wet plate photography.

Factory-made dry plates: In 1879, George Eastman, the founder of Kodak (originally Eastman Dry Plate) invented a machine to automate the coating of dry plates, thereby reducing their cost. A second advantage of the dry plate process was that since the photographer didn't need to make his own plates, the process could be standardized and mechanized, greatly reducing the cost and increasing predictability of the result. Although it removed a degree of control from the professional photographer, the cost savings was immense and enabled another wave of rapid expansion in the number of people who could take pictures.

Roll film: Eastman created the next disruptive innovation in 1884 when he invented roll film on a cellulose carrier (versus glass plates up to this time). This led to two great advances—the ability to take many pictures without reloading the camera and the development of motion-picture photography.

Kodak camera: In 1888, Kodak introduced the first inexpensive camera explicitly intended for amateur use. It was designed to use Eastman's previous invention of roll film, with enough capacity to take 100 pictures before reloading. The advantages that made it suitable for amateurs were the low cost, convenience of roll film, and elimination of much of the apparatus and skills that had been necessary to take pictures before this point.

Outsourced film-processing labs: In 1892, Kodak rolled out the marketing slogan "You press the button, we do the rest." Continuing the push downmarket, Kodak's customers could now take their exposed film to Kodak for the professional development and printing of pictures. This disruption, by eliminating the need for photographers to have their own darkrooms and mess with chemicals, further democratized photography, making the ability to take a picture almost universal.

The Brownie camera: In 1900, Kodak introduced the Brownie camera, a simple black box with a fixed focal length lens that sold for just $1. Twenty years earlier, a single photographic plate from Eastman dry plate was $5. This low-end disruption ushered in the era of mass-market photography. Not only was photography easy enough for anyone, it also became cheap enough that all could afford it, and even kids could own their own cameras.

Color photography, Kodachrome film: Kodak did not invent color photography, but continuing its long history of disruptive innovation, was again the first to create a consumer-friendly film product. Introduced in 1935, Kodachrome recorded a virtual color separation of red, green, and blue on separate layers of a single piece of film, doing away with the messy business of shooting multiple images through color filters and then recombining them into a single image at time of image processing. This enabled color movies for the first time, as well as color slide film—the first easy-to-use color photography process that could be employed by amateurs.

There were many, many sustaining innovations in between these numerous disruptive ones, such that Kodak was the leading company in photographic film, chemicals, and processing throughout the 20th Century. Like many other disruptors, Kodak grew so dominant that it suffered several anti-trust bouts with the Department of Justice for exercising monopoly market power.

The most significant of these resulted in the 1954 consent decree ordering Kodak to provide technical information and to license its photofinishing technology to competitors to break its near stranglehold on the photofinishing business. By 1976, 22 years after the consent decree, Kodak still sold 90% of film and 85% of cameras in the U.S. market, and it had more than 50% market share globally.

Significantly, Kodak invented the digital camera in 1975—about the same time it had reached its market power zenith. Despite inventing this next great advance, Kodak no longer possessed the modus operandi of a disruptive innovator. It was no longer a company with a vision of broadening the market through ever simpler and less expensive (and lower quality) formats. The Instamatic camera and film introduced in the 1960s was to be Kodak's swan song of photography dominance. There can be no doubt that had George Eastman been alive in 1976, Kodak would be the dominant player today in digital photography, just as it had been in film-based photography during the previous century.

However, the success of the Instamatic models gave Kodak such complete dominance of the consumer film and processing market that management seemed to shift away from a culture of being first with the next viable inexpensive format that would expand the market, to one of profit maximization and protecting its current market position. It is at precisely this point, when companies appear the strongest, when they are a virtual cash machine, when management believes they are unstoppable and can control industry progress, that they begin to be vulnerable to disruptive innovation.

Evidence: Though Kodak was first to create a digital camera, rather than see this as the next opportunity to offer low-cost photography to the masses and expand (and corner) the market, digital photography was viewed as a threat to its film and processing businesses, Kodak initially choose not to commercialize this invention, instead allowing Sony to release the first digital camera to market in 1981.

More insidious than squandering a six-year technology lead to a competitor, Kodak actively resisted rebranding, and it took a follower approach to the market, consistently playing catch-up with vendors who were more focused on digital photography as a business (and who weren't worried about the decline of film, chemicals, and processing businesses). They eventually got into the digital photography space, offering a best-selling camera, but despite this were never seen as a market leader, nor as the inventor of the technology.

Their cameras, though sold in large quantity, were a low-margin business, and Kodak had long since given up any opportunity to challenge Epson or Hewlett Packard for printing and ink supplies, forgoing most of the profit to be made. By the time Kodak introduced its first consumer inkjet printer in 2007, it was already more than 15 years behind competitors with a low-quality me-too product that didn't have either a lower price or any game-changing qualities— a strategy that disruption theory predicts will always fail. And it did.

Kodak filed for bankruptcy protection in January of 2012, having ceased production of Kodachrome film in 2009 due to plunging sales, and having lost money through most of the first decade of the 2000s with a series of desperate, failed "Hail Mary" strategies to save the company.

Kodak's peak market capitalization occurred in 1997 when it was valued at $28 billion—this at a time when the company was already incredibly weakened (although the markets didn't seem to understand this) and the seeds of its failure were already coursing through its veins, ironically the same year that Apple was mere weeks from closing the doors in bankruptcy. Steve Jobs returned to lead Apple to becoming the most valuable company in the world by 2012, through a string of ever more successful disruptive innovations the same year that Kodak failed.

The Financial Impact of Disruptive Innovation

Disruptive innovation is about the creation of economic value. The best way to understand this is to compare disruptors with a control group. For our purposes, we'll use the S&P 500 as a base.

Now, we know that any index adds new companies as they grow to prominence, and it removes others as they fail, shrink, or are acquired. When adding and removing members, the index takes great care to equalize the value of the replaced stock such that it does not change the value of the overall index on the date it is changed. This has two impacts when using it as a control group:

- Companies that have completely failed or continued to decline after being removed from the index are not reflected in the index's value. That means that the index value is more stable, but it also means that it is higher than it would be if you assume that the index is a proxy for overall market growth.

- Not only is the index higher than it would be if failed companies were reflected in the value, but the growth rate of the index over time is also higher, since once a stock is removed from the index, its subsequent decline has no impact on the index, while the stock that replaces it is generally a healthy one that rises.

For our purposes, these two considerations are worth noting, but they also make the comparison more than fair.

What we're interested in comparing over time is the growth rate of companies in the index. To get a true average growth rate, we also want to look at the index over a long period of time to smooth out bumps but not distort the data by a couple of anomalous years.

For simplicity (because the data is readily available), I use growth in dividends paid from 1960 to 2010. I am assuming that over the long haul, growth in dividends is a strong proxy for growth in earnings, and that over 50 years, the average growth in earnings should be almost the same as the average growth in dividends (even though in the short term, earnings growth often leads dividend increases).

This data is plotted in Figure 1-3. There are three growth lines shown. The squiggly dotted curve is the actual cumulative growth in dividends. It obviously varies quite a lot from year to year, but it shows steady growth approximating a smooth curve over time. Since 1960, the cumulative growth in dividends paid by the S&P 500 is 1214%, or stated another way, $100 in dividends in 1960 would have grown to $1314 by 2011.

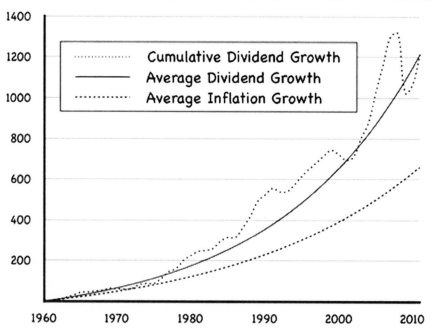

Cumulative Economic Growth 1960–2010

Figure 1-3. To arrive at a baseline for real economic growth of the S&P 500, we subtract cumulative average inflation growth rate (the dashed line) from the cumulative average dividend growth rate (solid line) to arrive at a modest 1.1% cumulative growth rate since 1960.

The solid line is a regression of the squiggly curve into a smooth one, and shows the average growth accumulation. Annualized, the average cumulative growth rate in dividends was very close to 5.2%.

The third (dashed) line shown is the cumulative average inflation (it too varied quite a lot year by year, but for this graph, I've illustrated just the smoothed average). Over time, we see dividend growth reassuringly outpacing inflation, with the annualized average inflation over these 50 years being approximately 4.1%. To get the real growth rate over this period, we subtract the cumulative inflation growth rate (dashed line) from the cumulative dividend growth rate (solid line) to arrive at a modest 1.1% real annual growth rate.

So, that is our baseline control group. America's most successful blue chip companies over the past 50 years have attained real growth averaging 1.1% annually. How does that compare with a disruptive innovator?

Apple Growth

Apple is an extreme example, but that's precisely because during the "return of Steve Jobs" era, it was a serial disruptor, bringing to market one game-changing innovation after another. A quick review:

- The iPod disrupted how we carry music and virtually killed off CDs.

- iTunes disrupted music distribution, killing off record stores and all the middlemen. By making legal copies of songs downloadable at a reasonable price to an easy-to-use integrated platform, iTunes greatly accelerated the end of CDs and other physical music recording products.

- The iPhone completely made obsolete anything that was just a cell phone, or even a "smartphone," by offering the first true handheld computer that did useful things in an easy-to-use thoroughly integrated form. Every smartphone today copies the iPhone interface to some degree—whether through a nearly identical look and feel, or due just to the general principles embodied in the iPhone. The two biggest players pre-2007, Nokia and RIM, are both on the ropes, completely disrupted by the iPhone.

- The iPad literally created the category for tablet computers, and it is rapidly disrupting desktop and notebook computer markets, as well as numerous other markets that benefit from a large format (compared to an iPhone) mobile computer you can easily take almost anywhere.

- Then, there is the revolution that Apple has created with their retail stores, not just redesigning what a store can and should be, but generating higher revenue per square foot than any other retailer anywhere.

- Finally, and least obvious, is how Apple has executed on a vision articulated by Jobs in 2007 of creating a set of products and a managing platform to support a digital lifestyle. The concept of consumer electronics products enabling a digital lifestyle is now implemented through the innovations described above,, with the Mac in its various flavors at the core of rapidly growing sales, while every other PC platform is in rapid decline.

Apple's market capitalization in 1997, when Steve Jobs returned as "interim CEO," when it was months from bankruptcy, bottomed out at $1.6 billion in July. At the time, it had approximately $1.2 billion cash on hand, therefore valuing all the assets, including products, factories, patents, and growth potential at less than $.5 billion. At the time of writing, Apple hovered around $600 billion in market cap with approximately $100 billion cash on hand, for a net value excluding cash of approximately $500 billion. That's 1,000 times greater than in 1997.[6]

At that value, Apple's P/E ratio is below 15, which is a ratio normal for a moderate-to-low-growth blue chip stock, not one of fastest growing and highest margin companies in the world. Apple could easily be valued at over $1 trillion today by the "high growth" yardstick used for many other tech companies. (Amazon, for example, on the same day as data was examined for Apple, was trading at a P/E ratio of 180, and the overall ratio for the S&P 500 is 20.8.) Apple has had such extraordinary growth that the markets don't know how to estimate and value future growth—there is no precedent for a company of Apple's size growing, and continuing to grow, at such phenomenal rates.

---

[6]In dynamic markets, it is very difficult to keep figures accurate and up-to-the minute, so rather than rewrite the story, I have added this footnote to update the figures just before publication of this book. The value of APPL fell back by nearly 40% by mid-2013 after Steve Jobs's death and with no significant new products being introduced, trading at a ridiculously low P/E ratio of around 8 (significantly lower than virtually any other blue chip stock), before a 7 for 1 stock split and significant dividend distribution was announced. With Apple Pay now available and Apple Watch expected in early 2015, the price for APPL has fully recovered and is again trading at near all-time highs for a total market cap of about $625 billion, nearly $200 billion more than the second largest company. At a current P/E ratio of approximately 16.5, APPL is still one of the most conservatively valued blue chip stocks. Though Apple no longer appears to be a serial disruptor, it is still a market leader with highly popular products generating extraordinary demand for new releases.

What I'm arguing is that even as the most valuable company in the world, and with the highest price ever for Apple's shares, it is still a very conservative valuation. And that is a heavily discounted P/E ratio for a company that has a compound growth rate of 158% annually over the past 15 years since Jobs returned.

Ordinary Disruptive Growth

So, let's agree that Apple is the exception. But, what's exceptional is how many times and how many different industries they disrupted. Even a single disruptive product can create remarkable growth during the period when a market is being disrupted.

In my practice, I use a tool called the Disruption Report Card to evaluate whether companies are disruptive based on their current market position and activities. Companies that the report card grades as disruptors have had a minimum annual growth rate of 40% while they are disrupting markets. Figure 1-4 illustrates the growth rate difference between the S&P 500 control group and disruptors.

Average Annual Growth Rates (%)

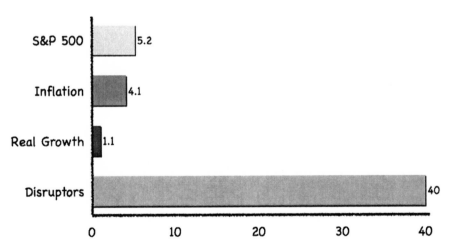

Figure 1-4. Disruptive innovators' average growth rates are more than 35 times the real cumulative growth rate of the S&P 500 since 1960. Since a large number of disruptors have been added to the index in recent years, and their exceptionally high growth rates (even as they become large companies with slowing growth, they still grow many times faster than the average) are embedded in the 1.1% cumulative real growth rate, it begs the question whether all real growth is driven by disruption.

Most actually grow faster than 100% compounded and the most successful exceed 200% and even greater multiples.

We further observe that the S&P 500 index includes many recent disruptors who, though often past their fastest growth years by the time they are added to the index, still perform at rates far above their long-established S&P index peers. That means that their growth is embedded in the growth of the overall index.

Just one example of the impact of this is Apple. *The Motley Fool* reported the analysis by Dan Sanborn of Ned Davis Research in April of 2012 that if Apple's growth was removed from the S&P 500, overall earnings growth drops from 7.8% to just 2.7%. Now imagine what would happen if Amazon, Google, Whole Foods, Salesforce.com, and few other highfliers were also removed. The impact of removing just these few strong performers is enough to flatline growth of the overall index.

And, it's even more dramatic when we look at Apple's contribution to the rise of the index itself. Since March of 2009, the increase in Apple's stock price accounts for 8% of the total increase in value of the S&P 500 index, according to Bloomberg. In earlier eras, Google, Microsoft, and Cisco had similar impacts to that which Apple is creating today.

The question it begs is whether all real growth is due to disruption. And, of course, that's why we care about building disruptive companies and products by design.

Summary

This chapter was a quick review of disruption theory, including:

- The Disruptive Innovation Model
- How to identify a disruptive innovation
- How to know that innovation is not disruptive
- Why market disruption happens
- Enabling factors that create disruptive opportunities
- How disruption is connected to economic theory
- The financial and business impact of disruption
- How disruptive innovation is a driver of growth

The purpose of this introduction was to lay the foundation for how to disrupt markets on purpose and to illustrate that although much disruptive innovation has happened by accident historically, it is a predictable phenomenon with repeating patterns that can be engineered by design.

Key Takeaways

- Disruptive innovations are powerful because they create abundance out of scarcity

- Disruptive innovation is a major, and perhaps the most important, economic driver of growth

- Disruption is not about technology (although it is often enabled by technology), but rather about the business model

- Not all innovation is disruptive; disruptive innovation is a very small subset of all the innovation and new product development undertaken

- Sustaining innovation is also necessary and important to realize the full economic benefit of disruption

In Chapter 2, we will delve deeper into the key concepts of disruption that you will later apply to design disruptive strategies for your business and its products and services.

Key Concepts of Disruption

We must learn to tailor our concepts to fit reality, instead of trying to stuff reality into our concepts.

—Victor Daniels

One of the unique things about disruption theory, when compared to alternative theories of innovation, growth, market formation, and economics, is how it originated from the study of an apparent market anomaly—a repeating narrative of small "David" startups beating large "Goliath" incumbents whose market advantages included size, money, and talent, as well as a wealth of knowledge and experience about the marketplace (i.e., their customers). In contrast with most business theories that try to "stuff reality into concepts," disruption theory is entirely derived from observing and recording the patterns that these business stories share.

The curious thing about this is that even though disruptive innovation resonates strongly as an explanation, many elements of the theory can seem counterintuitive when taken individually. The very tenets of the theory are a paradox: how can an "inferior" product consistently defeat "better" products in the market, or how can a business lacking market awareness, distribution, scale, and resources beat another that possesses all these advantages?

We know that in each instance, larger competitors appeared helpless to defend themselves, not because of incompetence but as a natural consequence of following "best practices." And, we can assume that all things being equal, the larger, well-established competitors are going to remain vulnerable precisely because they are optimized for efficiency and will continue doing what they do best. The goal, simply put, is to create the set of conditions that favor a disruptive outcome, even when doing so conflicts with intuition, conventional wisdom, and traditional business strategy.

The first chapter quickly reviewed some definitions, discussed what disruption looks like in the real world, laid out the basic theoretical framework, explained the market conditions that enable it, and finally discussed why it all matters. To move beyond simple post facto identification of disruption and use the theory to create disruptive products and companies, we need to more deeply understand the levers we can control to influence the market and increase the probability of disruption. To do that, we need to internalize the key concepts of disruption theory.

In this chapter, we dive deeper into the most important conceptual underpinnings of how disruption happens. In later sections of the book, we'll refer back to these concepts as a kind of short hand when explaining the processes and/or rationale behind the strategic approaches taken to design a business model and develop the right go-to-market plans.

The key disruptive concepts that we care about are:

- Disruptive potential versus disruptive
- Sustaining versus disruptive innovation
- Disruption Lifecycle
- Job To Be Done
- "Good enough"
- Competing against non-consumption
- Low-end versus new market disruption
- Innovation customers can use
- Exceeding market needs
- Sustainable cost advantage
- Fighting commoditization

Disruptive Potential or Disruptive?

To date, market disruption is a relatively rare event. Yet, listening to the media and to the numerous conference organizers sniffing opportunity, you'd think disruption was happening everywhere all the time, and that every innovator was disruptive. If you want to be successful at this, ignore the hype and don't believe your own press.

Since the intent is to help companies and products be disruptive, it's important to be more precise and differentiate between possessing disruptive potential and being a disruptive innovator. You aren't a disruptive innovator until you've actually disrupted a market, or until market disruption is well underway. That's the minimum criteria to wear the label.

To actually fit the theory you need to satisfy many more attributes. If it's clear that your strategy exhibits all or most of the identifying points of the "disruption fingerprint," and the key concepts described in this chapter are part of your product and market plans, then you have disruptive potential.

In particular, the concept of a "job to be done" is critical (see the high-level overview below, and full discussion in Chapter 4), and it must clearly be a job that the market is willing to pay for and that you either uniquely solve or have significant advantages over alternatives that make you the preferred choice. Until you have proof of that, it's best not to say the word disruptive outside of your company or in investor circles.

The paradox in claiming to be a disruptor is that it's a lot like being in high school and claiming to be "cool." The more you claim it, the less likely it is to be true. Remember that disruptive innovation is not a customer benefit or value. It doesn't solve any problem that the customer/market has. As a startup and/or potential disruptor, all your energy needs to be directed to meeting un-served or under-served needs and identifying jobs for which you are the preferred candidate for hire. If you do this, you still might not be disruptive, but you're a lot more likely to be successful.

Frankly, if you are asked, it's far better to say you have disruptive potential or that you're trying to embed the principles of disruption into your go-to-market strategy than to claim you are disruptive. Let others make that judgment and focus on your vision for the market.

For our purposes, we do care about whether you have disruptive potential (that's what this book is about, after all), but that discussion should be one that stays inside the boardroom and among the key executives determining product and market strategy.

I won't name names to make examples of anyone, but suffice it to say that the disease has spread worse than a virus through Silicon Valley. Virtually everyone who claims their company is disruptive a) doesn't even have a product yet, let alone customers, b) has little to no chance of disrupting any market, c) doesn't conform to the patterns of disruption theory in any way, and d) has greater than an 80% probability of failing in the market outright, because they aren't focused on the right things. In other words, they aren't even a little bit disruptive.

Save yourself the embarrassment, and let others make disruptive claims on your behalf.

Sustaining versus Disruptive Innovation

The theoretical difference between a sustaining and disruptive innovation was covered in the first chapter, but there are important subtleties that you need to understand. Technically, once your product is in the market and successfully gaining users, every enhancement after that point is sustaining. But, that *doesn't* mean that:

- You've disrupted a market yet, and therefore have a disruptive innovation on your hands

- Subsequent innovations can't continue the process of disruption; in fact, they may be necessary before disruption can occur

- You don't need sustaining innovations to expand the market for your product and secure the early wins you've made

Recall that the purpose of a sustaining innovation is to better serve existing customers or enable higher-end uses. They can also make your product "good enough" (as defined below) for adjacent market spaces through additional features, better quality and reliability, and so on, thus disrupting a new market niche.

This leads to two important ideas:

- Disruption is not a singular event, but a process. I like to think of a "Disruption Lifecycle" that includes both disruptive and sustaining innovations. This key concept is further described later in this chapter.

- An innovation can be simultaneously disruptive and sustaining. That's because disruptive and sustaining are both relative terms—disruptive is relative to the market that's being attacked, while sustaining is self-referential and relates only to the path of innovation that your product or category of direct competitors is on. This highlights the importance of positioning strategy (discussed in detail in Chapter 6).

The Disruption Lifecycle

Market disruption is not a singular event, but rather disruption has a lifecycle that is important to recognize so that we approach strategy properly. The *Disruption Lifecycle* is a natural extension to disruption theory that accounts for the following issues:

- Disruption can only be judged in the rear view mirror with certainty. Until a market has been disrupted, the best we can do is evaluate whether a product and related business strategy match the disruption fingerprint. Based on that, we can predict the likelihood that a potentially disruptive innovator will succeed (that is, the probability of market disruption).

- There are definite stages that a potential disruptor must go through to become disruptive.

- It may take several sustaining innovations to a product after its initial release before it becomes good enough to disrupt mainstream markets.

- A single product may disrupt multiple markets over a period of several years as new sustaining innovations (relative to the original target market) make the product good enough to compete for alternative jobs to be done (see "Job To Be Done," next).

- Execution is critical to cementing a market hold and maintaining it as the new incumbent. In fact, disruption is completed only when the innovator becomes the dominant incumbent in enough mainstream segments that it becomes the clear market leader.

Market disruption is not an explosion that immediately kills off competitors, nor is it a successful launch, nor is it the point in time when a startup discovers the right business model to drive the company forward. In fact, there is no precise time when something happens that disrupts a market, because it is a process that occurs over time, and therefore has a beginning, middle, and end. In other words, it is a lifecycle.

Although it is impossible to pinpoint an exact time of disruption, there is a point when disruption becomes inevitable, a tipping point past which we can say that disruption has occurred. However, that tipping point isn't always obvious at the time, and there is no guarantee that a potential disruptor will not make mistakes that enable a challenger to take their place. Typically this point of inevitability occurs when the market-leading disruptor is approaching a 20% share of the target market and is in a rapid growth phase (typically 50% per year or faster growth). The end point for a successful disruptor is usually between 40% and 80% share of the total available market.

Diffusion of Innovations

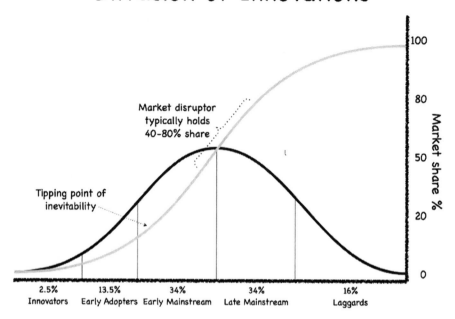

Figure 2-1. Everett Rogers described the path by which any innovation is absorbed and adopted into a market. Disruptive innovations follow the same general cycle, but start with tightly matched JTBDs and "must have" target segments, spiraling out in waves to users with similar desired outcomes and eventually to broader market segments. The reason the pattern unfolds this way is detailed in Chapters 4 and 5.

The Disruption Lifecycle begins with the familiar Diffusion of Innovations graph by Everett Rogers, which illustrates the overall pattern by which any technology is adopted and absorbed. Within that pattern, each version of the product that is "good enough" (often after multiple staged steps of sustaining innovations) to target a new micro-segment of consumers spirals outward from the initial group of users whose JTBD exactly matches the top outcomes delivered by the product (so called "must have" users) to broader groups of users with similar requirements and adjacent segments, and eventually similar, but not exactly matched, JTBDs. There may be five or six of these tightly wound spirals just to get through the Innovators and Early Adopters phases before the product becomes good enough for broader segments of mainstream users.

Job To Be Done

The "Job To Be Done"[1] is often considered the most important indicator and predictor of market disruption. This is partially correct. First, let's look at what it means and why it's important.

The phrase "Job To Be Done" (JTBD) is derived from a metaphor that likens the decision process used by a buyer to the process a hiring manager uses to hire a candidate for a job. How is choosing a product or service similar to hiring a job candidate?

The first condition to hire someone—and so obvious it's easy to overlook—is that there is a job opening to fill. Or, turned around, if you don't have something you need to get done, you won't hire anyone.

The second condition is that the situation determines what type of candidate is qualified for the position. For example, assume that you have a job posting for a new marketing director. Now, imagine three different scenarios:

- A new product has been developed for which there is no marketing support. The job will include identifying the right segments to target, positioning the product appropriately, developing core messaging, and hiring and managing a team to promote the product and support a direct field sales team.

- You are filling a recent vacancy created when the previous marketing director was fired. As you are drafting the job description, you realize that there is an opportunity to grow sales internationally.

---

[1]The phrase "job to be done" comes from the outcome-driven innovation (ODI) methodology developed by Strategyn Inc., which is described in detail in the book *What Customers Want* by Anthony Ulwick, Strategyn's founder and CEO. This work was also referenced by Clayton Christensen in his second book, *The Innovator's Solution*.

The key observation and insight behind the methodology is that customers buy things because they want to accomplish a specific goal or set of goals. That is, they have a "job to get done." Needs are the metrics by which customers judge suitability for a particular job and success in accomplishing it, but it is the job that is the core driver of purchase decisions, not the needs.

The idea of a job to be done is universal—all products, services, and solutions are ultimately "hired" to do jobs, whether the companies selling these products are aware of these drivers or not. Although it is true that all companies and products benefit from understanding the outcomes desired by the customer (jobs they want to accomplish), it is absolutely critical to the introduction of disruptive innovations.

Even when discovered by accident, as is often the case, identifying the job(s) to be done that are both high value and currently un-served or under-served by existing products is necessary for potentially disruptive innovations to gain a foothold in the market from which they can grow to become disruptive.

- You are increasing the marketing support for an existing product, and the primary driver in searching for a new marketing director is to take responsibility for building a presence in a new vertical industry segment.

Although the job title is the same for each of these situations, the qualifications and desired experience will be different in each case. In one case, you'll want demonstrated ability to build a team from scratch and think creatively and opportunistically about how to address the marketplace. In the second instance, fit with the existing team and culture will be critical, along with experience building markets in different countries. In the third case, you're going to want someone with specific experience and deep knowledge of the industry vertical that you're targeting.

Only in very rare instances would the same person be the ideal candidate for more than one of these situations. And the more variables we add to the decision—the company is for example a startup or *Fortune* 500, the product requires technical knowledge or is a purely nontechnical consumable, the budget is low versus whatever it takes to get the candidate you want, and so forth—the more the candidate must precisely match the job specification.

The key observation is that it is the situation that defines the right candidate for the job, not the category of person. It's exactly the same when looking for a product:

- You must have a job that you need the product for, or you won't buy it.

- The reason you need the product (situation and context) determines which product is the best match for the job.

Simply, you aren't going to "hire" a product unless you have a job that it's needed for. The product category is irrelevant, but the situational context in which it will be applied and the customer's desired outcome is crucial.

This idea turns traditional marketing and business strategy on its ear, changing how you approach everything from segmentation to positioning to messaging to business model development to distribution—absolutely everything is impacted. This metaphor and its implications are fully developed in Chapter 4, and how it impacts marketing strategy and the business model is discussed in Chapters 5 through 9.

Paraphrasing Theodore Levitt, the consumer doesn't want a quarter-inch drill bit, they want a quarter-inch hole. All product creators need to understand what the quarter-inch hole is for their product and why the customer wants it.

> **Tip** Marketing master Theodore Levitt tells us that customers don't want a quarter-inch drill bit; they want a quarter-inch hole. Most of us are accustomed to thinking in terms of customer needs; however, it can be surprisingly difficult to identify the jobs that customers are trying to get done with your product, especially without the right methods to capture and express these critical insights. How would you define the "quarter-inch holes" customers want from your product or business? Ask others to do the same and compare notes. Do you consistently describe the same JTBDs?

As noted, the JTBD is often considered the most important indicator or predictor of disruption. But we know that all products are hired for jobs, so simply being the best alternative to a job is not sufficient to predict market disruption.

Disruptive innovations provide alternative solutions that are not only better matched to the situation than the competition, but which also offer significant advantages that bring non-consumers to the table, such as a sustainable price advantage, simplicity and ease of use, or convenience. Disruptive innovations need to create abundance from scarcity and resemble the disruption finger-print described in Chapter 1.

In other words, the JTBD must be supported by other game-changing attributes. It should be used to focus the business model, market segmenta-tion, promotions, positioning, and other elements of marketing strategy for disruption to take root. One of the key takeaways from this book should be how you apply those concepts based on the JTBD to create a disruptive opportunity.

Being "Good Enough"

When a disruptive innovation comes to market, it is often dismissed by incum-bents as inferior, or derogatorily referred to as a toy. This is particularly true of low-end disruptive innovations.

Yet for any product to be disruptive, it must be "good enough" to satisfy the requirements of low-end consumers who are over-served by the currently available choices, and/or of non-consumers who are excluded from the cur-rent market because of price, complexity, required expertise, or other factors that restrict access.

In the "lean startup" approach to innovation, the concept of being good enough is the rough equivalent of the MVP, or minimum viable product. However, it is also more than that. As products evolve by adding performance charac-teristics, they become good enough to address larger subsets of the overall marketplace. If they do so while retaining a cost advantage (or another of the strategic advantages that expand markets), and better target the job to be done, then they will continue to disrupt new market segments and eventually displace incumbents in all categories except those serving customers with the most demanding performance requirements.

How do you know if a product is good enough? That's always up to the user, but it is much easier to tell when you're competing against non-consumption because anything at all is better than nothing if the price is right.

But ultimately, if you understand the situations where your product could be used and who would get the most economic gain, you can have a pretty good idea how much is good enough. In other words, if you've captured the right JTBDs for your market and properly prioritized them, "good enough" should be staring you in the face.

Being good enough to be a viable substitute or replacement for alternatives, or meeting the minimum requirement to target the key JTBD, is what we mean when we say "good enough" in this book. Most of the time, the existing marketplace will judge a good enough product to be inferior in key ways (at initial market entry), but in at least one important way, it exceeds the capability of incumbent solutions for the target user and JTBD.

Importantly, it is much easier today than it has ever been—because of the ability to quickly and inexpensively build Internet "apps" and release fast mini-products where you can get early users to try the product—to test and validate whether you've reached the "good enough" condition that enables the process of disruption to commence.

Competing Against Non-Consumption

When most companies enter markets, they look at conventional definitions of product categories. They target demographics rather than JTBDs, and/or they compete based on product features. As a result, they either copy existing players, or they add features based on the researched preferences of the presumed average consumer in the target demographic.

This competition against other players in a defined product category is competition for the existing consumers in a market, and it is the sort of competition that does not increase the size of the pie, but rather increases the number of players wanting a slice of the same pie. This is the opposite of what a disruptive innovator needs to do.

This "competing against consumption" usually favors the dominant incumbent, although it hurts everyone. What disruptors need to do is to compete against non-consumption and increase the size of the pie.

For every need that a product addresses, there are consumers who are left out of the market. The biggest reason is often cost—incumbent products are simply too expensive for low-end applications. Those potential consumers choose to do things manually or find awkward workarounds to accomplish the job they need done.

Note   Disruptors cannot effectively compete against incumbents on their terms. The rules of the existing market favor the current leaders—from control of channels to price to awareness to production volumes (and the lower cost that comes with them)—there are many, many barriers to market entry. The best strategy for a potential disruptor is to identify the non-consumers—all those who don't participate in the existing market—and understand why they don't participate. What's missing from incumbent solutions? Are they too expensive? Do they require specialized expertise? Are they too hard to source? Your best bet: Solve one or more of these problems and target the customers that incumbents can't or won't. Initially, you shouldn't even try to compete head-on for the market leaders' core customers. Along the way, you will create new market rules that make it hard for incumbents to compete with you.

But cost isn't the only reason. Products can be too difficult to use, require specialized expertise to operate, be available only through controlled distribution networks, impose technical blocks such as "digital rights management" (DRM), or possess a variety of other attributes that limit accessibility and shrink the market.

Products that target these users—the ones unable to participate in the existing marketplace—are said to compete against non-consumption. The advantage to the disruptor is that this is virgin market that incumbents are unable or unwilling to address.

Low-End versus New Market Disruption

I discussed the definitions for low-end and new-market disruption in the first chapter, but it's important to remember that the driver for each type is different and that the strategy needs to be different as well.

Low-end disruptions typically are driven by low-cost, inferior products (inferior relative to the performance dimensions valued by the existing market). New-market disruptions primarily are targeted at new segments (as defined by the JTBD) that are unserved by incumbent products. Disruptive innovations can be both low-end and new-market simultaneously, and these types tend to have the strongest market impact.

Innovation Customers Can Use

Innovators often fail to appreciate that a lot of innovation, especially in incumbent markets characterized by sustaining innovations, is unusable. Consumers simply can't keep up with the pace of innovation, and often never discover that many features even exist let alone learn to use them. For instance, it's estimated that more than 90% of the functionality in Microsoft Word is never touched by the average user, even when it would be useful. Only a very few experts know what most of the features are and how to use them.

When this happens, increased production costs can't be recovered by increased sales or premium prices; there is no improvement in differentiation that changes customer preferences, and profits narrow. For most people, the only reason to "upgrade" MS Office is to get the latest security updates, but this feels like hygiene, not a motivation to keep paying again and again for little to no new value.

■ **Tip** Innovations that customers don't use are a sure symptom of an engineering-led, inwardly focused organization that decides for customers what they need and what is best for them. Innovation that customers can't use is also usually a sign of a mature market where the majority of customer needs are over-served by all incumbent solutions. Disruptors avoid this problem by focusing their attention on high-value unmet or under-served JTBDs and targeting non-consumers. If all the possible JTBDs are adequately served and customers are satisfied with the performance of existing products, you're best to look for a different market to try to disrupt. Avoid the temptation to build innovations that are simply bells and whistles and don't improve the ability of users to accomplish their goals.

Thus, the concept of innovation that customers can use is critical, and it ties to the job the customer is trying to get done. In other words, when sustaining innovation targets deficiencies relative to the JTBD, it is innovation that customers can use. When we see previous disruptors failing badly in the market (Blackberry comes to mind), it is often because they are focused on innovation that customers don't want and can't use relative to the job to be done.

Exceeding Market Needs

The opposing concept to innovation that customers can use is that of exceeding market needs. This relates to the diagram illustrating the disruptive innovation model (shown again in Figure 2-2).

Disruptive Innovation Model

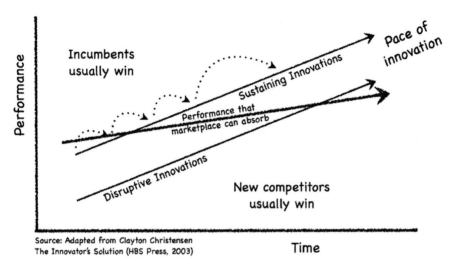

Source: Adapted from Clayton Christensen
The Innovator's Solution (HBS Press, 2003)

Figure 2-2. Although every market segment has a different line representing the performance that the customers in that marketplace can absorb, and therefore a different intersection with the pace of innovation line, eventually all consumers, even the so-called "power users," are over-served by all products in the market. After these lines intersect, all sustaining innovations will exceed market needs, and the only way to reinvigorate the market—to build new value and grow profits—is to introduce new disruptive innovations.

The line that is closest to flat represents the rate at which customers can absorb innovation. Typically, innovators create and introduce innovation at a much faster rate than the market is able to absorb it. When the lines intersect, this represents the maximum innovation that consumers are able to use in a given market segment, and past that point, all innovation exceeds market needs (even though the performance that customers can use also keeps increasing).

The important thing to remember is that this point is eventually reached for all products, but it can be deferred the longest if innovation is focused on the core JTBDs.

Sustainable Cost Advantage

Low-end disruptive innovations are generally characterized by pricing significantly below incumbent alternatives. Although disruption theory as originally described by Christensen et al. discusses the impact of price, low price alone is not a viable strategy in the long term. Competitors can easily match low prices if their products and costs are comparable, thus leading to price wars, which are usually lose-lose propositions.

A low-price strategy is therefore extremely difficult to sustain and the easiest disruption for incumbents to counter, *unless* your innovation of process or technology gives you a sustainable cost-of-production advantage, and hopefully, one that's patentable. If you have a sustainable cost advantage of 2-3 times or more, then low-end disruption is very defensible, and aiming for the lowest price that you can afford will almost always disrupt markets if you are satisfying a JTBD better than the alternatives.

This is why so many online software/services offerings are offered as freemium solutions—if you can offer something valuable for free and make money with upgrades or services, it can protect your market space from encroachment when it makes it difficult for alternative solutions to gain a foothold and sell anything profitably.

However, the important point to remember is that your cost advantage needs to be sustainable, at least for the medium- if not long-term. Once you face direct competition from larger incumbents, you'll find they are well-resourced and have deeper pockets. If they can match you on price, you're unlikely to disrupt them, and you will likely go bankrupt before they are seriously hurt.

Fighting Commoditization

Commoditization happens when multiple product offerings are undifferentiated in the consumer's mind based on their ability to perform the job that the customer wants to do. This doesn't mean that the products in a category aren't different, but that there is no perceived added value in choosing one versus another.

Commodity purchase decisions are made almost entirely on price and availability, and therefore commodities have very low sales margins. In fact, "low sales margin" and "commodity" are almost synonymous in most people's minds for this reason.

Fighting commoditization is a generic concern of business, and not specifically a "disruptive concept." However, disruptive innovation—innovation focused on a unique JTBD that people are willing to pay for—is the best way to fight commoditization. So much so that when we refer to fighting commoditization, what we mean in this text is coming up with innovations that have disruptive potential.

The key to this is again focusing on the JTBD as the basis for differentiation. Differentiation that focuses on attributes that help the customer do the job better—rather than on having the most features, or creating features that are different just to be different, and which the customer doesn't value—means that at the point of decision there is a preference for your product, regardless of its price. Price then becomes a concern only if it is too high relative to the "reference price." (See Chapter 7 for explanation and discussion of the reference price concept.)

Summary

This chapter completes a quick review of what disruptive innovation is with a deeper dive into some of the key conceptual underpinnings of the theory.

The goal has been to provide readers with a primer (for those unfamiliar with the constructs of the theory) or a refresher focused on the important reproducible elements that we hope to create on purpose.

Key Takeaways

- No single factor indicates market disruption in process. Disruptive innovation is the result of a complex interplay of several factors and market conditions.

- Identifying high-value jobs that the customer needs to do that are under-served in the current market, and have the potential to create new markets to compete against non-consumption, is the most important beginning point for any company that wishes to create a disruptive innovation.

Chapter 3 will conclude the foundation needed for the balance of this book by examining how to apply the theory (Chapter 1) and key concepts (Chapter 2) to create a predictive model that allows us to identify the products most likely to be disruptive.

Does Your Idea Have Disruptive Potential?

Probable impossibilities are to be preferred to improbable possibilities.

—Aristotle

Logically, disruptive innovation shouldn't be possible.

Think about it: A small, underfunded startup with ideas that one or more larger companies reject as being inferior or having too small a market to care about comes from nowhere to upset the old order. Once a disruption has taken hold, the larger, established company—with ready access to billions of dollars, thousands of people, world-class research teams, control of distribution channels, and immense marketing resources—is unable to fight back while the disruptor takes control of the market and becomes the new dominant incumbent.

Yet, Aristotle understood that the impossible often happens—we simply need to know how probable it is and place our bets accordingly (quite literally if you are an investor in disruptive innovation or a hopeful disruptive innovator).

It's time now to conclude the fundamentals of disruption theory by taking the principles of the first two chapters, including:

- Christensen's model describing the market disruption process
- Disruption fingerprint analysis, and
- The key concepts of disruptive innovation

to learn how to make accurate predictions about the likelihood that a product, service, or business model has disruptive potential and how to identify the key factors that increase or decrease the probability of disruption (disruptive strengths and weaknesses).

Importantly, even with the best technology, a breakthrough product, rave reviews, or a previous track record of success by the inventor(s), disruption is not a certainty. (Those conditions may actually lead more probably to the opposite outcome of market failure.) That's because none of those factors are directly relevant.

For example, the track record of the founding team only influences one attribute affecting the probability of disruption—namely the likelihood of strong execution. But, this only matters if the product has disruptive potential to begin with.

Why Predict Disruption?

I discussed in Chapter 1 the economic value of disruption and its financial impact, both on the innovator and on the market incumbents who are disrupted. In that analysis, I showed how disruptive innovators grow faster, dominate their markets, eventually own the largest market share, generate the largest profits, and therefore command the highest valuations.

The predictive power of correctly assessing the probability of disruption occurring, or that a company or product has disruptive potential, is therefore enormous. Predictive assessments can be used to:

- Plan strategy, finance, marketing, business model, and product decisions as well as determine which investments to make and how large they should be (startup founders, board, and advisors).
- Adjust strategy to compensate for elements of the business model or product strategy that aren't disruptive (management team and founders).

- Determine investment strategy—when to go long or to sell companies in your portfolio or when the business needs strategic assistance to create disruption (investors and VCs).

- Understand the best strategy to defend your turf and remain relevant (companies facing market disruption).

Making Predictions

The reason I have given the subject of predicting disruption its own chapter and made it a major focus, is that many maintain that disruption is not predictable, and that it can only be observed after the fact. Given the economic importance of disruptive innovations, that would be a sad conclusion. Fortunately, the naysayers are wrong, and that makes this subject worthy of further exploration.

In asserting that disruption is not predictable, they are saying two things. First, that they don't understand (or possibly aren't convinced by) the model of disruptive innovation. Second, like most people, they don't appreciate the difference between a probable outcome based on a predictive model and an assertion of fact.

But, if we can't predict disruption and use the theory to become more effective at innovation, then the theory would have little practical value outside of taxonomy, and classifying types of innovation to be studied and catalogued.

Note Contrary to the opinions of skeptics and some pundits, market disruption *is* predictable. In fact, the primary value of disruption theory is in its power to predict when disruptive innovations are likely. This chapter—and book—shows how and why.

I'm going to ask you to suspend disbelief about the disruptive innovation model a little while longer (assuming that you believe it to be an accurate representation of how disruption happens, or you wouldn't still be reading this book), and to consider later how we use it to affect the outcomes we desire. However, I want to consider the notion of probability just a little bit here, so that our goals are clear.

Not Just Possible, Highly Probable

While this will be obvious to anyone who works in the fields of statistics, actuarial science, econometrics, or even in the gambling industry, it bears repeating because creating disruption by design is an exercise in maximizing probability. Our goal is to create conditions that increase the likelihood of disruptive success, not to promise that you will be disruptive if you follow this guide.

This matters because predictions often end up being incorrect when the assumptions they are based on turn out to be wrong or change. When a prediction is wrong, it doesn't invalidate the model—in fact, the model predicts that unlikely outcomes will happen sometimes. You will find at times that execution of a disruptive model is counterintuitive, and that it is hard to stay the course because peers, investors, and even your own shoulder homunculus tell you it can't work. That's when you need to believe in the model and cast your bets.

Put another way, if there is a 90% probability that a particular outcome will occur, then 10 times in 100, it will not occur. Even though I suspect that most entrepreneurs are mathematically inclined enough to understand this, it's also true that entrepreneurs tend to be optimists with high levels of confidence in their own abilities and assessments of market opportunities. After all, with a startup failure rate exceeding 95%, if you based the decision to be an entrepreneur strictly on probability, no new companies would ever be started.

While we lack certainty regarding disrupting markets, the good news is that there is a very high degree of predictability when you have accurately modeled the contributing factors that influence it—much higher in fact than anyone's ability to predict the success of any particular startup. But even creating the perfect scenario for disruption, there are still many factors we cannot control. For example, something as simple as a startup with high disruptive potential deciding to accept a buyout offer from an incumbent can thwart disruption.

Other mostly uncontrollable factors that we know can influence the outcome include economic externalities, government interference, legal issues, emerging technologies, competitive actions, access to financing, the management team, network effects, and market ecosystems. So, the strongest statement we can make reads something like "90% of the time, when these conditions exist, this outcome occurs, and here are the variables that could cause it not to occur." It's sort of like predicting elections, or the likelihood that your next child will have red hair, or the direction of the stock market. You must always keep in mind the disclaimer—"past performance is not a *guarantee* of future results."

But Don't Worry About Lack of Certainty

Although I could belabor this point at length, I'll continue now with the framework used to identify and predict disruptive opportunity, but with the caveat that whenever I say "do x and y will happen," I am not stating a fact, but rather making a prediction that has an associated degree of uncertainty. If you are interested in a more in-depth discussion of how probability is used to make predictions, I suggest you watch this video where Nate Silver discusses modeling of sports and elections at a Google event.[1]

On a continuum, disruptive innovation is much more predictable than sports, somewhat less predictable than poker, and a bit less predictable than elections.

Methodology for Making Disruptive Predictions

The following steps outline the general methods we use to make disruptive predictions.

Validate Existence of an Addressable Market Scarcity

As I noted in Chapter 1, disruption is caused by the radical distortion of the supply and demand curve that occurs when abundance replaces scarcity. If there is no market scarcity, or you lack technology or processes to mitigate it, then disruption cannot occur.

To validate scarcity, look for market behaviors that indicate a shortage of something. Are prices too high? Is an entire industry characterized by bad service and the constant drone of customer complaints? Are available products difficult to acquire or hard to use, pushing consumers to use nothing or substitute less than adequate solutions? Now ask whether the solution, business model, or new technology that you imagine can address the scarcity, and write down how.

If the answer to this requirement is "no" or "there isn't one," then there's no need to proceed any further, as you already know that the probability of disruptive potential is near zero.

---

[1] http://youtu.be/mYIgSq-ZWEO. See also Billy Beane and *Moneyball* at http://youtu.be/-4QPVoOUIzc.

Assess the Job To Be Done

Assuming that you have identified an addressable market scarcity, you next need to assess and accurately encapsulate the JTBD. To do this, we need to understand

- The function of the product

- Who its intended user is

- How the user will apply it to uniquely solve a problem (address an unmet or underserved need)

All of these feed into the core reason the purchaser decides to choose our product.

Let's use the iPod as an example. Its function was to store digitized music in the form of MP3 files, making access and playback intuitive and trivial. The intended users were unsophisticated (non-technical) consumers who wanted portable music—the mass market. The unmet need was to be able to carry a sizable portion of their music collection (if not all of it) with them everywhere without requiring physical media such as tapes or CDs.

The JTBD was enabling an element of consumer digital lifestyle in a music player making it simple and elegant for average people—or, as Steve Jobs put it at the introduction—and how consumers might say it—"carry my entire music collection in my pocket."

Unspoken, but equally important, was the fashion aspect of the iPod as a signal that its user was a cool style leader. (The physical design of the product embedded a key part of its job to be done, and was part of the support for a high price point.)

For our purposes here, this is a radical simplification of how jobs the consumer is trying to get done are assessed. I deal with this critical step in depth in subsequent chapters, especially in Chapter 4, "What Should My Product Do?" In retrospect, it may seem trivially simple to describe what jobs a product like the iPod is designed to accomplish; however, capturing the right core jobs and knowing whether they have disruptive potential is far from obvious at the time the product is being specified and designed.

If you have difficulty believing this, ask yourself the question, "if the iPod was disruptive, why were the various MP3 players that preceded it to market not disruptive?" If it was obvious at the time, others would have already satisfied the job consumers wanted to hire a digital player for, and Apple would not have enjoyed the absolute market dominance that they did.

What we care about most in evaluating the JTBD is whether by serving a different set of needs, the product requires discontinuity. Although the initial quality and compression of digital music files was substantially inferior to CD-based music, there was certainly no way you could have accomplished the goal of carrying your music collection in your pocket using CDs or any prior platform.

Tip   All products are "hired" to do jobs. Disruptive products make it easy to accomplish jobs that are poorly served by incumbents, and tend to be much closer matches for what the consumer actually wants to get done. By accomplishing this, they create abundance from scarcity. It's not about breakthrough technology or having an "insanely great" product. It's about what business has always been about—solving a problem or addressing an unmet need. Strive to understand deeply the jobs your customer is trying to get done and especially the jobs they struggle to accomplish.

Is the Product Viewed as Inferior by Incumbents in the Market (or Likely to Be)?

The marketplace as it exists has many embedded assumptions about quality and what consumers value. Products that disrupt are often viewed with disdain or as inferior by the incumbents. If you're lucky, competitors will dismissively view you as irrelevant (not even in the same market).

When the iPod was introduced, CDs were still king, and portable CD players were how music was played on the go. MP3 players existed, but the category was very small and mostly dismissed as irrelevant because they were hard to use, played poor-quality sound because of very high compression rates and poor CODECs (compression/decompression algorithms), and were mostly used by techies who knew how to "rip" CDs and get them from their computer to the player.

Moreover, the music industry viewed consumers of these players with contempt, taking the view that they were "pirating" music (in many cases, users did download songs which they hadn't paid for from sites like Napster because the music industry refused to make digital copies available).

Although Apple's iPod was superior in many ways to existing digital music players, it was clearly viewed by the market incumbents as being in the "inferior" camp—another MP3 player that didn't sound as good as real CDs.

Primary Segment Targeted

Referring again to the disruption fingerprint, the best segments for initial market entry by a disruptor are considered undesirable by incumbents. This can be because the market is:

- Low-end/poor (consumers with little money to spend)
- Low margin
- Needs are overshot by the minimum, cheapest product offered, so they mostly don't participate in the existing market
- Small niche (and/or low to moderate growth potential)
- Lacking skills/expertise to use product
- Comprised of non-participants in existing market

On most of these measures, the iPod would not score well as a disruptor. However, at the time of introduction, the MP3 player market was miniscule compared with the CD market, and those who ripped CDs or downloaded music from Napster were viewed suspiciously at best, and as outlaws/lawbreaking pirates at worst.

Consequently, most makers of CD players (the incumbents) viewed MP3 players as an undesirable market. Sony had an entrant in this market, but never invested in it, nor was able to make it successful, probably because of internal politics viewing CD players as the real market.

Are There Unmet or Underserved Needs that Incumbents Can't Address?

When targeting a disruptive innovation, it's important that in addition to the "disadvantages" (the attributes that incumbents would judge as inferior), there are benefits that they are unable to provide without changing their technology platform or business model. This increases the likelihood of being ignored by incumbents while giving the disruptor a clear differentiation. These unmet needs are often (or should be) directly related to the core JTBD.

In the case of the iPod, clearly it would be difficult, if not impossible, to take more than a couple of CDs with you for portable use, and many users of portable CD players, such as joggers or people working out at the gym, might carry just one CD with them. MP3 players also had the advantage of not skipping due to physical stress (jumping up and down, running, or getting bumped).

Carrying your music collection in your pocket was definitely an unmet need of the market, and one that the incumbents could not address with the old technology.

Importantly, this unmet need is almost always paired with a seemingly insurmountable problem (inferior attribute), so in the case of the iPod at the time it was introduced, it was not easy for the average consumer to load MP3 players with music, nor were there readily accessible sources of legally downloadable music. In fact, the music industry had just finished their collective assault on the popular file-sharing site, Napster, and had succeeded in shutting it down. That would have appeared an insurmountable problem to incumbents, as well as appearing like an unattractive market to sell to.

So, although there was a definite trend toward digital music and players, this did not look like a mainstream market to the incumbents and they stayed out. Of course, with the introduction of iTunes and later the ability to legally download virtually any song you wanted for 99 cents, that changed, but it was too late for the previous incumbents to catch Apple's "music collection in your pocket."

Pricing

In general, the price must be below the market "reference price"[2] for a product to become disruptive. In practice, the disruptor needs to have at least a two to three times price advantage and a sustainable cost-of-production advantage that enables them to maintain a below-market price over the established players.

---

[2]The *reference price* is how much consumers expect to pay for a product in relation to other competitors and the previously advertised price.

When making buying decisions, especially when considering a replacement or substitute for their usual alternative, consumers assess value by comparing the price of the good with an "internal reference price": namely, the price that they would usually expect to pay or what they think the product is "worth," using all previous data.

Much research and analysis has been done to understand how the reference price is established by the buyer, with the best estimate being a narrow range of prices around a perceived median price. Everything with a cost higher than the reference price is perceived to be relatively high priced (expensive), and everything below the reference price is perceived to be relatively low-priced (inexpensive). The reference price for different individuals may be different depending on their awareness of alternatives and how frequently they buy goods in a particular category.

The reference price, how it is established, and how the consumer perceives value, quality, ease-of-use, and various other attributes are critical to establishing price for a disruptive innovation, so we will address this concept in much more detail in the pricing chapter of this book.

The probability of disruption increases as the price advantage increases such that an order-of-magnitude price differential (incumbent price = 10 x disruptor's price) virtually guarantees that the innovator will disrupt the market if their product is "good enough."

In absolute terms, the iPod did not have a significant price advantage over portable DVD players. In fact, by the time iPods were introduced at $399, CD players had dropped in price to a range of $50 to $75.

The brilliance of Apple's positioning was in talking about the price advantage per song versus the price advantage for the machine. So, while the iPod was five to six times more expensive than a portable DVD player, the cost of the machine per song it could contain was $5 on a CD player versus $0.40 on an iPod.[3]

By changing the point of reference, Jobs not only was able to demonstrate a greater than 10 times price advantage, he also drove home the primary value proposition of 1,000 songs in your pocket.

■ **Note** A substantial and sustainable cost-of-production advantage, which enables lower pricing versus incumbents, almost always results in market disruption. It is possible, but rare, for more expensive products to be disruptive, and it most often happens when the new platform has a different feature set that more closely targets the core JTBD, or when the price comparison can be shifted to a different unit of measurement, as Apple did with the iPod.

Such a strategy doesn't always work (shifting attention to a different unit of measure), but in this case the other benefits were so strong that it worked. (We would not have initially given the iPod a great score on price as a disruptive factor, but Steve's sleight of hand was once again effective.)

Outsider to the Industry

Particularly with new-market disruptive innovations, disruption comes from outside the industry. This seems to happen about 90% of the time, although it isn't a universal truth.

---

[3]This book can't do justice to the brilliance of Steve Jobs' product positioning and his skill in first establishing what competition he wants you to compare his products to, and then showing his pricing strategy most effectively. We recommend readers view the keynote address where Jobs introduced the iPod (http://youtu.be/Mc_FiHTITHE), and in fact, all the keynote addresses where Jobs introduced new Apple products. The iPad introduction begins at approximately 11:30 of this video clip, and the price positioning begins at approximately 13:18.

There are several reasons why, but one of the most powerful is that disruptive innovations often require alternative distribution channels that otherwise upset the ecosystem of partners, suppliers, retailers, and distributors that incumbents all depend on. Often, that's because the new product doesn't require these intermediaries and/or because it gets its price advantage by going around them and passing the savings directly to the consumer.

It's also the case that incumbents are busy competing with each other on features and price, offering products that exceed that market's needs. New market disruptors often come to market with radically different technology or solutions to accomplish the same end, while low-end disruptors target the customers whose needs are simpler, and who won't pay or can't afford the higher prices charged by incumbents.

In all of these cases, disruption favors the industry outsider, so when scoring probability of disruption, we add some weight to the score if you're an outsider, and reduce the grade somewhat more if you are an insider.

Again, using our iPod example, Apple was an outsider to both the music industry and to the consumer electronics industry. As an outsider, they viewed the business differently than the incumbents and played by different rules.

Apple, for example, focused on music portability (1,000 songs in your pocket), and cared much less about quality of sound. CDs clearly sounded much better, but the inconvenience of carrying around all that physical media made it easier for teens and 20-somethings, and their comfort with digital media made it easy for them to trade off quality for usability.

Use, or Doesn't Use, Existing Channels

As described previously, the disruptor will typically not use the existing channels if there is a choice. Channel partners of the incumbents have a vested interest in the status quo, and will often block changes necessary to reduce cost or that remove (disintermediate) them from the chain.

Incumbents will generally avoid causing disruption in their channels to prevent the risk of losing sales, but the disruptor has nothing to lose and everything to gain by going around the channels or going direct to the consumer.

If a potential disruptor is using the existing channels, this will generally reduce the probability of successful market disruption. If the potential disruptor can effectively reach the customer without using existing channels, then the probability of successful market disruption is enhanced. This factor is somewhat context dependent, and a weaker predictor than many of the others.

iPods were sold through traditional electronics retailers. However, the primary channels were direct (from Apple's website), and later through its own chain of retail stores. More importantly, in conjunction with iTunes, filling the iPod with music completely bypassed existing music distributors and record stores, relegating them to a small niche role in the business. This played a strong role in their disruption of the industry, since the existing channels had no role to play and couldn't block Apple's assault on the music business.

■ **Tip**   Disruptive potential is enhanced if you can bypass the usual sales/distribution channels. Not only will the existing distribution channels resist you if you are perceived as a threat, but incumbents will be protecting them and not looking for reasons to provide easier routes to products in your category.

Has One or More "Usability" Advantages

Usability advantages are focused on the ability of the intended user to derive the promised benefits. They include:

- Ease of use

- Simplicity versus complexity of design

- Convenience or accessibility (usually driven by centralized versus decentralized use of the product)

- Amateur-level skills required (anyone can use versus skilled professionals only)

- Flexibility (a single version of the product can be applied in several different ways)

In most cases, these usability attributes are less valued by existing users than by a new underserved segment, and may even be viewed derisively by existing users. (For example, "That product isn't good enough for professional use.")

Disruptive innovations will tend to have at least one of these advantages, and sometimes several of them. The iPod, for example, had several—it was much easier to use than previous MP3 players, had a trivially simple user interface design, offered more flexibility to use in a variety of different scenarios versus CD players, and was extremely convenient ("your music collection in your pocket").

Is the Primary Competitor Non-Consumption?

Marketers and consultants will tell you that there is no such thing as a product that has no competition, and to a degree, they are correct. If there are no competitors for what you do, that probably is for a very good reason—consumers don't have a need to do what your product provides.

However, competition isn't always obvious, and in the context of disruption, we care much more about the alternatives that a consumer might consider when they have a "job to get done," and one of the competitors is often "doing the job manually." In other words, the consumer will often choose no product if their need isn't addressed cost-effectively or simply or conveniently enough by the available alternatives. In disruption theory, we describe this as competing against non-consumption.

When there is an underserved segment of the market whose needs are unmet by any of the alternatives, who cannot afford a product to address their needs, or who lack the expertise and skills to use any incumbent solution, and you specifically target these constraints, then you have an opportunity to compete against non-consumption.

That means, in that segment, you essentially have only "do nothing" as a competitor. If your solution crosses the threshold of being good enough, affordable, simple, and accessible, and the only competition is to buy nothing, then you have a much higher probability of achieving market disruption.

Using our iPod example one last time, there was no alternative to carrying your music collection in your pocket (the job to be done) that was simple enough to use (compared to other MP3 players), affordable, and convenient, so it also scores very high on "competing against non-consumption."

■ **Tip** Identify the non-buyers of current offerings and ask why they don't participate in the market. Do they have a different JTBD? Are there constraints that exclude them? In many markets, there are more non-consumers than there are consumers, so focusing on their needs can both be a larger opportunity as well as the path to market disruption.

Assessing Disruptive Strengths and Weaknesses

Coming up with a prediction is just the first step in assessing disruptive potential. In order to come up with a plan, you'll next want to evaluate disruptive strengths and weaknesses in your current position (or in the position you want to attack). Though not a comprehensive set, the above factors are certainly among the most important and common influences. A few others will come up as we go through the steps to creating disruptive innovations by design.

Assessing how important your disruptive strengths and weaknesses are relative to your market context is a bit more difficult and implies a firm grasp on the job to be done. For right now, we won't go into detail regarding how we assess which are the key strengths and weaknesses, but suffice it to say that it is necessary for developing a strategy so will be covered in the coming chapters.

The strong disruptive levers that we have a lot of control over include:

- Pricing/cost of production advantage
- How precisely matched your product is to a job to be done when there are unmet or underserved needs
- Whether you can compete against non-consumption
- How likely it is that incumbents will view you as a competitive threat

There are also environmental factors to consider, which may be beyond your control. These include:

- Regulatory/legal issues
- External economic events (stock market collapse, terrorist attack, earthquake, or war)
- Access to growth capital
- Competitive response
- Alternative innovations

Predicting the iPod as a Likely Disruptive Innovation

Looking back, the market dominance that the iPod has enjoyed makes it fairly obvious in retrospect that it was a disruptive innovation. However, we could have easily predicted this outcome at its introduction. If we take a simple grading scheme to consider each of these factors, the iPod evaluation would look like the "report card"[4] below.

To simplify illustrating this example, we can think of this as a school report card and take a simple average of these individual grades to come up with an overall assessment. Doing that, the overall grade for the iPod is just slightly below an A. If you knew nothing of the iPod's absolutely dominant market success, you would still predict that the iPod was going to be a strong disruptor with a high degree of confidence.

---

[4] This "report card" summary for the iPod is for illustrative purposes only. A more rigorous approach that assesses the influence each factor has on the probability of disruption is taken by Innovative Disruption's *Disruption Grader* tool described later in this chapter.

The analysis is a bit more rigorous to come up with a real prediction, but since all the factors are strongly positive for the iPod, this is a pretty good approximation of what we'd do, and it gives quick "thumb in the air" guidance. All that's lacking for a more thorough evaluation are probability assessments, factor weighting, inclusion of several "special case" variables, and a subjective assessment of factor relevance.

iPod "Disruption Report Card"

Factor	Grade
Job to be done	A+
Product viewed as inferior by incumbents	A
Undesirable segment targeted	B
Unmet/underserved needs that incumbents can't address	A-
Pricing	B
Industry outsider	A
Doesn't use existing channels	B
Usability advantages	A+
Competes against non-consumption	A
iPod Final Grade	**A-**

What you should notice in this evaluation is that the "gee whiz" technology embedded in the product is irrelevant to disruption. What is important is how the technology is applied to solve a problem (the job to be done) and how strongly the business/marketing strategy and business model match the disruption fingerprint.

The conclusion? If you're looking to predict disruption, don't look at technology, look at how it is applied. Remember, there is no such thing as an inherently disruptive technology, despite the widely held misconception to the contrary. Disruptive innovation is not a technology phenomenon, but a market pattern, and that is a crucial distinction.

▒ **Note well**   Disruptive innovation is not a technology phenomenon, but a market pattern, and that is a crucial distinction.

Importantly, there is no way through creative design processes or brainstorming gimmickry to come up with disruptive hypotheses that are guaranteed to lead to products that disrupt markets. Such design thinking is a great way to come up with clever and novel ideas for innovation, but boring ideas can also be disruptive.

We need to remember that the objective hasn't changed—we still need to figure out where the quarter-inch holes are needed, not try to make quarter-inch drill bits into solutions for every customer need.

Free Grading Tool: Create Your Own Disruption Report Card

As noted above, the iPod "report card" example that is used here was abstracted somewhat to show the general principles used to grade the probability that an innovation is disruptive. I used a familiar product example that I hope most people can relate to so that the thought process makes sense.

As a complement to this book, I have created Disruption Grader,[5] a free online tool that generates a Disruption Report Card based on data you provide in response to a set of questions. Disruption Grader is a simplified (slightly less rigorous) version of a tool I have used in my consulting practice to generate Disruption Report Cards. It's not quite as accurate as having a disruption expert work through the assessment with you in detail, but it's close enough that you should find it valuable to perform a self-assessment and get a prediction of your own disruptive potential.

One caveat: when evaluating whether or not a product has disruptive potential, context matters. Market context, competitive alternatives, what users expect, the nature of a market scarcity and associated JTBD are all critical. Interpretation of the fingerprint criteria relative to your offering, market trends, and even timing make a difference in assessing disruptive probability. To a certain degree, the more you understand the principles of how disruption happens and the things you can do to maximize your likelihood of success, the more accurate your grade will be. Nevertheless, it should provide you with a useful benchmark and guidance as you work through this book to create disruption by design.

Summary

Our goal in predicting disruptive innovation is to create a measurable level of objectivity and a self-assessment benchmark that we can evaluate progress against and use to develop strategies that increase the likelihood of achieving market disruption. It's critical to be aware that prediction implies probability

---

[5]Visit http://www.innovativedisruption.com/disruption-grader/ to run Disruption Grader. It is a free tool, but it requires a valid email address to receive a full report.

and that predictions of success or failure can be affected by factors beyond our control. That said, the more you are aware of the variables of probability, the better chance you have of succeeding.

Your disruption report card enumerates the factors you need to pay attention to, and the assumptions that your business model is (or should be) based on. If your goal is market disruption, you must take Andy Grove's "only the paranoid survive" admonition to heart and be vigilant in monitoring all the key factors that could change your hoped-for outcome.

If the assumptions embedded in your report card change, so may your grade and the probability associated with your disruptive potential. For that reason, it's especially important to have a deep understanding of the job to be done, and to realize that if your understanding of that changes, or market feedback from users tells you it needs to change, you'll want to reevaluate your report card and your strengths and weaknesses and then adjust your strategy on the fly, and constantly if necessary.

This chapter completes the first section of this book—a quick overview of the key concepts of disruptive innovation and how to predict it. We're now ready to jump into the core how-to guide that takes these concepts and applies them to product and marketing strategy and development of a suitably disruptive business model for your product.

Key Takeaways

- Predicting whether an innovation is likely to be disruptive has a large economic value for investors, startup entrepreneurs, and companies whose products may be disrupted.

- Perform a disruption report card assessment to score the probability of market disruption and to understand factors that favor and contra-indicate disruptive potential.

- Disruptive strengths and weaknesses indicated by a disruption report card provide the insights needed to create strategic plans for products, marketing, and investment, as well as to design a business model.

In the first section of Disruption by Design, I reviewed disruption theory, the key concepts underpinning disruptive innovation, the ties to economic theory, and how to predict when market disruption is likely. In the next section, I tackle the process of creating and executing a disruptive business strategy. In Chapter 4, I begin by looking at the most important question you need to answer, namely, what should your product do?

Designed for Disruption

What Should My Product Do?

We thought that we had the answers
It was the questions we had wrong

—Bono

*If there are no **stupid** questions, then what kind of questions do stupid*
people ask? Do they get smart just in time to ask questions?

—Scott Adams

Often the dumbest questions are the ones that yield the greatest insights. They are "dumb" because they seem so obvious, and no one dares ask them fearing people will think they are stupid. Usually it's just the opposite and the stupidest mistakes happen when we don't ask questions; especially the question "Why?"

Why are you building a product? Why does it do what it does? Why are the planned features on the requirements list?

Okay, so you don't usually have a blank slate. You already have a product, and it has a defined set of features. A product manager with an existing product will talk to existing customers, do traditional market research, examine competitive solutions, and draft a Marketing Requirement Document (MRD). To this mix, they'll add internal ideas from R+D, and then evaluate the development costs of the features and the projected sales volumes that these capabilities will drive. After running the spreadsheets and optimizing for lowest cost and greatest revenues/profits, the feature list for the next product is set.

Even if you don't already have a product in the market space you're targeting, the process isn't usually that different. Competitive products are examined to determine a baseline market entry requirement and expected pricing, and although you'll be looking at a few features to differentiate, little else changes from this standard process.

These are the formal "good" processes. More often than we're willing to admit, and especially in small and startup companies, it is completely seat of the pants. The person running the show trusts his or her own intuition, personal needs and wants, and observations. They act as a benevolent dictator, deciding for customers what they "need." If they take input from customers, it is usually:

- The company that buys/spends the most whose opinions are sought out if it is a B2B product—they pay the bills after all, and are likely the most demanding of attention, or

- A laundry list of assumed middle-of-the-market requirements imagined by users in focus groups who've never seen or tried to use what you intend to make if it's a consumer-oriented product

And those are the "good' scenarios: often, the product "requirements" are determined in an even less reliable way through requests from channel middlemen, which are interpreted third hand by the development team who may never talk to a real customer.

But, did anyone ask what *should* your product do? What single thing does it do better than any other alternative for the price?

Is this the right product to deliver to the market? If you believe so, why? And, how do you know? Seriously—how do you know?

What's Wrong with the Traditional Process

No matter how product innovation is conducted, it is usually wrong. The facts speak for themselves:

- Of approximately 1.5 million patents currently in effect and in force in the United States, only about 3,000 of them are commercially viable according to Richard Maulsby, director of public affairs for the U.S. Patent and Trademark Office (USPTO). "It's a very small percentage of patents that actually turn into products that make money for people," says Maulsby.[1]

- A Canadian research study evaluating the market success rates of over 1,000 entrepreneurs whose inventions and ideas had been assessed by the Canadian Innovation Centre prior to going to market found that 93% of the polled inventions never got to market. Of the 1 in 14 that did make to market, only 40% of those (2.8% of the original total) produced positive returns. All the rest—60% of those that made it to market—lost money. Only seven of the innovations achieved significantly above average returns.[2]

- According to Cincinnati-based research agency, AcuPoll (quoted in *Forbes* magazine), 95 percent of new products introduced each year fail. This new product failure rate is virtually the same at large companies and small.[3]

- $260B is wasted on product development in the United States every year (2010 estimate) due to new product failures, according to Rob Adams in his book *If You Build It, Will They Come?* Worldwide, he estimates that the figure is in the trillions.[4]

[1]"Avoiding the Inventor's Lament," *BusinessWeek*, November 9, 2005, http://www.businessweek.com/printer/articles/256666-avoiding-the-inventor-s-lament?type=old_article. Accessed March 24, 2012.

[2]Åstebro, Thomas, "The Return to Independent Invention: Evidence of Unrealistic Optimism, Risk Seeking or Skewness Loving?", *The Economic Journal* 113 (484), 226-239, January, 2003.

[3]Laurie Burkitt and Ken Bruno, "Brand Flops: Ford, GE, Coca Cola Know Hype Can Hurt New Products," *Forbes*, March 21, 2010, http://www.forbes.com/2010/03/21/microsoft-sony-exxon-apple-coke-ford-xerox-conde-nast-cmo-network-brand-flops.html. Accessed March 26, 2012.

[4]Rob Adams, *If You Build It, Will They Come?: Three Steps to Test and Validate Any Market Opportunity.* Hoboken, NJ: John Wiley & Sons, 2010.

What's wrong with our product-development processes? They fundamentally start from the wrong premise. They assume that the status quo is correct. They assume customers can accurately articulate what they need. (Hint: They can, but not in the way most people think.)

They assume that if the competition has it, we need it too. They assume that all the people who aren't buying our products (usually the vast majority) are exactly the same and have the same needs as those who are.

The question that is almost never asked is, what exactly is the customer trying to accomplish by seeking out a product to buy? Why are they searching for a solution? What problem are they trying to solve and what's the best way to solve it? What alternatives do they have to solve the problem? What deficiencies are there in current alternatives to solve the customer's problem, and when faced with all the different alternatives, why do they or should they choose yours over the alternatives?

At the point a buying decision is about to be made, why will this product be chosen over the available choices looking at the customer from the store shelf? What would an ideal solution look like if it existed?

These questions have nothing to do with the competition, the current feature set and its presumed benefits, or what engineers think are cool features to build.

They are the "dumb" questions that we often think are too obvious to ask. That's because the embedded assumption in most innovation is "if we build it, they will come." Or, it's better than what we had before, so customers will naturally prefer the better product. But clearly the data doesn't support that conclusion.

Note   You have to ask, at the most basic level, why the customer is seeking a solution. What are they trying to accomplish by buying your product that they can't do any other way? Why should they choose you over all the available alternatives? The customer never asks whether you have the most features or benefits, nor is the result they are looking for defined by what the competition is selling—these are irrelevant when the customer is thinking about their desired outcome.

The Job Candidate

Now, let's think for a second about something that may seem completely unrelated to product development and innovation—hiring a new employee. Let's ask another dumb question: How do companies decide that they need a new employee?

One or many of the following conditions are likely true:

- The current person doing the job is failing and needs to be replaced.
- There is an unexploited opportunity to increase revenues that requires a new person to go after.
- The company is missing a critical skill set to increase revenues, reduce costs, service customers, or build product.
- More productivity is required to satisfy demand, and current staff is working at maximum ability.
- The previous person quit.

In other words, there is a job to be done that requires hiring a new person. If there isn't a job to be done, a company won't create a hiring requisition. Seems obvious, right?

So let's assume there is a job that needs to get done. How do we choose the right candidate?

The following steps will usually occur:

- Define the requirements of the job.
- Assess current and future needs based on expected growth or decline of the business.
- Define the skills and qualifications required to perform the job and meet the requirements.
- Identify qualities and attributes needed and desired in potential candidates, including what constitutes a good cultural fit.
- Create a "straw man" of what the perfect/ideal candidate looks like.
- Identify the minimum acceptable qualifications to make a hiring decision.
- Assess how much it should cost to hire the right person and assign a budget.
- Perform a cost justification.
- Conduct a search for candidates.
- Interview candidates to assess their qualifications.
- Choose the person who best matches your need.

So, what does conducting a search for a new hire have to do with designing products? Conceptually, it *should be* exactly the same process, because no one chooses to spend money on a product until they have a job to get done.

Paraphrasing former Harvard professor Ted Levitt, people don't buy quarter-inch drill bits, they are trying to find a way to get a quarter-inch hole. Conceptually, when we are searching for a product to buy, we are conducting a hiring process to find the candidate who can best satisfy our desire for a quarter-inch hole. And, if there was a better, cheaper, easier, safer, cleaner, or more convenient way to accomplish that goal than a quarter-inch drill bit, that's what we would choose.

Often, we are trapped by what we assume the solution to a problem is because that's how it's always been done. Because of that, conventional wisdom is that our competitors are other drill bit makers if that's what we make.

From the customer's point of view, nothing could be further from the truth. If they could get the same quarter-inch hole with a punch tool, or a laser, or a chemical process, or by creating materials that have holes in them already, to name a few possible alternatives, and one of those was faster, more convenient, less expensive, or safer—whatever qualities are most important to the consumer—that's what they would choose.

■ **Tip** From the customer's perspective, it's the result that's important, not the product.

The Job To Be Done (JTBD)

None of this discussion so far has anything to do with disruptive innovation. There's a reason for that: innovation is not about inventing new products, but about better meeting customer requirements, however that might be accomplished.[5]

---

[5] I noted earlier when JTBD was introduced as a key concept of disruption in Chapter 2 that the insights behind "Jobs To Be Done" theory were originally expressed by Anthony Ulwick, and documented in his book *What Customers Want: Using Outcome Driven Innovation to Create Breakthrough Products and Services,* New York: McGraw-Hill, 2005. The idea of JTBD is universal—it applies to all products and all innovation. However in this chapter, I drill down to focus specifically on how it is applied to create disruptive innovations and why. Tony's company, Strategyn, employs a proprietary and patented methodology he calls Outcome Driven Innovation (ODI), but there are many variations of JTBD-based innovation in use today. The important thing is that you focus on capturing the real jobs, and then use the principles described in this book to uncover and sort out the disruptive opportunities from the innovation opportunities that are purely sustaining and best left to industry incumbents to pursue.

All product developers and marketers need to first consider what jobs customers need to get done to come up with the best solutions, but—and this is a very big "but" —incumbents can get away with not asking these questions and taking the more common and lazy path, because they will continue to sell products based on their brand awareness, reputation, distribution channels, advertising and promotional strategies, and other marketing activities, all things being equal.

For incumbents, the folly of not understanding what the customer's JTBD is becomes truly apparent only if a competitor is doing a substantially better job at it, or if a disruptive innovator is on the horizon. In fact, as we discussed earlier when reviewing the "Disruptive Innovation Model," as long as innovation continues along a sustaining path, incumbents have a huge advantage over new market entrants, precisely because:

- There is a risk to changing.

- Perceived switching costs may be high.

- If there is no reason to change, we tend to stick with what we already know.

- Incumbents have much greater strengths and resources for sales and marketing.

- Incumbents have already optimized operations to be able to sell higher volumes at lower cost.

Disruptive innovators, on the other hand, cannot succeed unless they know or can uncover a JTBD that their solution is a substantially better fit for than incumbents. Potential disruptors need to know what the JTBD is, and then serve it with laser focus to establish a market beachhead from which they can expand.

Importantly, the JTBD is not what makes an innovation disruptive (remember that creating abundance from scarcity is the primary driver of disruption), but it's impossible to succeed at disrupting a market without having a JTBD for which you are the best job candidate. So, the question we need to ask as innovators is how do we know what jobs people need to get done?

The notion of a job to be done is more subtle and a bigger idea than simply "satisfying needs," which every product does at some level. Because we are most familiar with a traditional needs (or requirements) analysis, the difference can be confusing. This is often the hardest thing to grasp for disruptive innovators, so I will interrupt the train of thought and offer a couple of examples that should help illustrate what this important concept is all about.

Can an Air Freshener Be Disruptive?

Procter & Gamble's air-freshener, Febreze, is fascinating because it started its life doing almost everything wrong, the way most "big company" new products are introduced to market. It was a product designed for spraying on draperies that reeked of cigarette smoke, a smelly sofa that was frequently inhabited by a wet family dog, or a room where cats had done their thing on the floor. The problem it addressed was removing odors from homes made smelly by daily habits and the environment, which were trapped in the environment itself.

Unfortunately, this was a made-in-the-boardroom problem. Although it seems reasonable to imagine that people are embarrassed and repulsed by these smells and would want to get rid of them, in the real world, the people who most needed to fix this problem didn't believe that they had a problem to fix. In the real world, people build up tolerances to smells the more they are exposed to them, and may even associate that "wet dog" smell with positive feelings.

So, while any visitor to such a home might be hit in the face with detestable odors and wonder how people could live that way, the person who lives there has masked the smells in their mind and has no idea that their house smells like smoke or cat pee. And, even if they could smell it a little bit, they certainly didn't perceive their house to be unclean and in need of a new kind of air freshener product. A little spray of perfumed air freshener would replace that odor anyway, and seemed like the natural and superior thing to do.

When P&G launched Febreze as an odor-killing unscented spray in the mid-1990s, with ads targeting the homeowner's love for their pets but hate for their smell, there was no resonance in the market with this messaging. (Might they have done better to target visiting friends instead?) It was a complete dud in the market, with sales falling each month, rather than growing.

Air Freshener Category History—The Context Febreze Was Launched Into

Importantly, but unrecognized as an issue, Febreze was a new entrant in the crowded air freshener category. The first modern air fresheners were invented and brought to market in the late 1940s, and by the 1990s were a well-established category.

Powered by aerosol technology using chlorofluorocarbon (CFC) propellants that had been developed by the military in the Second World War to spray insecticide, these early air fresheners depended on perfumes to mask odors, just as had been done for centuries without technology for dispersing the masking smell. Over time, a variety of different ways to mask odors had been introduced to market, from aerosols to atomizers to candles and incense to wicking.[6]

Febreze was different from the older generations of freshener products because it used a new compound, cyclodextrin, which employed a property of its molecular structure to bind with organic molecules that emit smells, thereby neutralizing the smells rather than covering them up.

Its other critical property was that it could be sprayed on fabrics without doing damage or leaving discernible traces. This was important because organic compounds such as cigarette smoke, body odors, and cooking oils tend to collect in fabrics in a house, from draperies to bed sheets to clothing to furniture upholstery, which means that masking does not have a long-term impact. Eventually, perfumes dissipate and lose their effectiveness while the odor-causing organics remain unaffected. As the perfumes wear off, the smell re-emerges, just as bad as before and perhaps a little more stale.

Diagnosis of Launch Failure: What Went Wrong?

Clearly looking back, Febreze's odor-binding and killing technology is superior to odor masking (at least conceptually it is—Febreze has not eliminated competitive alternatives from the market). But, that would not have been obvious to anyone who didn't try it or realize what the advantages were and why.

With the JTBD being imagined rather than observed, there was nothing to make these advantages compelling—the people who most needed the product didn't recognize the need, or they were happy using perfumed fresheners that had always been good enough for the job. More than good enough actually—it was a mature, over-served market with literally hundreds of different perfumed alternatives and ways of dispensing them.

On market entry, Febreze tried to differentiate by talking about the features of spraying on fabric and being odorless. But these technical advantages would have looked like disadvantages for the job of odor-masking (air freshening)—it seems an odd idea to spray chemicals into your furniture, and it's asking a lot of a typical homemaker to understand the product chemistry and how and why it is different and better.

---

[6]Air Wick, as the name implies, literally used a wick to draw perfumed oils up from its reservoir.

Given all this, and knowing that incumbents have an advantage over new entrants if they are competing for the same job with a sustaining innovation (relative to existing products and their performance at "freshening air," Febreze was a sustaining innovation), the month-by-month declining sales figures were entirely predictable after the launch promotions had run their course.

Accidental Disruption

The patented chemistry that made Febreze work was the result of a very substantial R&D investment, and Procter & Gamble was understandably reluctant to abandon their failing product without giving it one last "college try." Sending a team of researchers into the field, P&G observed that there was an anomalous group of avid users who were not only repeat buyers, but also increasing their use of the product. This scenario is laid out in a *The New York Times* article[7] by Charles Duhigg that details the work of behavioral researchers in understanding habits that influence purchasing decisions.

The company was perplexed and sent researchers out to the field to try to understand what was happening with happy users of Febreze who were using lots of it, and what was different about them. Did they have more sensitive noses? Were they more "anal" about cleaning? Were they more socially embarrassed about the smells when visitors came over?

Out in the field, in the homes of the happy repeat buyers of Febreze, it was discovered that these homemakers had built spraying into their regular cleaning habits, but surprisingly, the reason was not to freshen the air. These users were not eliminating bad odors per se, but rather spraying after their cleaning was finished.

They were using the spray as a part of a completion ritual, signaling that the room was clean—like putting a bow on a wrapped gift. Psychologically, the spraying ritual was acting as a reward for finishing, so when the bedroom was finished being cleaned and tidied, a quick spray of Febreze on the comforter was the icing on the cake. When the laundry was clean, a spray of Febreze confirmed it. When the living room was cleaned and the sofa vacuumed, Febreze was the finishing touch.

Its odor-neutralizing strength would have kept the room seeming fresh and clean longer, but these users did not perceive their homes to be dirty or in need of de-smelling—just the opposite. The spray at the end was the piece de

---

[7]Charles Duhigg, "How Companies Learn Your Secrets," *The New York Times*, February 16, 2012, http://www.nytimes.com/2012/02/19/magazine/shopping-habits.html. Accessed April 16, 2012.

resistance—a finishing detail to signal being done and get that little endorphin high that comes with completing something.

The happy ending for Febreze is that P&G discovered this counter-intuitive behavior, and built this notion into their marketing. Sales exploded, to the point that it is today a best-selling $1B franchise.

The now familiar ad template shows a giddy, self-gratified housewife who has finished the cleaning, sprays a shot of Febreze, and closes her eyes to breathe in the warm fuzzy feelings. Or, more prosaically, a quick spritz when the task was complete was the reward for finishing—the idea being to associate the product with habit formation and the good feeling of being done with the work and knowing that things were clean. In other words, rather than promoting it as a cleaning product, they began promoting it as something you should do after cleaning was complete.

The gist of the *NYT* story was how statisticians and behaviorists are decoding habits and using them to sell to us, and the Febreze story is just a small piece of it. However, what's interesting from a market disruption perspective is the contrast of the original launch of Febreze with the ultimate conclusion.

What Was Different the Second Time Around?

At product introduction, conventional wisdom and conventional marketing supported Febreze. Conventional market research would have identified the market size for air fresheners and confirmed that most people would prefer their homes to smell cleaner (a common symptom of bad market research is "confirmation bias," where people selectively remember things that confirm what they already believe to be true, or in this case, remember how much they dislike the smell in everyone else's home even when they don't recognize it in their own).

Research and sales forecasts would have identified a sizable market share that could be captured with this differentiated freshener and used as the justification for product development.

Launched with conventional research and conventional messaging tactics and marketing strategy, Febreze was just another incremental and sustaining cleaning innovation, but one that in the minds of consumers was different enough to cause concern. This positioning deficiency was the cause of declining sales, and would have led to product cancellation but for the behavioral research conducted post-launch in the field.

The most important hidden piece of this story—the part that is so obvious in retrospect that it's easy to miss—is that Febreze needed to find a unique job that consumers needed to get done that it did better than any available alternative. The reason it was better than alternatives was tied to the chemistry advantage and unique properties of this product, which was important to owning the position in the consumer's mind.

But the chemistry was proof of the compelling advantage in being hired for the job, not the reason to hire it. In other words, marketers initially positioned Febreze as an air freshener because they didn't understand the "job" that consumers were hiring it to do. By positioning it this way, they sold it as a commodity into a crowded market, and the only way to win that game is with the lowest price.

After the behavioral research uncovered that a loyal core of avid users were using it differently from those who stopped using it after trying it once or twice, they were able to decode a very different job to be done—not by conducting surveys or by buying market-size data, but by observing the way they used it, including when, how, where and why.

They noticed that a quick spray at the end of cleaning a room created a habit-forming ritual that said "I'm done. This is clean and fresh and I can move on to the next room." The job to be done for Febreze was to be a reward, and a signal of being clean, after you were done, rather than a cover-up of something shameful.

By precisely targeting the job that the consumer identified with, they created positioning that is virtually impossible to dislodge them from.

Febreze is an interesting example, because although other attributes of the disruption fingerprint need to be present to achieve disruption (and Febreze also has those), this case demonstrates how the same product can come to market competing as a sustaining innovation, and lose, or be positioned for the correct job to be done, and win.

■ **Tip** It's the consumer's perspective that matters, not yours and not your competitors'. To learn this perspective, don't listen to what they say, but rather watch what they do. Observing and understanding consumer behaviors—the how, when, where, and why attributes, and especially the things they have trouble with—is often the key to unlocking the true unique JTBD for your product.

Ethoca: A Private, Closed Social Network?

Ethoca is a provider of fraud management services for e-commerce.[8] In the beginning, the founders of Ethoca had a brilliant and simple insight: if Walmart knew that a credit card had just been used fraudulently at Amazon, that information would be very useful in stopping fraud from occurring at Walmart. Taken to the extreme, if any merchant could know about good and bad transaction data anywhere in the payments network in real time, virtually all fraud could be stopped.

The trick to accomplishing this feat was to build a secure private hub and social network for banks, credit card companies, payment service providers, merchants, police agencies, and any other parties involved in processing transactions, and then get everyone to join. With a strong network effort, the more organizations participating, the greater the benefit to all in the network.

The idea makes intuitive sense and is much like other networks. If there are only two people with a telephone, only one connection can be made to have a conversation. If three people have telephones, there are four possible connections. With four telephones, there are 11 possible ways to connect the parties. And, the growth in value grows exponentially the more people there are with phones.

E-commerce fraud is a very large and growing problem. There are many sophisticated predictive analytics tools available using a variety of different approaches, and they catch more than 98% of all fraud. But that doesn't mean the problem is solved. The remaining fraud that slips through is still a multi-billion dollar drain on US-based e-commerce, and that much again for the rest of the world.

While effective, these tools are not cheap, and most merchants subscribe to several of them because they're good at different things. On top of that is the appropriately named "insult rate," which is the frequency with which a legitimate customer is denied because of a false positive risk assessment generated by the anti-fraud tool.

---

[8]In the interest of full disclosure, Ethoca was a long-time client of mine I advised and worked with for about five years. I am also a small investor in Ethoca. This story details the early years before Ethoca's technology found a compelling job to be done, and how and why it can be very difficult to subscribe users to an idea that is beneficial in the long run if you can't identify a unique JTBD that targets non-consumption and provides value that can't be achieved any other way. Since Ethoca introduced its highly successful Alerts service, it has grown in partnership with many of the world's largest banks and credit card associations, and has leveraged its technology platform to address other critical JTBDs, including the revolutionary Order Rescue service, which enables merchants to recover revenues from orders mistakenly identified as fraudulent.

The net is, fraud costs online merchants three ways:

- **Direct fraud losses.** This includes the cost of stolen goods, shipping costs, transaction processing costs, and chargeback fees. And, if merchants suffer too many charge-backs, the credit card company (Visa, MasterCard, Amex, and so on) can cut off their card acceptance privileges, which has the potential to destroy an online business.

- **Fraud-management costs.** This includes the cost of tools, databases, internal software tools, and staff to man-age anti-fraud efforts and spot check (manually review a percentage of flagged transactions that the tools may not give a definitive yes/no indication for).

- **Lost revenue.** Whenever there is a false positive, or the merchant decides that the cost of taking a risk is too high and decides not to accept a transaction that was actually from a legitimate customer, revenue is lost. And those customers are not only inconvenienced, they are unlikely to return to a site that refused to sell to them, and will often spread the negative news that they were treated poorly by the unwitting merchant. I've done as much myself.

There is also an indirect but insidious cost to fraud, and that is the number of people who refuse to shop online because they fear their card being compro-mised. Every time the news reports that hackers have broken into a database and potentially stolen millions of credit card accounts, it creates fear that inhibits online shopping despite the fact that the vast majority of transactions occur without problems.

What we take from that is that fraud is a huge problem, and even though we're getting better at stopping it, as more and more commerce moves online, the total amount of online fraud is continuing to grow. Many parties, from financial institutions to the credit card brands, to the merchants and consumers, have an interest in stopping it because it affects everybody.

So Ethoca's fraud-busting private closed social network solves a really big problem and should be a massive hit in the marketplace, right? You'd think so, and so did everyone Ethoca talked to in the formative days of the company.

The Network Problem

The classic network problem, especially in a B2B context, is this: how do you get people to join before the network is sufficiently large to provide value? Going back to the Walmart/Amazon example, these are two very large online retailers, representing approximately 8% of total e-commerce revenues between them in 2011. Yet that still means 92% of sales are happening elsewhere, and while the overlap between their customer lists is probably growing over time, a very large number of Walmart customers don't shop at Amazon and vice versa.

So, on any given transaction, the probability that Amazon's data could help Walmart to accept or refuse a sale, or that Walmart's data could help Amazon is pretty low. No doubt, there would be numerous matches, but a network that includes just the two of them is probably more trouble than it is worth. It's a little better with three members in the club, but still not of real value.

What's more, the sales data we're talking about is the crown jewels for most retailers, and potentially high risk to share. It's easy to imagine troubling scenarios (a competitor gains access to unmasked customer files and starts data-mining through it, or the personal data associated with millions of transactions isn't properly secured and gets out to the Internet, causing embarrassment and liability and potentially other problems), and no matter how improbable, these worst-case nightmares are the sorts of things that keep security experts and e-commerce executives awake at night.

Of course, the probability of linking and matching both fraudulent transactions and good customers goes up as the network grows, but businesses need assurances of value to invest their time and resources in any solution, and something that may yield a return at some uncertain point in the future is going to be pretty low on the project priority list for most companies. Even offering the opportunity to join the network free of charge (as Ethoca did in the very beginning) doesn't solve this problem, because there is still a cost to connecting and providing data to the network.

The point here is that even with a clear need, an obvious potential benefit, a real technical solution, and plenty of capital to grow a company and build a product, there is still no guarantee that you will be able to introduce a disruptive innovation, or even a successful niche product. The thing that is missing from this scenario is a job that the new technology does better than any available alternative.

As "superior" a solution as a global merchant network might be theoretically, existing predictive analytics tools already stopped well over 98% of all fraud. A promise of stopping 99% of that fraud, or even 99.9%, would not be sufficient incentive to incur the cost of switching from a solution that is already working pretty well, even if imperfectly.

The most difficult problem to overcome was the notion that the long-term vision of making online shopping the safest kind of shopping where fraud is virtually nonexistent was not the job that customers needed to hire a product to do. In fact, for that job, Ethoca's service was possibly the worst candidate for hire out of the starting gate, lacking not only a network of partners to share fraud data with, but also even the most rudimentary of analytics capability when compared with the well-established competition in this market space.

Four Years to the Epiphany

As Steve Blank[9] has articulated extremely well, startups are not mini-versions of big companies. Rather, they are temporary organizations whose purpose is to experiment, fail fast, stir, and repeat until they either discover a repeatable business model that will enable a real company to rise up and thrive, or run out of cash trying.

This is true of all startups, whether they have disruptive potential or not, but to realize disruptive potential, one key element of the business model is critical—namely the discovery of a *unique* job to be done that dramatically changes the basis of competition and/or creates a new market, replacing scarcity with abundance.

With Ethoca, we knew there was an opportunity to create abundance—to offer merchants greater real-time visibility into fraud attempts, more knowledge of which transactions were safe and which were potentially risky, and ultimately offer a safer online shopping experience to customers. In the long run, this would reduce the "payment friction"—the necessary steps to challenge, test, and accept or reject transactions, resulting in lower costs for everyone and happier shoppers.

The question was how to bootstrap the network. What unique or underserved market need could this service address that no other solution could? How could significant value be delivered, even with a small number of network participants? Was there a subset of the market for whom no existing solution offered a good enough or affordable fraud deterrence alternative? Or, was there another even better job that a network such as Ethoca's was the ideal candidate for hire?

---

[9]Although not directly relevant to disruptive innovation, Steve Blank has authored a couple of books that should be on every startup entrepreneur's bookshelf for easy reference including *The Four Steps to the Epiphany: Successful Strategies for Products that Win*, Pescadero, CA: K&S Ranch, 2007, and a book he co-authored with Bob Dorf, called *The Startup Owner's Manual: The Step-by-Step Guide For Building a Great Company*, Pescadero, CA: K&S Ranch, 2012.

These deceptively simple questions are perhaps the hardest to answer when you are in the trenches, simultaneously trying to build the core technology, find customers even before you know what you have to offer them, tell a compelling story about your vision, and mold your technology into one or more products. It is even more difficult when you have a multi-sided market where each network participant has a different motivation for joining and receives benefits at different times and at different scales.[10] Many companies have a similar challenge. Google and Twitter have each faced similar questions in their formative years and consumed enormous amounts of investor cash before discovering a sustaining business model.

In Ethoca's case, several alternatives were pursued, from selling traditional predictive analytics solutions, to outsourcing fraud analytics and decisions for specific high-risk businesses, to simply going out and asking merchants to join and contribute data to the network based on a promise of future benefit from collaboration. With varying degrees of success, none of these achieved the hoped-for market breakthrough.

Despite having a unique technology platform and approach to solving the fraud problem, Ethoca was having trouble identifying a job for which it was the best or only candidate available for hire. For the routine predictive analytics merchants were looking for—how risky is this transaction and should I accept, reject, or manually review the order?—there were lots of well-established tools focused on building a risk model and the complex mathematics and rules behind predicting which orders were safe to accept. Ethoca, in short, was not competitive in that market as an off-the-shelf solution.

100% Certainty Is a Compelling Difference

Because I'm discussing an anti-fraud solution, I need to be a little circumspect in what I disclose, so some details in the conclusion to the Ethoca story must be kept to a high level and what is already in the public domain, or glossed over. However, I can say that the solution to the question "what job should Ethoca be hired for?" came in collaboration with a card-issuing banking partner, and it came about because of an opportunity created by the transition from face-to-face shopping to e-commerce.

If you think back to a time pre-1995, when almost all retail shopping was done in person at stores, the needs for transaction processing of sales was quite different and dramatically simpler. A customer would decide what they wanted to buy, take it to the cashier to check out, and offer cash, check, or credit card to pay.

---

[10]In Chapter 7, there is a detailed discussion of pricing strategies for multi-sided markets, and how price can be used as an important lever to bootstrap the network.

Most cash registers, if they were connected to a computer at all, were simple devices for holding the day's receipts, totaling and reconciling cash at the end of the day and sending the day's sales either at intervals or shift changes during the day or as a single bulk (batch) transaction to the mainframe or local store server at closing. If paying by credit card, a physical impression of the card would be made in triplicate with the customer getting one copy to take as proof of payment and for reconciling their statements at month-end.

The fraud check was comprised of a visual inspection to verify that the signature on the card matched the signature on the payment receipt. Larger stores had electronic terminals that could capture the data on the magnetic stripe on the back of the card, and would sometimes authorize by telephone with the issuing bank to verify available funds and that the card was valid and not compromised. If the bank authorized payment and the signatures matched, the customer would soon be leaving the store with the merchandise.

Once the customer left the premises, and it turned out that the card had been stolen, there was little the merchant or bank could do to recover either the goods or the payment—the successful fraudster was literally home free. Even in the more recent years, as merchants increasingly had payment terminals connected to the banks enabling electronic authorizations, if the card was not yet reported stolen, the fraudster would have been next to impossible to catch after they left the store with their ill-gotten gains.

As shopping has increasingly moved online, a different pattern has emerged, and from it, a non-obvious opportunity.

One of the reasons that fraud detection systems are so much more sophisticated for e-tailing is because the shopper isn't face-to-face with the merchant. Therefore, without the ability to verify a signature or identity, the merchant must rely on predictive systems that analyze patterns of good and bad transactions. Essentially, they are making highly sophisticated guesses about whether the shopper is a real customer or a thief. But as often as these systems make accurate predictions (and they are highly accurate), they still make mistakes.

Occasionally, fraudulent orders slip through, and occasionally merchants reject legitimate orders. Neither is a good outcome, but neither is avoidable when you have to guess and factor in to your guesses how much risk you are willing to accept.

It may be stating the obvious, but orders taken online also need to be processed differently, particularly for physical goods. After the order is accepted and verified, a package needs to be assembled and shipped to the customer. This means forwarding the order to the warehouse where items are picked from inventory, packed for shipment, coded, and labeled with handling instructions, followed by submitting a ticket to the shipper (usually electronically) to pick up the package and deliver it. This usually takes at least one day with the most efficient systems, and can require a week or more depending on the nature of the order, whether goods are in stock, delivery method chosen, and so on.

This latency—the time between when an order is placed and when the customer receives it—turns out to be very important for fraud prevention. This has to do with how banks detect when credit cards have become compromised.

At some time, almost everyone who uses a credit card frequently has received a phone call out of the blue from their bank asking them to review a series of recent charges, and to confirm that they were indeed made by the cardholder and are legitimate. What has happened is that the bank's internal fraud systems have detected an unusual pattern—maybe a lot of purchases made in a short period of time, or a very large purchase of high-risk items such as computers or jewelry, or maybe you've been traveling and made some purchases away from home. Or perhaps you used your card at a merchant whose systems were known to be compromised and from whom a large batch of card data was stolen and appears to be in use by fraudsters.

The bank is asking you to verify that the purchases were in fact made by you, or to deny that you made them and identify them as fraudulent, at which point they will cancel your card and issue you a new one.

Often this will happen after a few successful fraud attempts have already gone through the system, because until there is a suspicious pattern, there is nothing to challenge and validate, and of course, the whole point of credit cards is convenience, so it certainly doesn't make sense to challenge every transaction if there is no reason to do so.

This is where the time gap between when an order is received and when it is delivered to the customer becomes very important in e-commerce. If merchants who got authorizations and accepted and processed an order based on that could find out that a card had in fact been compromised quickly enough, they could stop the order in process. Even while on the delivery truck to the fraudster, the order could still be cancelled, and the goods returned to inventory, all without incurring either a direct fraud loss or chargeback fees.[11]

---

[11] When the real cardholder challenges purchases that are proven to be fraudulent, the charge is reversed and online merchants are assessed a processing fee for the chargeback, since unlike card-present transactions, merchants have to accept the liability for fraud, even if the bank authorized the transaction.

As I explained to begin this discussion, most banking and card payment systems in use today were designed to support traditional offline commerce (pre-e-commerce). There was no time gap since goods were paid for and carried out of the store in real time. As a result, the opportunity to catch fraud after an order has been processed couldn't have been anticipated, and banks generally don't have any way to cost-effectively determine which merchants were affected and distribute that information to the affected parties on a timely basis.

You might surmise that this is the eureka moment—when Ethoca's network found a job for which it was not only the best, but the only candidate. So perfect a fit, it could have been tailor-made for the purpose of taking the banks' and card associations' knowledge of compromised cards, sorting all the inputs by affected merchant and securely distributing the information in real time—in time to stop fraud, even bad transactions already on their way to the fraudster.

The Job Is What You're For, Not What You Do

I've deliberately described this story the way most people would think about it—by features, functions, and what the product does. When considering what job needs doing, though, this is the wrong way to think. When a person is hired for a job, they are selected based on what they are expected to accomplish and how their experience and aptitudes are likely to help the employer achieve those goals, not because of their skills per se.

The same is true when we buy products. We don't care so much about what the product category is and what features it has, but rather whether it is a good solution to accomplish our goals. In other words, the context and the application are critical.

Ethoca's network was indeed designed with functions to detect and stop fraud, but that was not the reason that customers selected it. Remember, the job of mitigating e-commerce fraud was already being done pretty well, with just a little more than 1% of bad transactions getting through the system.

The unique job that made Ethoca a compelling no-brainer was the fact that the network was not *predicting* the possibility of fraud, but was actually able to tell a merchant with *100% certainty* that a credit card had been compromised and cancelled, and that any transactions associated with that card would result in fraud losses and chargebacks. In so doing, it was able to take advantage of the latency between when an online order is placed and when it is delivered, enabling merchants to stop fraud losses even after their probability-based analytics tools had given the green light.

When Ethoca issued a fraud alert, no decision was necessary on the part of the merchant—they could immediately detect where the order was in the fulfillment process and stop it or call it back. Secondarily, they could also use this data to fine tune their predictive analytics tools to preemptively stop other fraudulent orders in the future, both confirming when the predictions had been right as well as identifying mistakes.

After a prolonged period trying to fit a square peg into a round hole, suddenly Ethoca's network was able to show how it could do something no one else could do. It was able to stop merchant fraud losses, even after the order had passed fraud checks. It was able to eliminate chargeback fees on these orders, because merchants could cancel orders and issue refunds to the cards with the certainty that the orders would bounce back if they didn't—even if the goods had already been delivered to the fraudster, at least part of the total loss could be prevented.

Banks also saved money on processing chargebacks and earned goodwill with merchants who had long wished they could get access to this information. In short order, Ethoca became the last line of defense, effectively "corralling the horses after they'd left the barn." In a matter of months, virtually every e-commerce merchant of any size had adopted Ethoca's alerts and integrated them into their processes, most major card-issuing banks had joined the network, and the major card brands also joined to contribute their data.

Ironically, Ethoca's original vision is rapidly becoming possible as for the first time, there is visibility across banks and card networks and fraud vendors and payment processors, linking fraudulent actors to their behaviors in ways that couldn't previously have been detected, and this is creating new product opportunities in other areas no one else has been able to accomplish, such as recovering revenues lost due to rejecting good orders.

Finding a Job That Needs to Be Done

These stories illustrate the need for a compelling JTBD. Particularly for new market entrants and startups, finding the right JTBDs is essential to success. Of course, we've already pointed out that all products are acquired for JTBDs whether their creators understand that and employ that knowledge in their product design and marketing processes, or not, and that usually many products (in mature categories for sure) compete to be hired for the job.

What's different about potential disruptors is that they usually provide the only solution for a unique JTBD that the market doesn't currently address, but for which there is both a sizable need and market opportunity.

This raises two important questions:

- How do you find a unique JTBD?
- Could the post-facto discoveries by Febreze and Ethoca of their JTBDs have been known before they went to market, or even before they designed a product?

I'll come back to the second question at the conclusion of this chapter, and focus now on the first: finding a unique JTBD.

Source of Jobs

It is perhaps easiest to start with where jobs for products are not found. For example, inventors don't create jobs. Nor do brainstorming committees or R&D labs. Marketing departments don't create them. Not even product managers.

This all seems obvious when framed from the perspective of where jobs are not. Yet surprisingly, these sources are exactly where most companies look for ideas for what products to develop, enhancements needed to existing products, and products that haven't been created yet. But, JTBDs can be found in only one place. That is, in the things your prospective customers are trying to accomplish.

Tip JTBDs aren't created by inventors, marketing departments, or product managers. They are uncovered (not created) by researching what your potential customers are attempting to accomplish. Disruptive innovators target the high-value but unfulfilled JTBDs and outcomes that customers need solutions for.

One critical insight about the nature of a "job" is necessary. I've said before that jobs are not the same as product features, nor are they the same as benefits. Jobs deliver outcomes. Jobs are therefore processes or transformations. They are the means by which an input becomes an output or a result.

Understanding this, we can find jobs that need to be done many ways, including redirection of traditional research techniques to this purpose:

- Web-based questionnaires
- Telephone surveys to ask customers how they accomplish the task today

- Behavioral research: watch customers try to accomplish tasks, recording the steps, and identifying where they have difficulty

- Anthropological research: study the customer's environment, including how they use it and the things in it to accomplish goals

- Anecdotal research: Record customer stories about how and why they use certain products to accomplish their goals

These are intended as a short list of examples, not as an exhaustive set of methods. The method is less important than its ability to capture the things you need to know to document the job fully, which depends both on the job and how well understood it already is. Generally however, the more direct the research method, the more likely it is to yield good results.

Tip Being on site with customers and watching how they do what they do and asking them why while they're doing it will outperform a telephone survey 9 times out of 10 (and the 10th time, the telephone might be just as good, but not better). Customers will simply tell you more when you are face-to-face and showing active interest, and when you have the benefit of body language to react to. However, if telephone surveys are the best you can do, they're better than nothing.

The things you need to discover to capture the full JTBD include:

- The process or transformation that the customer desires

- How success is measured

- How it is done today

- Context of use

- Performance metrics

- Importance/priority of the job

- Opportunities to improve the result

- Economic value of the job

- Job frequency (how often the job is performed in a given unit of time)

The data you collect here isn't just to fully define the JTBD, but also to prioritize the most important opportunities and help size the "real" market. In fact, traditional market research is notoriously bad at accurately sizing markets by looking only at product categories and existing patterns of consumption and guessing how much share of that existing space can be captured. The only way to size disruptive opportunities is by fully understanding the job, including who needs it done and how much economic value there is in performing it differently (and therefore how much of your solution could be sold).

Identifying Alternatives—How Is the Job Done Now?

When gathering data about jobs that customers are trying to do better, there are two factors that stand out as the most important to consider. These are what things are difficult, inconvenient, expensive, productivity bottlenecks, or completely unsupported by tools today, and the economic value of providing a better solution.

While it's important to understand how the job is accomplished today, it is critical not to be constrained by product categories that exist, but to look at what needs to be accomplished holistically. This is because the JTBD is the closest thing to a constant (jobs can change, but tend to evolve very slowly over time), but how it is accomplished is constantly undergoing revision as technology, resources available, cost constraints, social trends, and environmental factors change.

Take the simplistic example of needing same-day transportation from New York to Atlanta. Knowing that the job is to make a sales presentation but be back in time to attend a recital that your daughter is giving that evening matters, because it means that an alternative is to use web-based tools to deliver the presentation online. On the other hand, if the job is to attend a funeral, but be back in time for work tomorrow, then the only suitable alternative is air travel. In other words, same-day travel is not the need, but one possible solution to each of the jobs, and you can appreciate that only if you see the whole job in context.

Part of collecting data about JTBDs is the identification of tools and products commonly used by customers to complete the job, and analysis of the strengths and weakness of these relative to what the customer is trying to accomplish. Are there steps that are completely unsupported? Are the available tools less than a good fit, or suboptimal solutions given current technologies? Where is the customer making trade-offs and compromises that they would prefer not to have to make? Could the job be made easier or less expensive by collapsing or automating several steps with technology?

Creating a Job Description

Just as creating a job description is a critical step when hiring a new employee, the job description is also critical for innovation. It is the tool that helps identify opportunities to improve how things are done and where there are unmet needs for which new products can be created.

Although documenting the JTBD for a product is a little different, and definitely more formal in structure than a job description for hiring a person, the intent is much the same and the process is somewhat analogous:

1. Collect job information

   - Conduct job analysis to document the key expected results

   - Identify inputs, outputs, context, and constraints

   - Document job purpose

2. Task analysis

   - Identify and list the critical tasks that have to be carried out to prepare for, execute, and finish the job

   - With each task, answer the question, what is the customer trying to accomplish and why is this task part of the job process

   - Rank the importance of the task, and how well served it is today

   - Identify products used to perform the job, which tasks they support, and the degree to which they are a good enough solution for the requirement

   - Record the frequency with which each task is performed

   - Perform cluster analysis of tasks to determine logical groupings by function and/or by how different customer types value them

3. Identify key performance criteria

   - What must be accomplished for the customer to judge the task successful

   - What metrics are used to monitor successful performance

   - What qualitative standards must be met

4. Create JTBD description(s)

JTBDs are really just related collections of desired results. The binding of expected results into jobs is dictated by a natural clustering of things that are important to one type of customer versus another—the core reasons why they would choose solution A or solution B. In that sense, the results, or desired outcomes, are the atomic units of the job.

When documenting tasks, the best place to start is in the middle—the execution steps—to understand the core reasons the job is being done and how. Then, look at the steps taken to prepare (that is, planning, gathering materials, starting software, and things needed to get the job done), and the steps taken to finish the job (that is, log output, clean up, put tools away, and things required to ensure the job was successfully completed). As these steps are recorded, you should ask whether you are looking at an anomalous case (steps peculiar to this customer only, or a subset of customers) or if the step is part of the general process that applies to everyone.

In order to be useful as a language for innovation and communicating about product development, customers, marketing programs, and so on, desired results should be expressed in a consistent way with a common syntax and grammatical structure that includes in each statement:

- What is being acted on
- The context for action
- The type of change
- How the result is measured
- The nature of the improvement relative to how it is performed now

So for example, a desired result statement for driving a car might read: "Eliminate blind spots when changing lanes on the highway." Using this form helps to ensure that you haven't inadvertently included solutions to the jobs in the job statements, and that some jobs aren't over- or undervalued because of the differences in how you stated them.

It's easy to imagine that this result might be bundled with a number of other safety-oriented concerns when driving, which would be evident when you cluster groups of people by their desired results. The ultimate JTBD might be to offer the safest car for highway driving for people who tend to make long trips and/or for nervous drivers.

When you write out your desired results statements and JTBD, they should not include any specific solution in the statement. The example of same-day travel from New York to Atlanta discussed previously illustrates why. After drilling down deeply enough to discover the reason for same-day travel, it quickly becomes apparent that this is not the real need, but one potential solution to the problem, and that the best solution is different depending on what I'm trying to accomplish (the JTBD).

In practice, it can be difficult to see the difference, and separate the two, especially if you listen to the customer and they state that their need is for same-day travel. One way to get around this blind spot is to always ask "why." In this case, when you ask why it is important/necessary to travel to New York and back to Atlanta on the same day, you discover that the real job is either a making a sales presentation or attending a funeral in New York, and that in one case, modern technology makes travel unnecessary.

Many companies have made themselves vulnerable to being disrupted by listening too closely to their customers, but not observing their actions (what they do, not what they say) and asking why. When you ask why, it becomes much more difficult (though not impossible) to inadvertently include the assumed solution in your desired results statements. If possible solutions are embedded in the result statements, you risk missing the real JTBD and not seeing the opportunity for disruptive potential.

Organizing Your JTBD Requirements

After collecting the full set of desired results, they need to be scored as "innovation opportunities" as a first step in sorting out which have disruptive potential. For any innovation, disruptive or not, the quality of the opportunity is a function of how important the documented tasks are to successful completion of the job, and the degree to which existing products address the need (data gathered during task analysis).

Relative to the "good enough" principle (see the key concepts in Chapter 2), you will want to sort these observations into three buckets:

- Jobs for which available solutions are not good enough. For these jobs, you will typically observe that the customer has a high degree of frustration or difficulty in completing the job to the desired standard, or that the quality of the outcome is subpar.

- Jobs for which available solutions are just good enough.

- Jobs that are grossly over-served with high-performance products that are too expensive, complex, feature rich, and so on.

Having sorted the jobs this way, do you see any gaping holes (poorly served job requirements), or opportunities to apply proprietary technologies for large productivity gains or cost savings? Or, could a radical simplification provide a good-enough solution for a dramatically lower cost? If not, it may be prudent to stop now and look for a different problem to solve.

Sorting Out Disruptive Potential

As I've noted a few times in this book already, it's worth remembering that conceptually, the customer is always hiring a product to get a job done, and therefore, whether it was a conscious part of product planning and design or not, all products have jobs to do. Understanding the jobs that your product does best and which ones customers prefer your product for is therefore essential to maximizing effectiveness of your product marketing. That's true whether your product is based on a mature technology with little innovation happening, whether you are introducing sustaining innovations, or whether your product is disruptive.

This bears repeating because while I've biased the job collection and documentation process described in the preceding paragraphs toward finding disruptive potential, none of what I've described here would be significantly different for any product. Now it's time to prioritize the jobs you will work on satisfying according to disruptive potential. So, what are we looking for?

Let's start by looking at the three buckets of opportunities organized in the previous step.

Over-Served Jobs

When a job is over-served, it usually means that the products available to support that job have a technology core that hasn't changed significantly in recent memory, or belong to a mature category that's been around for a long time, and there are likely several alternatives available to hire that are generally undifferentiated in the consumer's mind.

This lack of differentiation (commodity status) exists even when the available products may be different, because the important thing is not the feature set, but that the customer doesn't perceive any difference in the value for their job. When this state exists, products generally have a surplus of features that customers rarely use, and even "the best" cannot sustain a higher price.

It may seem counterintuitive, but over-served jobs are usually the low-hanging fruit and often present the easiest opportunities for low-end disruptive innovations. The key questions to ask are:

- Is there a segment of the market that opts out because existing products are too expensive or require too high a level of expertise to use?

- Can a radically simpler solution be designed that accomplishes the highest priority tasks for a fraction of the cost?

- Can we obtain a sustainable cost-of-production advantage of at least two-three times through a new process or patentable technology?

- Could the job be done a different way, perhaps by skipping steps, automating the most difficult parts, or by using a new immature technology?

The most important attribute for low-end disruption is the ability to substantially under-price incumbents. Thus, it is extremely important that you have a low-cost advantage that's not easily duplicated by incumbents and/or that you target a market that doesn't value the high-end features that incumbents provide.

If you are lower quality, targeting low-margin consumers that incumbents can't reach, and have a unique low-cost technology advantage, it becomes almost impossible for incumbents to compete with you without undermining their existing product lines. Your goal is radical simplicity, fewer features, under-performance, low price, and a product suited for undesirable customers.

 Tip   Targeting "undesirable customers"—the ones incumbents in the market can't or don't want to reach because it would undermine their existing product lines—is an excellent market entry tactic for a low-end disruptive innovation.

Available Solutions Are "Good Enough"

When the JTBD is neither over- nor under-served, but available solutions are just good enough, then there is usually no disruptive opportunity, even if the jobs could be done better. There may well be several incremental opportunities for sustaining innovations, but these enhancements favor incumbents, and it is in their interest to provide them and to defend their turf. Better is not disruptive.

As an innovator searching for opportunities to gain a market beachhead and upset incumbents, it's best to ignore the JTBDs in this bucket (unless you can combine/integrate them into a bigger job that the consumer desires).

Under-Served Jobs

Generally, under-served jobs are where market incumbents spend most of their development efforts creating sustaining innovations to make their products "good enough." Most of the time, this makes under-served jobs a bad place to look for disruptive opportunity (disruptive opportunity is enhanced by "asymmetry of motivation"—that is, it is more likely when incumbents have no incentive to fight), but this isn't always the case.

Incumbents tend to innovate in a straight line, and they rarely introduce products that would lower their margins, change the core technology that their products are based on, or accomplish the JTBD in a novel and completely different way. It's also the case that sometimes jobs are under-served because:

- The need hasn't been recognized
- No suitable solutions have existed to address the problem

For example, we couldn't print professional-looking documents at home until we had affordable personal computers, easy-to-use word processing software, and cheap inkjet printer technology. The JTBD was always there, but the best alternative we had before all these things existed was creating a document from scratch with a typewriter.

Under-served disruptive opportunities look different, however, from over-served ones. Generally, the result will not be a low-end disruption, but a new-market disruption. This is especially true when technology has advanced, but the market ecosystem of distributors, suppliers, creators, and feeders is tied to an old form factor.

Apple's iPod was a prime example of this. Music listening, storage, retrieval, searching, sharing, and cost were all constrained by the physical media of CDs. Thus, the consumer's real JTBD was severely under-served and digital music files created many new possibilities to accomplish the consumer's desired results.

It took not just the vision of a digital lifestyle, but an outsider's incentive to break the old system of selling CDs and vinyl recordings in record stores. The new system also provided an all-encompassing alternative ecosystem through iTunes, legal downloads of safe (not virus-carrying) music files of predictable quality, and an easy-to-use device and process for getting music onto it.

For Apple, the iPod and iTunes were a new-market opportunity, and Apple never tried to compete at the low end. In fact, the first version of the iPod was significantly better than the many digital music players already in the market, as well as higher-priced. It served the real JTBD differently, including solving the distribution, pricing, ease-of-use, legality (licensing), storage, portability, search, and access problems that traditional forms of music had in a digital world. While the music quality was lower than a CD (for a while), it turned out that this wasn't the reason most people hired music and music-playback devices. Most of us wanted access to a large selection of our music wherever we were, in a convenient, portable, and stable form, and this was the job the iPod did better than any available alternative. Incumbents were busy trying to compete on music quality when most consumers felt quality was already good enough and were prepared to sacrifice a bit of quality temporarily to serve the primary jobs for music playback better.

The important point here is that you can't introduce products with disruptive potential by competing directly against incumbents with "better" products in the same category that share the same channels, suppliers, and constraints, even if the JTBD is under-served. Incumbents will fight back, and most of the time, you will lose. The best you may be able to achieve is to carve out a market niche, but you won't be disruptive.

But you can attack under-served markets if you change the game, and if your product requires (or is better supported by) new channels and ecosystems that are incompatible with the old. And while new-market disruptions like this are harder to find and create, they have much greater power in creating long-term market dominance.

When looking at JTBDs in the under-served bucket, the key questions to ask are:

- Does the new technology have the potential to fundamentally alter market dynamics? Does it require different channels and ecosystems to address the JTBD?

- Is the new technology incompatible with existing methods of supporting the JTBD?

- Can several jobs be combined into one to satisfy the real outcome the customer wants in a more convenient way, obsoleting incumbents' core technology?

- Are incumbents incentivized to fight for your market beachhead or to stay out or abandon it because margins are too low? Asymmetry of motivation is a good indicator of disruptive potential (incumbents more likely to flee than fight).

In general, disruptive opportunities are harder to find and realize in under-served JTBDs than over-served, so the answers to these questions are critically important. If you don't have the right answer for all of them, the probability is much higher that your product is a sustaining innovation than disruptive. On the other hand, new-market disruptions for under-served JTBDs tend to be more defensible in the long run and to generate higher returns.

What Customers Will Buy

Disruptive potential can be realized only if customers desire your product and are willing to buy it. Often what customers will buy comes down to the business model and accessibility (is it easy to get?). If you are addressing the JTBD as the customer sees it, these things are actually part of it, but for now I will confine remarks to the product itself.

In general, the following things are true:

- The economic value of using your product must exceed the cost of acquiring, learning, and using it.

- If you are replacing incumbent products, the switching cost cannot exceed the economic value of using your product, even if your product is substantially lower cost to acquire and use.

- Customers will always prefer products that come closest to satisfying the complete JTBD (desired results) from start to finish versus point products that do a small part of the job better.

- It requires a sustainable cost-of-production advantage versus incumbents of at least two-three times to price your product attractively as a potential disruptor. Less than that, and you may be successful as a niche product, but will not overtake the market leaders as the new mainstream solution. If your cost advantage is 10 times or greater, you may be able to disrupt markets based on price alone.

- When markets are over-served, you have prima facie evidence of a JTBD that customers are willing to pay for. Often you will find that the non-consumers of potential solutions outnumber those willing to spend money for over-priced incumbent products. If you can address the core JTBDs of non-consumers with a radically simplified product that is easier to use and much lower cost, you will succeed in attracting both non-consumers and over-served customers of existing products.

- When markets are under-served, you must either target solutions that are uneconomical or undesirable for incumbents to provide, or create game-changing solutions that consolidate bigger JTBDs in a simpler way. This is usually the domain of technology-based, new-market disruptions. If you have accurately identified and prioritized the most important JTBDs and come up with a novel solution that your target customers will find affordable, it will sell even if it is higher priced than incumbent solutions (think of the iPod and iPhone). It must still represent good value when compared to the reference price of a comparable solution (set).

- Satisfying the JTBD is the surest way to create products that customers will buy. Designing solutions that do not address the core JTBDs or that offer me-too functionality with a different user interface based on misinterpreted customer demands is the least reliable way to create successful products (although this is more common than thinking about better ways to deliver the quarter-inch hole that the customer desires).

So, can you know what customers will buy? The answer is a qualified "yes." You can know what your target customers will buy with a fairly high degree of confidence, as long you've followed these principles, and what you've designed and built sticks to the most important and unserved or under-served JTBDs.

The reason the answer is qualified is that you can't control external variables—potentially competitive products being readied for market at the same time as yours, running out of cash before finishing your product and getting it to market, financial meltdowns, currency crises, and political upheavals—all of these and other things that can't be predicted can affect your results.

However, the odds improve substantially from the 1–2% success rate described at the beginning of this chapter to somewhere in the range of 75–80%. That's true whether you end up being disruptive or not, and the reality is that the number one factor that impacts success or failure is being able to sell what you've created.

Can You Always Know the JTBD Before Going to Market and/or Before Designing a Product?

Some practitioners of JTBD theory believe that the JTBD can be fully articulated with the right methods, and that no latent needs exist or will surface if you've properly solicited and recorded all the desired results. From their perspective then, the needs addressed by the examples of Febreze and Ethoca discussed earlier in this chapter were entirely knowable beforehand, and the solutions provided could have been designed precisely to address these JTBDs. This is only partially true in my experience, and these examples help illustrate why.

Let's start with Febreze. What if prior to creating an odor-killing product, researchers had gone into the field and observed cleaning behaviors of homemakers? Might they have observed that potential users had a finishing ritual that gave an endorphin rush signaling completion of the job? Might they have realized that this under-served opportunity was the key to designing a product and marketing campaign that linked the product to habit formation?

In this case, I will offer a solid "maybe." It would have taken very keen observation of how other products were used and intense questioning about the reasons for each step of the cleaning JTBD. Further, it would have taken decoding a pattern that no one seemed conscious of. That's like making a discovery as big as electricity or gravity, but without the strength of physical properties and cues that made those discoveries possible.

So, it is possible that "certifying completion" could have been discovered as the core JTBD for the yet-to-be-created Febreze, and that the go-to-market introductory campaigns could have focused on how Febreze satisfied this desired outcome. However, I also think it is stretching credulity to suggest that it would have certainly been discovered and 100% accurately defined and articulated such that R&D could have created the necessary product, and marketing could have created the necessary rollout strategy. As a new-market disruption, this was a subtle behavioral JTBD that could easily have been missed, even by expert anthropological researchers and behavioral scientists.

And what about Ethoca? Its private closed social network was surely the best and most ideal solution to the problem of secure hub-and-spoke communication between parties with mutual interests in stopping fraud. There could be no better solution to distribution of compromised card data as alerts to merchants, helping to defeat fraud even after bad orders had successfully passed through the systems. Technically, if you knew of this problem, Ethoca's network is exactly what you would have designed.

Unfortunately, the JTBD in this case needed to surface after the technology was built. It could have been ascertained from merchants that it was highly desirable to get this information in near real-time from card issuers. The costs of fraud losses and the economic value across the entire payment chain could have been determined. However, unless you knew of the latency problem and the reason it existed, this precise solution would not have been designed.

Ethoca actually represents a special case of a general technology solution that can be applied to several desired results effectively, but which needs to be built first and then matched to the highest value market opportunities. Part of doing so also involves creating appropriate business models to address those opportunities. Ethoca is not alone in this—some of the largest, most successful disruptive innovators have started the same way. Consider companies with names like Google, Facebook, and Twitter. These are products for which applications and business models needed to be discovered and fine-tuned in the marketplace, and for which no JTBD analysis a priori could have identified the best opportunities.

There are a few defining attributes of products such as these:

- Broad general-purpose technology that can be applied many different ways
- Network-based
- Often supported by multi-sided markets (contributors, users, and payers are often not the same, subscribe for different reasons, and get different value propositions from participation)
- Solve really big problems

So, the net is that most of the time, you can uncover most of the JTBDs and target your product, market, and business model strategies to maximize disruptive potential. In a few special cases, especially with new-market disruptions, it can require putting the technology out there and discovery of the best opportunities in conjunction with customers. Nevertheless, the process of finding JTBDs and prioritizing them based on the importance of the opportunity is a necessary part of creating disruptive products by design, whether done in initial pre-product planning, or immediately after the technology is released to the wild and early adopter customers begin to be interested in applying it.

Summary

I began this chapter by talking about the extraordinary failure rates of new product development—failure rates that are only a bit better for established companies than for startups. In the end, these failure rates can be attributed largely to hubris and an unwillingness to ascertain what the customer's real JTBDs are. While incumbents can usually survive product failures and market misfires, potential disruptors cannot. Discovering and understanding your customer's JTBD is critical, and one of the top three or four predictors of potentially disruptive success.

You must think of your new product as a job candidate, and you must understand the results your intended customers desire and why your candidate has the highest probability of delivering those results. In fact, as you'll see in subsequent chapters, everything from segmentation to positioning to pricing—every bit of creating a winning market strategy and business model (by design)—depends on it.

Key Takeaways

- Knowing the unique jobs to be done (JTBDs) that your product can serve better than any other is the key ingredient in designing a disruptive strategy.

- Identifying the high-value jobs to be done that are underserved in the current market and that have the potential to create new markets to compete against non-consumption must be the disruptive innovator's mission and mantra.

- Low-end disruptive innovations most often come from targeting over-served JTBDs.

- New-market disruptive innovations most often come from under-served JTBDs and new technologies that have a big general-purpose application.

- The least likely place to find a potential disruptive innovation occurs when customers consider existing solutions just "good enough."

- You can know what customers will buy if you don't let your own biases and ego get in the way of discovering the real JTBDs.

This chapter introduced the idea of uncovering and documenting JTBDs to provide the necessary inputs to product development, and how to choose which JTBDs have the best potential for market disruption. In the next chapter, I continue the theme of applying the discovered JTBDs to create a disruptive market segmentation strategy.

Segmentation

The hardest thing when you think about focusing, right, you think, well, focusing is about saying "yes." No. Focusing is about saying "no." And, you've got to say "no, no, no." And when you say "no," you piss off people.

—Steve Jobs

Most economic fallacies derive from the tendency to assume that there is a fixed pie; that one party can gain only at the expense of another.

—Milton Friedman

I've started this chapter with two quotes from important business visionaries that may appear unrelated. Perhaps they even seem a little contradictory.

One of the most difficult tasks that startup entrepreneurs have—much harder than building a product—is effective market segmentation. That's because market segmentation is about saying "no." Infinitely more difficult than saying which potential target customers you intend to pursue, it is about saying you aren't going to pursue the majority of them, at least for now.

To many who have estimated a total available market worth tens of billions of dollars that they intend to capture a 10% share of, segmentation is going to feel like cutting off their leg to save their toes. It feels like they are forgoing potential revenues on purpose. The paradox in market segmentation is that if you don't make choices about what to say "no" to, you will sell a lot less—and maybe even fail outright.

Some of the difficulty in appreciating this comes from Friedman's observation—the belief that marketing is a zero sum game, and that every sale that someone else makes is a sale you lose. That's true only if you are losing sales for which your product is the best job candidate for hire, or if yours is a commodity that offers no differentiated value in the mind of the customer. If you are selling a commodity, then you haven't been paying attention (or this book isn't for you); if you are the best candidate for hire, customers will come back to you when they are dissatisfied with the alternative.

Disruptive innovators know that the size of the pie is not fixed, because their whole raison d'etre is to create a bigger pie. The secret to disruptive segmentation, and successfully growing the pie, is absolute focus on the jobs to be done (JTBD) for which your solution is best matched.

Why Segment Markets?

Market segmentation is the science (many in marketing would have you believe it is the art) by which the complete universe of potential buyers is divided into subsets of customers with similar needs and characteristics. There are two primary reasons to segment markets:

- Segmentation enables scarce development, marketing, and sales resources to be focused on the areas that are of greatest value to your business. This is especially important for startups that have the disadvantages of few customers, no brand awareness, high market education costs, and less cash to spend than established competition.

- When properly grouped, segments respond in similar ways both to your product and to your marketing promotions. That results in more effective and efficient product development and marketing.

These two reasons can be summed up as higher revenues and lower costs, or as the answer to the command to do more with less. Along with positioning and pricing, segmentation is one of the most strategic functions a marketer (or often a founding CEO) performs.

So, at this point you're probably thinking "I've been to business school and got my MBA. Where's the news?" And, even if you haven't got an MBA, you probably think you know what segmentation is about because it's so much a part of popular culture.

But that's exactly the problem. Humans instinctively categorize groups and assign stereotypes to them. We toss around terms like the "youth market" or "soccer moms" or "aging boomers" and assume that everyone we tag with this group name is the same, and that these categories are therefore valid segments for marketing purposes.

But if you want to be a disruptor, you need to leave the inaccurate stereotyping and poor segmentation strategies to the big incumbents you're trying to disrupt. You need to work with meaningful segments whose members view your product as a must-have, and that means avoiding the use of lazy, dumb labels.

"Soccer Mom" Is a Meaningful Category Only If You're Selling Soccer Products for Kids

There is no such thing as universal categories called "soccer moms," "youth market," or "aging boomers" with homogeneous (a fancy word for common, uniform, or a standard set of) needs and preferences. At best, these are imperfect proxies that have a correlation to the attribute that you really care about.

In other words, most segmentation strategies based on demographics (age, income level, sex, where you live, education level), psychographics (attitudes, values, personality types, interests, lifestyles), or behavioral characteristics (loyalty, frequency of use, habits) are simply wrong. This may be the most controversial statement I make in this book, so let me repeat it: the kind of segmentation you're taught to do in business school and that's practiced by the majority of marketing organizations is wrong, inefficient, wasteful, and even harmful.

Incumbents do things this way. Disruptors can't afford to.

Note The ineffective segmentation strategies employed by most marketers, especially incumbents, lead to inefficient and wasteful efforts that do harm. This is a weakness that disruptors need to exploit.

Most Market Segmentation Is Done Wrong

Despite the preceding strong statements and inflammatory heading, I am not saying that segmentation is done wrong and is therefore worthless. Quite the contrary—it's worth noting that even bad segmentation offers some value in focusing, messaging, identifying prospects, and so on. Large companies tend to have the resources to support broad market segmentation, even when this means poor targeting. It's not great, and it's certainly not efficient or maximally effective, but it's better than nothing.

In fairness, we have not had the tools, techniques, and technology needed to slice market segments more precisely, but that was then and this is now. In today's world, there is little excuse for continuing with these bad habits and imprecise targeting.

Let's go back to first principles and look at the objective of segmentation, and why getting this right is so important to disruptive innovators. The ultimate goal is identification of a group of customers who agree so strongly about what they value that the same product will appeal to all members of the group. If you can identify such groups, you can sell them the same product using the same marketing tactics and they should all respond similarly.

That's the generic goal of all marketers. Assuming you've followed the advice in Chapter 4 (What Should My Product Do?), you want much more than to simply appeal to group members—you want a perfect match between your target and your product. That's the audience that views your offering as essential and as the only solution to their needs.

So, ask yourself: if you're a soccer mom, do you buy the same vehicle as every other soccer mom? Does your family eat the same foods? Do you wear the same clothes? Do you buy the same cell phones?

Probably the only thing that you will strongly associate with that all other soccer moms do is related to supporting your kids playing soccer. Buying them soccer gear. Socializing with other soccer moms at the practices. Watching and recording games. But even those things aren't universal.

In fact, if you do fit into the category of soccer mom, there's a good chance you bristle whenever you hear this term because you don't consider yourself or your needs identical to every other soccer mom. You don't drive the same vehicles. You don't take the same vacations. Your kids aren't the same ages, so you can't even count on Chuck E. Cheese for a restaurant choice after the game.

What that means is that for any given demographic, psychographic, or behavioral category, a significant percentage of group members in that category will not respond the same way to your product or its promotion. Many may even have the opposite reaction you hope for, finding the features unimpressive and/or the promotions offensive.

Many professional marketers even acknowledge this, saying they know that 50% of the dollars spent on marketing are wasted—they just don't know which 50%. In fact, for many products it's more than 75%. You can, and must, do much better.

Do Any Categories Make Sense as Segments?

Of course this begs the obvious question, if none of the typical segmentation strategies are right, how do you partition a market? Do any categories work, and if so, how do you go about finding them?

It helps to understand why the usual segmentation approaches are what they are. The truth is, laziness has much to do with it.

Modern marketing management grew out of consumer-oriented advertising in the 1950s and 60s. Traditional media outlets (TV, radio, newspapers, and magazines) all collect data to categorize their consumers by age, sex, race, location, income levels, and other demographic classifications. Business media track business size, revenues, executive level, buying authority, job titles, and so on.

Because the data exists, it's easy to define categories based on these attributes. With a little more information, it's easy to create psychographic profiles based on stereotyping, and to track existing customer behaviors such as loyalty.

Though traditional advertising is just one arrow in the marketing quiver today, and often the poorest and most expensive marketing choice for many products, we continue to use the categories defined by advertising media because it requires no additional effort, and we know what to expect (sort of) when we chose the 16–25 year old audience, or Hispanic males.

That makes it both convenient, and the path of least resistance, especially when trying to explain how you intend to reach your audience to those approving the budgets. But "easiest to do" doesn't mean the most effective, nor the segments most likely to buy your product, nor does it necessarily allow you to stay out of the crosshairs of incumbents while targeting your initial market entry points. Gaining market traction as a disruptor requires that you maximize all of these to the extent possible.

The second factor is that the alternative—segments based on truly homogeneous groups of prospective customers—isn't something you can just go out and buy a list for. Minimally, it requires deep knowledge of needs and behaviors—for example, because Nike was founded by a distance runner and a performance-oriented and highly competitive track coach from University of Oregon, they knew where to find people interested in performance footwear targeted at distance runners and understood the characteristics and behaviors of that segment.

The closest that traditional segmentation approaches have come to getting it right is what is referred to as "needs-based segmentation," but even armed with consumers who have supposedly common needs, marketers find that these segments are heterogeneous in nature, do not offer any better insights into (predictable) customer behaviors, and are therefore difficult to target.

That's because "needs" aren't the same as "expected results," and that brings this discussion full circle.

The Assumptions Embedded in Your Product

To effectively segment a market—to identify the subsets of the market that agree on what they value so strongly that the same product appeals to all group members and will therefore respond similarly to marketing campaigns and messaging—requires understanding what it is that makes that group of customers different from any other. As discussed in the previous chapter, there is only one thing that effectively differentiates a group of customers from any other. They are all trying to get the same job done. They want the same quarter-inch hole and have the same performance metrics for success.

Although we aren't trying to persuade incumbent product managers that they too need to apply JTBD theory to better segment their markets, the truth is that this notion is just as universal for segmentation as it is for defining what your product should do. But products that have an established brand reputation and identity, strong market awareness, existing channels to reach consumers, and relatively large budgets based on their market share can afford some inefficiency and laziness in their targeting. The truth is, you don't have to worry about that because they don't believe their processes are broken, so they aren't likely to fix them. That's good for you because it gives disruptive innovators an opportunity to gain the upper hand right out of the starting gate.

Incumbents also benefit from overlapping Venn diagram slices because they are addressing much broader swaths of the market, so as long as there isn't a more targeted solution for the job to be done, some of the lost potential due to poor segmentation can be masked.

A potential disruptor that segments the market based on imaginary targets—made-up classifications that sound good in the boardroom, but in reality don't exist—is likely to grab a small piece of the pie at best. At worst, it will fail to secure the early customer wins needed to grow a new market. In other words, they not only won't disrupt, they stand a good chance of being one of the 9 out of 10 "walking dead"—companies that do just well enough to stay alive, but never achieve their potential—if not outright market failure.[1]

The essence of disruptive segmenting is about identifying the most compelling uses and users who will achieve the greatest value from your product. Those initial customers need to be passionate and excited to carry the message about your product to the rest of the world. Many users will simply see a cost advantage or a slightly improved way of doing what they were doing before. These aren't the users you want to start with.

---

[1] In *Crossing the Chasm* (New York, NY: HarperBusiness, 1991), Geoffrey Moore identifies segmentation as the key to first identifying early adopters and then jumping "the chasm" between the visionaries who typically inhabit the early adopter growth phase to early mainstream users. Some have said that the Internet changes everything and that there is no longer a need to segment markets. The evidence suggests otherwise: segmentation is as important as ever, and perhaps even more important with the explosion in innovation that has happened as barriers to entry, especially cost barriers, have created ever smaller niches and orders of magnitude greater competition for customers. Poor segmentation will sink a potential disruptor, and, as Moore illustrates, can prevent companies that make it that far from crossing the chasm and fulfilling their disruptive destiny.

You need to find the customers who are so engaged and happy that you created your product that they identify with it (as if they created it themselves) and feel an emotional attachment to it. They can't help promoting it to others.

> **Note** The first target segments for a potential disruptor will view your product as "must-have" and identify with your product so closely that they feel an emotional attachment to it. Customers from those segments will promote it to others quite naturally and without prompting.

By definition, these are the people for whom your product is an exact match for the job they need to get done, and for whom the results prioritization that you did when you were designing for unmet and underserved requirements (see Chapter 4) aligns perfectly.

No other solution will do as good a job for them at achieving their goals, and in most cases these are the customers who would rather buy nothing than not have your product. That's important, because as we've described in the Key Concepts (Chapter 2), competing against non-consumption is one of the most important pattern attributes that define the early stages of disruption.

Identifying the Best Market Segments for Disruption

In addition to using the JTBDs to identify primary target customers, there is one additional thing you need to do to differentiate between categories of users in order to have the most effective segmentation strategy. Even within groups of potential customers who all need the same job done, there are variances in why they want to get the job done and in which results matter the most. To finalize your segments, you need to sort out these differences, which you will later use to develop key messages, design marketing campaigns, choose the right media, and ultimately reach the target customers.

In effect, what you are looking for are micro-segments that prioritize the importance of the results you deliver differently. Ideally, prospects in each of these micro-segments will view the unique capability that you offer as "must-have." This idea is illustrated in Figure 5-1.

Outcome-based Microsegmentation Strategy for Disruptive Market Entry

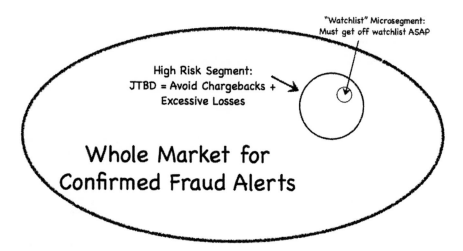

"Watchlist" Microsegment: Must get off watchlist ASAP

High Risk Segment: JTBD = Avoid Chargebacks + Excessive Losses

Whole Market for Confirmed Fraud Alerts

Figure 5-1. A micro-segmentation strategy drills down to a narrower target than even the required JTBDs, identifying the most important outcomes or desired results that motivate customers to buy based on the job they need done. This idea is illustrated for Ethoca's Confirmed Fraud Alerts (discussed in Chapter 4). The entire market for Confirmed Fraud Alerts consists of all e-commerce merchants. A key job to be done for the high-risk segment is to cancel orders that have already been screened and accepted when the bank has confirmed that a card is compromised. For merchants who are at high risk, this service prevents excessive fraud losses, chargebacks fees, and processing costs. Within this JTBD segment is a micro-segment of retailers who are at risk of losing their card acceptance privileges because their chargeback rates are too high—they absolutely must stop every possible chargeback, and they must get it under control quickly, even if the fraud can't be stopped, or their business is at risk (because they won't be able to accept payments). For this Watchlist Micro-Segment, Ethoca's Confirmed Fraud Alerts is a "must-have" service

Methodology

Marketers will recognize the Market Attractiveness/Competitive Position Matrix illustrated in Table 5-1. For the purposes of determining the best segments when trying to enter the market disruptively, you use the same form but different criteria to evaluate the desirability of each alternative target.

	Points	Ethoca Alerts
Segment Attractiveness factors		
High Value Unmet Needs (must-have features)	10	10
Total Addressable Market	5	5
Target Market is Over-served	3	3
Opportunity Trends	3	3
Projected Market Growth Rate	2	1
Total Addressable Segment Size	2	1
Total	**25**	**23**
Competitive Position factors		
Compete Against Non-Consumption	12	12
Asymmetry of Motivation	6	4
Sustainable Production Cost Advantage	3	2
Relative to Alternatives, Simpler + Target Low-end	4	4
Total	**25**	**22**

Table 5-1. For the purpose of illustrating use of this table to identify the best target segments, I've used values based on the Ethoca network and the "Watchlist Micro-Segment," used as an example. The left column of figures is the total number of points available, and the right-most column of figures shows how Ethoca's solution stacks up. When inserting values in the table for each micro-segment, be very conservative, and if you aren't sure, give yourself fewer rather than more points. This evaluation shows that this micro-segment is one of the ideal sweet spots to target for a disruptive market launch (see Figure 5-2, Best Segments for Disruption).

These criteria (explained in the next paragraphs) are used with the simple scoring tool above to rate each possible segment for attractiveness and competitive position. The weight of each criterion is built into the points allocated for that particular measure.

Segment Attractiveness Criteria

High Value, Unmet Needs ("Must-Haves"). This is the most important factor in evaluating segment attractiveness for disruption. Looking at each of your core JTBDs, which desired outcomes are most important and to which subsets of customers? Rate the degree to which each segment views these needs as both unmet and "must-have." Starting with 10 points if no other alternative exists for addressing these critical requirements, deduct 2 points if at least one other solution partially addresses this desired outcome, and 5 points if several alternatives exist in the minds of customers. If customers consider it nearly a must-have, but not quite, deduct 2 points, and if it is just nice-to-have, deduct 5 points. If it is a judgment call whether a segment views the capability as must-have or that alternatives to satisfy the need exist, deduct the points (you don't do yourself any favors with a falsely high score).

Total Addressable Market (TAM). This is everyone who has a need to get the job done, whether they are currently unserved, using a competitive product, or satisfying the need with an alternative solution not traditionally considered a competitor. Even though you will be targeting one or more smaller segments initially, if you are successful you will eventually spread into adjacent markets likely taking a smaller percentage of each than if your JTBD profile was a perfect match for their needs. Because your closing efficiency will drop as you face competitors for the JTBD, it's important that the TAM is at least $1 billion. Give yourself 5 points if the TAM is greater than $1 billion, 3 points if it's greater than $750 million, 2 points if it's greater than $500 million, and 0 points if it's less than $500 million.

Target Market Is Over-Served. This is somewhat counterintuitive, but if there are many well-established incumbents, most of whom offer more functionality than their customers need, then their cost structure is likely high and many customers would be happy with a less complex solution that costs significantly less. This usually has two corollaries: there are prospective consumers who don't participate in the market because of the high cost and complexity of existing products, and it also is a clear indication of a large TAM to eventually reach as your disruption moves upstream. Give yourself 3 points if the market is over-served and the products in it have become largely undifferentiated commodities with more features than customers are able to use. Give yourself 0 points if you are targeting a market that's already being disrupted from the low end. Give yourself 1 or 2 points if you are somewhere in between these two extremes.

Opportunity Trends. Do external environmental variables positively influence the growth potential of this market? For example, is the public becoming increasingly concerned about product safety, or do changing demographics automatically grow your TAM? Legal, political, socio-economic, technological, cultural, and international trends should all be considered for how they impact the desirability of your solution now and in the future. Give yourself 3 points if trends are highly favorable to your product's market entry and growth, 2 points if overall positive but not exceptional, 1 point if trends are neutral, and 0 points if trends negatively influence your market.

Projected Market Growth Rate. The best markets for disruptors are rapidly changing and growing. If the projected growth rate in your market exceeds 10% annually, give yourself 2 points. If it is growing but less than 10% per year, give yourself 1 point. If the market is stable, and slow or no growth is expected, give yourself 0 points.

Total Addressable Segment Size (TAS). Here, you care only about the segment defined by the JTBD that you are considering targeting. A good niche segment can be profitable on its own, and can provide you with the references and resources to expand into adjacent segments. Ideally, the total addressable size of your initial segment should be $50 million or more. If the biggest and best niche you can identify for market entry is $10 million or less, you may be building a niche product that forever occupies a small place, and not a disruptive one. Give yourself 2 points if the TAS for your target segment is greater than $50 million, 1 point if it is between $10 and $50 million, and 0 points if it's less than $10 million. If you plan to distribute your product as a freemium solution, your total addressable segment size in users should be no less than 1 million (if it's a consumer product). Give yourself 2 points for a TAS of greater than 10 million users, 1 for 1–10 million users, and 0 for less than 1 million. In B2B multi-sided markets, the target sizes depend on who is paying and on the value of the exchange between participating parties. I recommend you either come up with your own rating for these special cases or consult with a specialist.

Competitive Position Criteria

Compete Against Non-Consumption. As Wee Willie Keeler[2] famously said, "hit 'em where they ain't." The best competitive position to be in is when the only competitor for the JTBD is using nothing, or you are targeting a market that is too low margin or otherwise undesirable or unattainable to incumbents. If you can, find a segment that's left out of the current market because incumbent products are too expensive, too difficult to use, too complex, inaccessible, require professional expertise beyond the skills of most users, or a variety of other reasons. These are excellent market entry points for disruptive innovators to hit the ground running and dominate. It also gives you a chance to work out other parts of your strategy, such as positioning,

---

[2]In the early days of professional baseball, Wee Willie Keeler was a diminutive star who hit way above his size. Just 5'4" and 140 pounds, Willie had a career batting average of .341 over a 19-year span, and he hit over .300 13 years in a row from 1894 to 1906, ranking him in the top ten in his league every one of those years. The last six of those .300+ years were during baseball's dead ball era—balls were used until they were soft and the stitching was coming apart, and they did not yet have the cork centers or tightly wound string that give modern balls more "pop." Pitchers also had the upper hand with spitballs (made illegal in 1920) and much bigger ballpark dimensions, which made it nearly impossible to hit home runs. Willie's highest career batting average of .424 in 1897 still stands today as the highest ever for a left-handed hitter. When asked by Brooklyn Eagle writer Abe Yager what his secret was to hitting, Keeler famously replied, "I have already written a treatise and it reads like this: 'Keep your eye clear and hit 'em where they ain't; that's all." His hitting advice rings true to disruptive innovators today, who do best when they compete by avoiding the competition. (Abstracted from American Society for Baseball Research biography of Willie Keeler. http://sabr.org/bioproj/person/074d42fd . Accessed November 26, 2013.)

price, messaging, and distribution, since you will know that if there is a problem, it isn't because of competition. Give yourself 12 points if the segment currently does not have a solution to the problem you solve, 8 points if there is a partial workaround solution or indirect competition, 4 points if you have a single direct competitor, and 0 points if there are multiple solutions available to this segment.

Asymmetry of Motivation. If incumbents view this segment as unimportant and not worth fighting for, they will be more motivated to flee or stay out of the segment than to fight for it. If you have followed the advice in this book regarding what your product should do, and have a cost advantage that allows you to price below a level that is profitable for incumbents, then your motivation to fight for the market will be high. This asymmetry of motivation will cause competitors to leave the segment if they made the mistake of trying to get into it, or stay out, leaving you with an easy beachhead to take while you build your market strength and portfolio of references. Give yourself 6 points if incumbent competitors are more likely to leave the market than fight you, 4 points if they are likely to put up a weak fight but aren't competitive, 2 points if there are multiple weak competitors, and 0 points if you face direct attack by a strong competitor.

Sustainable Production-Cost Advantage. If you have a patented technology or unique production process that gives you a sustainably lower cost to create your product than competitors, enabling you to price your products at 50% or lower of incumbent pricing, then you have the ability to support a low-end disruption strategy. The larger your cost advantage, the more effective you are, as greater numbers of consumers will be willing to give up performance or features for price, and incumbents cannot simply lower their prices to match yours. If the price is low enough, your product may also become an alternative option in markets not currently considered competitive. Give yourself 3 points for a 10x cost advantage, 2 points for greater than 2x cost advantage, 1 point if you have an advantage but it is less than 2x, and 0 points if your price advantage is less than 50%.

Relative to Incumbents, Simpler and Target Low End. If incumbents view your product as inferior, or even as a "toy," but it is functional and offers benefit to segments concerned about complexity and ease of use, then you have an advantage that incumbents may not be able to match without hurting their brand image. Simplicity is a virtue, but don't equate that with low quality. If you have a radical simplicity advantage based on a completely different approach to solving the customer's problem, give yourself 4 points. If you are simpler, but have reduced performance as a result on key attributes that would make your product more appropriate for consumers rather than pros, give yourself 2 or 3 points depending on how much you've sacrificed to be simpler. If your product is simpler, but sacrifices important capabilities to reduce complexity, give yourself 1 point. If you have not improved usability relative to incumbents, and are neither less complex nor easier to learn, give yourself 0 points.

Complete Table 5-1 with your rankings for each micro-segment opportunity, and total them when you're finished to determine your overall rating for segment attractiveness and competitive position. To finish your analysis, plot the values on the Best Segments for Disruption graph (see Figure 5-2).

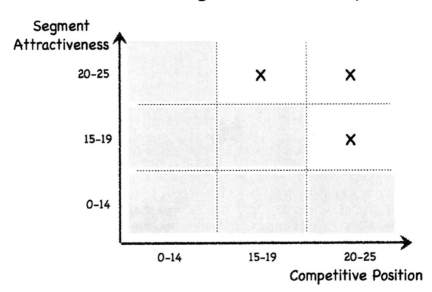

Figure 5-2. As you rank micro-segments for targeting, the only ones you should consider in the beginning are the three marked with Xs in the upper-right corner of this graph. The rankings in this chart are displayed for what I've labeled the "Watchlist Micro-Segment" for Ethoca's Confirmed Fraud Alerts service in Table 5.1, and are shown here as the dot in the upper-right corner. The graph shows that this is an ideal segment for initial market entry. Ethoca had more than one strong micro-segment, and you likely will too. In this case, targeting will be driven by where you have early success and connections to help you sell.

The Best Segments for Disruption

When you've plotted the values from your Segment Attractiveness/Competitive Position matrices, it becomes immediately obvious which micro-segments are the best ones for you to target as a disruptive innovator. Referring to Figure 5-2 , note that the only segments suitable for initial market entry for a disruptive product are those marked with an X and, ideally, you only want segments based on jobs that fall in the upper-right corner.

The segments that are one below and one to the left are good for second- and third-priority niches, and should be considered for initial market entry only if you don't have any targets in the upper-right corner. (But be aware that this isn't a good sign for disruption. Hopefully, if you have to target one of the secondary niches, your rank places you very near the edge of the upper-right section.)

The greyed-out segments are suitable only when you have successfully taken all those marked with Xs and are ready to enter mainstream markets. Initially, you should stay out of them, almost categorically, because in almost all cases you will be fighting against a much better resourced incumbent who is motivated to protect that segment against encroachment. Once threatened, such competitors are more likely to come after you in segments that they would ordinarily stay away from.

Avoiding Incumbents' Bread and Butter

In the previous section, I advised you to avoid the greyed-out segments in the Best Segments for Disruption graph. If your company has the wrong kind of investors, or management that believes the style of business planning taught in MBA programs is appropriate for a disruptive startup, they will often push you to go after these segments, precisely because they can see large verifiable dollars being spent there today and want you to go where the money is.

Tip One of the worst market-entry mistakes you can make, if you are potentially disruptive, is to go after existing mainstream segments where incumbents are strong, unless you have a huge cost advantage and can win on low price alone. It will limit your growth potential, rile incumbents, and provoke competitive battles you probably cannot win. Even if you can price below the competitive alternatives, it's better to initially target segments that incumbents view as undesirable or low-end and are currently unserved.

That is usually the worst mistake a potential disruptor can make, as it will forever limit your growth potential, and almost certainly ensure that you do not go on to disrupt those markets. So, here I amplify that message with several reasons why you should never directly target a core segment of the incumbent market as an initial beachhead:

- Incumbents are highly motivated to defend their turf

- Incumbents are much better resourced for a war of attrition

- Your actions alert them to your presence and intent to target their markets

- Incumbents have inertia on their side—customers will almost always choose the known and established product over an unknown that is "better" or "different"

Your only "safe" strategy to launch an attack against incumbents in a core segment as an initial target is low price, and you need a huge cost advantage to be able to price sufficiently below incumbents so that price alone can be a deciding factor. But, even if you are a low-end disruptor, it is still preferable to find an unserved segment of undesirable customers (to the incumbents) to target for initial market entry. That's because you want to defer a direct fight until you have established market success and a reputation that will carry you forward.

One other thing to consider is that if you do target a mainstream segment, you may get lucky and succeed in carving out a niche simply because you are better-focused and provide superior service when compared to incumbents. But you will always be playing on the incumbents' home field, and from this vantage you have little hope of changing the rules of competition.

At some point in your evolution, your product footprint will expand to adjacent markets, including core segments of incumbents. But the time for that is when your product has successfully established itself in defensible segments where you own the JTBD, you have solid references and enthusiastic users to leverage, and your product has improved sufficiently to be viewed as "good enough" (in the Key Concepts sense described in Chapter 2) for new sets of jobs. When this happens, you will likely have generated considerable market momentum and positive stories that will help the mainstream users in those segments see you as a safe choice.

Summary

It should be fairly obvious at the conclusion of this chapter that the process of segmenting a market when you have a potential disruptive innovation on your hands, especially as a startup company, is very different from conventional segmentation strategies. As noted, it would behoove incumbents to use JTBD-based segmentation as well, because it creates more homogeneous groups of potential customers with the highest probability of responding to your product enthusiastically.

It also makes those segments more receptive to your marketing, which leads to much higher sales success rates. Fortunately, few incumbents will ever do things this way, and that gives you the upper hand.

Remember as you choose your segments that the purpose is not to create a perfect emulation of this model, but to increase the chances of your success by focusing on the attributes that matter most to your prospective customers. As you define micro-segments to target, they need to be big enough to matter—it's hardly worth doing if the universe of potential users is just a handful—but small enough to be manageable.

Key Takeaways

- A strong segmentation strategy is as important today as it has ever been, and it is critical for increasing the probability of successful market disruption.

- Segmentation is as much about saying "no" to some opportunities as it is about saying "yes" to others. Often, what you say no to is even more important than what you say yes to.

- The unique jobs to be done (JTBDs) that your product serves better than any other are the key to defining highly targeted segments for disruption.

- For initial market entry, drill down into the JTBDs to identify micro-segments that value desired results differently. The more precisely you target these results in your marketing to the micro-segments, the faster they will become your customers.

- Avoid targeting segments that are important to incumbents until you are well established in areas they are not interested in, or for which they have a poor solution.

- When you have multiple choices of micro-segments to target, use the principles of Asymmetry of Motivation, Competing Against Non-Consumption, and best match with High Value Unmet Needs as your guide in prioritizing.

Segmentation is the first step in developing your disruptive marketing strategy. The next plank in your strategy is positioning, which is discussed next in Chapter 6.

Positioning

Nothing is good or ill but by comparison.

—Islamic proverb

Everything is compared with something, even if that something is (doing) nothing. Understanding this simple and fundamental idea is the Eureka insight that tells us why positioning is strategically important to product marketing generally, but never more so than when you are trying to disrupt a market.

We perceive and understand the relationships between things, especially similarities, differences, and rankings. Beyond a few absolute reference points, everything we know is relative. Moreover, everyone perceives things a little bit differently, based on our experiences, preferences, prior knowledge, and current circumstance.

Ironically, from our own perspective, we assume things are exactly what we perceive, and there is a tendency to unthinkingly assume that everyone else perceives the same things that we do. Yet, when we are forced to think about it, we can recognize that what is to one person the sweet smell of spring air is to another the choking pollen that provokes violent allergic reactions and asthma.

In the same room or even in the same bed, men will generally perceive that the temperature is too hot while women perceive it as too cold. A delicious dry red burgundy to one is a chalky, acidic unpleasant drink to another. Even when you appreciate and love the wine's flavor, when you drink it with fish, it can leave you cold, while with a fine steak, it is sublime. And after eating something sweet or salty, it can be an absolutely unenjoyable waste of money.

And, can anything be as subjective as art? A masterwork to one can be boring, tacky, or repulsive to another. If you want to start an endless argument between classic rock lovers, try posing this question: "Which is the better and more influential band—the Rolling Stones or The Beatles?"

Not only do we live in a world with no absolutes, what we know, or think we know, changes over time. The world is flat, then it's round. The earth is the center of everything, and then it's a planet in orbit around the sun, which is moving in a galaxy, which is itself hurtling at crazy speeds outward in an expanding universe.

People who were once possessed with evil demons that only high priests could exorcise, with an invocation to God to push aside Satan, are now seen to have been mentally ill, physically diseased, or perhaps high from eating some wild mushrooms. Newtonian physics is replaced by relativity and quantum mechanics. A ninth planet, Pluto, is discovered—or is it an asteroid, a Kuiper Belt object, or perhaps a dwarf planet?

If all my elementary school science tests were re-graded, I'm almost certain I'd be 10% smarter than I appeared at the time, even though my answers haven't changed.

Perception Is Reality

In fact, perception is more real than reality. We know that what we believe can influence what we see and how we interact with the world around us. Perception is how we decide what our interactions, needs, and desires are. So, metaphysically speaking, is any reality more real than what we perceive, even if it's different from what others perceive?

Positioning is about influencing the consumer's perceptual map, helping to build anchor reference points and relationships, understanding, and preferences. When you position a product, you are telling the market what you want to be compared with and why yours is the best solution to solve the customer's problem. The problem for many entrepreneurs and product managers is that this notion doesn't sit well with them. They aren't interested in being compared with alternatives, but rather they want to stand on their own merits.

Note Because each of us perceives the world differently, each of us has a different version of reality. Positioning is about influencing the target consumer's perceptual map, establishing a frame of reference for understanding, and occupying a unique place (position) in the customer's mind.

So why do it? Because if you don't identify what the product is and who it's for effectively and communicate that clearly, the customer will do it for you. Worse, the marketplace, analysts, media, and your competitors will all try to do it for you, leading to a dog's breakfast of confusion about your place in the market and why customers should choose you for jobs they need done.

It's All in Your Mind

To get to a workable definition of positioning and why it is a key ingredient in establishing a disruptive innovation, I begin by reviewing a few insights from cognitive science. It's a slight detour, but it will be helpful in understanding why we create positioning strategies and what the objectives are.

While the human brain is still largely a mystery, over the past 50–60 years we've begun to peel back the first layer of the onion of secrets. Psychologists, behavioral scientists, and even marketing researchers have studied how we take in information, the nature of memory, how and why we make decisions, what factors trigger action, how we associate related and disparate bits of data, and how we perceive the world around us.

In this discussion, I'm going to assume that you are a founding executive of a potentially disruptive startup, but not necessarily a professional marketer. You may even have a healthy dose of skepticism about positioning and why we do it.

That's okay—marketers have given us lots of reasons not to trust them, so skepticism is probably warranted. For now, I'm just going to consider how the brain perceives, stores, recalls, and uses information.

Brain Basics

What we've come to realize is that while in some ways our brains are able to process literally mind-boggling amounts of data and reach conclusions and take action so fast that we don't even know we're doing it, in other ways, our capabilities are quite limited and primitive when compared to modern computing technology. For example, while we have immense storage capacity, we can still have a great deal of difficulty remembering and retrieving specific facts, such as "did I take my blue pill this morning?" or "where are my car keys?".

On the other hand, we can remember exactly where we were and what we were doing decades ago when significant events happened and how we felt at the time. Sometimes, something as simple as a smell can instantly dredge up memories we'd forgotten we had and make them so real we're instantly transported to another place and time.

While we can store a lifetime of memories, real-time processing of data is relatively limited. We get confused if required to prioritize two equally important things that are both novel at the same time. For example, it is extremely hard to talk on the phone while driving and pay attention to hazards on the road such as potholes or cyclists or another driver who suddenly stops in front of us. And, while we sense all simultaneous inputs, our short-term memory lasts only about 15 seconds, after which point, if the data isn't either brought to the fore for action or moved to long-term memory, we have huge difficulty recalling it.

The brain uses short-term memory to hold sensory inputs, to aid in processing what to do about urgent threats, and to assess our immediate needs for action and response. The rapid decay of short-term memory appears to be a defense against information overload. So, clearly short-term memory (often referred to as "working memory") is about sensing and reacting and it operates on a "use it or lose it" model.

Long-term memory is about pattern recognition, adaptation, and recalling important facts for later use. We assume that because it must last a lifetime, it is more precious and that's why not everything gets lodged there. But the question is, how do things move from working memory to long-term storage and why?

Selective Perception

Perception is the process of taking in sensory inputs and attaching meaning to them, or how we use short-term memory combined with what's already stored in long-term memory to make decisions and/or choose what new things get stored for the long term. I say *choose* because we can control some of this intentionally, but most perception happens subconsciously, without us even realizing we're doing it.

■ **Note** The brain actively resists saving new information for the long term through a layered series of perceptual filters. Knowing these hurdles and what the brain is programmed to allow to get over them is key to understanding what a positioning strategy must accomplish, the advantages that a disruptor has, and why positioning is both valuable and necessary for marketing success.

Cognitive psychologists have shown that our brains actively resist moving data to long-term memory (which may help to explain why you're still having trouble absorbing everything I said about JTBD theory in Chapter 4, and why I keep repeating it). In effect, we have layered filters ("cognitive biases") to prevent data that isn't important enough from getting into our brains. "Selective perception" is what we call these cognitive bias hurdles, and it impacts both short- and long-term memory.

To compound our difficulty in understanding how all this happens, each of us is different—with our genes and our life experiences (nature and nurture) impacting how we perceive. When you consider that two people can be together experiencing the same event and view everything about it through different filters, it's truly a wonder that we can agree on anything.

There are four specific, progressive selection filters that have been identified. Data must get through all four in series to make it to long-term memory. They are:

- **Selective exposure.** We actively choose what things to do, and therefore what experiences to be exposed to via likes, dislikes, and preferences. (Do you go to school or to the concert?) Much selective exposure is also random or by chance.

- **Selective attention.** Once exposed to inputs, we selectively choose what to pay attention to. (Do you listen to the lecturer in class or think about the cute girl sitting in front of you?)

- **Selective interpretation.** We decide whether each bit of input is meaningful and important and whether it fits with our existing beliefs, attitudes, and models of the world, and therefore whether it is worth keeping. (If you believe in Biblical creation as the explanation for the origin of the world, you will tend to discard or refute data to the contrary.) Have you ever wondered why it's so hard to get people to do things a different way, or to change someone's political views, even with immense contradictory evidence?

- **Selective retention.** After passing through all the other filters, only a portion of what we want to keep is retained. (Do you remember the 10 most important identifiers that make up the Disruption Fingerprint? Hint: See Chapter 1.)

On top of all these, our memory degrades and becomes distorted over time. We've all had the experience of remembering things that didn't actually happen that way and of losing key data points, even concerning very important and significant events. For example, have you ever forgotten, or almost forgotten, your anniversary or your mom's birthday? Don't worry; you aren't alone.

The vast majority of things that are available to be perceived never make it past these hurdles to the brain. In fact, each filter blocks the majority of inputs that get to that stage. Even when the thing being blocked is good for us.

Is the challenge that a disruptor faces in reaching consumers and having them remember and/or acknowledge what you do starting to come into focus? Actually, the challenge is the same for everyone, but amplifying the challenge for potential disruptors is the fact that consumers lack familiar frames of reference with which to perceive and understand the value that a disruptor brings to the table and why it's important.

Fortunately, disruptive innovators also have a natural advantage in getting their message through these filters—I'll describe why shortly—if they understand how.

What Gets Through the Filters?

Humans are programmed to reliably allow a few things through the filters of selective perception. You might guess some or most of them:

- Sex
- Fear
- Surprise
- Shock
- Humor
- Strong emotions
- Associations/connections with things we already know or have experienced
- News

Interestingly, there is one category of occurrence that always breaks through and persists, so much so that it has a name: "flashbulb memories."

Flashbulb memories are exceptionally vivid in detail and are so-named because in our minds they are like a snapshot that includes where you were, what you were doing, the time of day—literally everything from the important to the trivial. You may never have heard the term, but you will certainly recognize the concept in the context of shared experiences.

Note "Flashbulb memories" are vivid, persistent, and strong memories created instantaneously at times where the elements of extreme surprise or shock, high importance or consequence, and strong emotion occur simultaneously, such as when you experience a disaster. They offer key insights into the importance of using the right perceptual keys to get past our brain filters.

Collective flashbulb memories are those where virtually everyone can recall in detail similar stories as a universal shared experience, such as when you first heard about JFK being assassinated (if you're old enough).[1] It's noteworthy that most collective flashbulb memories are disasters.

Psychologists theorize that three major elements have to coincide to create these strong, vivid, persistent memories: extreme surprise/shock, consequentiality/importance, and strong emotion, which explains the connection to disasters, especially in the TV age.

There are also more localized and personal flashbulb memories. Typically, people remember with equally vivid detail their first serious car crash, the first time they had sex, starting their first job, their first child being born, and so on. These demonstrate that positive events can also register as flashbulb memories, although they often have a lesser element of surprise and greater personal significance and emotional impact.

Looking back at the list of things that we are programmed to allow through our selective filters, it's clear that most of these keys are experienced simultaneously in a flashbulb memory, which is why they are so strong and persistent. Flashbulb memories are an interesting anomalous pattern that demonstrates just how important these keys are in making it past the perceptual gatekeepers to lodge in long-term memory.

Memory Retrieval

Although we tend to think of human memory as the biological version of computer memory, it should already be clear that people do things quite differently—that we are selective and biased in what we remember, that our emotions and time can distort memories, and that there are even contexts in which we can create false memories. Not surprisingly, we also access and retrieve memory differently, and that is tied to the principal ways we use it to navigate the world.

There are two principal modes of memory retrieval, and they function differently. They are *recognition* and *recall*.

---

[1] Iconic collective flashbulb memories from the Baby Boomer generation forward include:
- Kennedy assassination
- Lunar landing and man on the moon
- Nixon impeachment
- John Lennon assassination
- Black Monday global stock market crash
- Challenger disaster
- Berlin Wall coming down
- Princess Diana death in violent car crash
- 9/11 attack and the collapse of the World Trade Center towers

Recognition is primarily about processing and interpreting patterns and is operating most of the time subconsciously. It works by associating current sensory perceptions (i.e., what you are hearing, seeing, tasting, etc., now) with events or physical objects that you have previously experienced, comparing the present with past knowledge and sizing up the differences.

So we quickly recognize that something we see is an animal, that the animal is a dog, that the dog is a German shepherd, and that its behavior suggests that it is friendly. This highly specialized function of our brain even includes an area dedicated to facial recognition (which is one reason that body language and expression are so important in communication).

Recall is a different process. It involves remembering facts, experiences, or objects that are not present. In recall, the brain directly accesses information in memory to reconstruct a mental image, concept, or detailed information.

For example, remembering a person's name or visualizing how to throw a football 50 yards down the field at the right speed and trajectory to drop in the receiver's hands at just the right moment both use recall, as does remembering the alternative routes you can use to get from home to work or the grocery store.

In both recognition and recall, brain scientists believe that memories are reassembled in real-time from various elements stored in different parts of the brain. In other words, we don't have a single place where an image of last Christmas is stored. Rather, the memory is stored as a neural network of data points, and the retrieval of it involves traversing the same nerve pathways that the original memory used to lodge itself in the brain. This distribution of memories across the brain may explain both the durability of memory (damage to one part of the brain or to one part of a memory doesn't impact other parts of it) and also why we can be 95% right, but still lose or confuse pieces of a memory over time.

Importantly, what this enables people to do that computers can't is to directly (rather than sequentially) access memories based on direct links to questions or external cues, assess the meaning of what we are sensing instantly, and react appropriately.

It also enables us to know without searching whether we know or can know the answers to certain questions. For example, the brain instantly knows that the question, "Where is the dog's car parked" is absurd, that there is no answer, and that it doesn't have to engage in a search for the data. We know this because we hierarchically link facts into classes, subsets, and patterns and infer answers from these patterns. This instant and usually subconscious process is better known as *stereotyping*.[2]

An important implication of the way that memories are stored and recalled is that different triggers get the memories out of our heads more effectively and efficiently.

There are three main ways that we recall memories:

- **Serially.** The ability to remember things chronologically, or as a list of things in series. Although we can generally remember many items in lists, there are frequent encoding errors in order. We often forget list items or substitute similar items. Serial data tends to degrade over time (we remember lists better in the short term than the long term), and we have better memory for short lists than long ones. Seven is the maximum number of list items that people can reliably remember. We can usually remember the top three things in a list, and their rank, if the list is meaningful to us. We can almost always identify the first item in a list.

- **Cued.** Memories are cued verbally, numerically, or visually, or by a variety of sensory stimuli. So, even when we cannot recall all the items in a list serially, the right cue will often trigger recall. Cues can be other items in the list (e.g., we can't recall the third item until we've said the fourth), mnemonic values, sounds, smells, or other learned pairings.

- **Free.** As the term implies, no order or cuing is involved. This is the slowest and hardest type of recall, and even without cuing or being asked to recall the list in order, people tend to more easily recall the first item (primacy effect), the last item (recency effect), and adjacent items in a list (contiguity effect). In other words, our brains impose order and remember some things better than others based on their position in the list.

---

[2]The term "stereotype" often has a negative connotation, especially as it comes into play with prejudicial treatment of classes of people based on disabilities, skin color, age, and so on. But it's important to note that stereotyping is a natural process and an extremely important tool for survival. If we had to think through the characteristics of a grizzly bear or great white shark linearly by assessing a complete list of all their attributes and make rational decisions about what we should do if we encounter one, it would likely be too late by the time we arrived at a conclusion. Stereotyping gives us the ability to recognize general patterns and classes of associated attributes all at once, focus our attention only on the small subset of differences that differentiate a pit bull from a border collie, for example, and then react accordingly.

We're now ready to start applying what we know about the brain to create an effective (disruptive) positioning strategy.

Positioning Strategy Basics

When the concept of positioning[3] was first described by Al Ries and Jack Trout in a series of articles in *Advertising Age* in the early 1970s, it was a time of great upheaval. The Baby Boomer generation was coming of age. The Vietnam War was ending. The United States and Russia had engaged in the cold war space race, culminating with the first lunar landing and a man walking on the moon. Marshall McLuhan had declared that the "medium is the message," and it's not clear that even he realized how right he was.

The OPEC cartel acted as one to raise oil prices and control supply, creating the world's first oil crisis, which in turn lead to a decade of "stagflation." Most homes were getting their first color TV, and the Watergate scandal was exposed. We witnessed, on live TV, impeachment hearings that would result in the first and only resignation of a U.S. president, even as Richard Nixon declared, "I am not a crook".

By today's standards, the pace of change was probably slow, but this was the generation that coined the term "future shock," and which was increasingly bombarded by ever-accelerating change and hyper-communications. It was the first time when we began to appreciate our own limits to absorbing information, managing it, and using it.

The late 1950s through the 1960s was the "Mad Men" era — the golden age of advertising. It's when marketers began to realize the need for greater sophistication in how they crafted messages. More science, less art. More measurable impact, less "any ad will do."

Product marketers were realizing that their claims of "new and improved" weren't enough to sell more soap. The new idea of positioning strategy was introduced as a way to break through the clutter and the information overload. A second, and equally important, goal was simplifying marketing communication to enable it to get past perceptual filters and into the intended customer's consciousness while still capturing the essence of a product's uniqueness and value to the intended user.

---

[3]My intent in this chapter is to summarize the importance of positioning to disruptors, while updating the theory and highlighting what's different and how to take advantage of those differences. If you are interested in all the nuances of positioning strategy, the original book by Al Ries and Jack Trout is still a good read and highly recommended. Ries & Trout, *Positioning: The Battle for Your Mind* (New York, NY: McGraw Hill, 1981).

Positioning strategy has come a long way in 40 years and its goals are better understood. If anything, the ideas that Ries & Trout introduced are even more valid and necessary today.

Principles of Positioning Theory

Think of the human brain as an old-fashioned pigeon-holing system. Each bit of information, every memory, resides in its own pigeon hole, and no other knowledge can reside in that place (yes, it's actually stored as a neural network pathway, but for our purposes, it's more useful to think of it as a unique physical place). Information has a "position" that it owns in your brain— indexed by descriptive cues that retrace the pathways by which the memory was originally stored to perceive, retrieve, and understand what the thing is and what its purpose is.

Because each of us perceives uniquely, the positioning of every concept, thing, or experience is created by and unique to each individual, and critically depends on what gets through our selective perceptual filters. Left completely to ourselves, each of us would position everything slightly—or a lot—differently, depending on the attributes that break through our filters. Even for shared flashbulb memories, the position in the mind is something that each of us creates and controls individually.

As implied by my quick review of brain science and how we store and retrieve knowledge, the job of the product marketer is to influence and help define the creation of those pigeonholes or positions. Marketers must ensure that consumers can access that pigeonhole at the time they are ready to make a purchase decision and can recall the most relevant bits of information relative to the customer's job to be done, or desired outcome.

Importantly, and contrary to the way most people view it, the strategic marketing discipline of positioning is not something done to the product, but rather it's how we navigate the pathways of the mind to create a lasting and relevant perception for the product. It's subtle, but it's a different idea that bears repeating—a successful positioning strategy happens in the consumer's mind. It is a simplification of what value(s) the product provides, not something a crafty marketer does to the product.

■ **Tip** Keep in mind that the goal of positioning is to create a unique pigeonhole in the consumer's mind that you, and only you, can occupy, enabling quick retrieval based on the right cues.

The purpose of positioning is to assist the brain in making connections that map a unique JTBD to your product (create a pigeonhole), and establish retrieval cues, so that at the point of making a decision, the knowledge of your product is recalled.

What does this imply?

If "Coke is the real thing" (the original, the first, the authentic soda)—*nothing else can be*, unless it displaces Coke from that position, which is nearly impossible to do. Notice that I used a tagline that Coca Cola first introduced in 1969. It hasn't been actively used in exactly that form in its advertising for nearly 40 years, yet we still remember it and identify it with Coke.

Part of the reason for that is that the slogan captures a truth that resonates: Coke was the original, it is the leader, and it is perhaps the best-known brand in the world (although Apple and Google are giving it a run for the money).

Similarly, if you hear the phrase "ultimate driving machine" (performance, quality, precision engineering, and unmatched driving experience), most people will automatically associate that with BMW, even if they can't afford or aren't in the market for one. If you think about any brand that has a strong identity, it also has a strong position that it owns in the mind.

Likewise, Google is search. (And, if you're on the corporate marketing side, it's also analytics and intention-based advertising.) It's a position so strong that we say, "I'm going to Google that" when we mean we're going to search for something online, even if we use a different tool to do it. By the same token, Amazon is online retail, and is the first place most people look when they want to buy something online.

Positions can be just as strongly negative and have the same near permanence. For example, a marketer might have described the Ford Pinto as a small, stylish, economical car; a subcompact class vehicle designed to compete with the Japanese small cars when it was introduced to market.[4] In fact, its tagline was, somewhat ironically, "the little carefree car."

---

[4]In fact, this was very close to Ford's positioning as a tough, dependable, economical "back to basics" car for the youth market. Ads were designed to recall Ford's original philosophy of building solid cars that the working man could afford, and related it back to the Model A. Follow this link to view the original commercial for the Pinto: http://www.youtube.com/watch?v=HA99GsXC3wI. Accessed: January 20, 2014.

Unfortunately, the car didn't live up to Ford's claims, and what most of us remember about the Ford Pinto (even today, more than 30 years since it went out of production) is how the gas tank exploded when the car was hit from behind. Here's the crash test that verified the problem, and seared very different positioning of the car in our minds: http://www.youtube.com/watch?v=1gOxWPGsJNY. Accessed: January 20, 2014. What stuck with us was "too small, unsafe, gas tank explodes when hit from rear." It clearly demonstrates that positioning is in the mind of the consumer, not something that marketers can do to a product.

Unfortunately, the enduring position that the Pinto occupies is "gas tank explodes when hit from behind," thanks to bad decisions designed to save $11 per car according to Ford's internal cost/benefit analysis. (Third parties offered fixes that cost far less, but even Ford's relatively high cost assessment of $11 is shocking when you consider how small the added cost to the vehicle versus the lives that it cost and the damage it did to the Pinto marque and the entire Ford brand.) An entire generation of consumers thought of Ford as the company that compromised safety to save a few pennies—a consumer-defined positioning that cost many hundreds of billions of dollars in lost sales.

After nearly 40 years and immense effort at improving their quality, Ford has largely repaired its reputation, but if you ask anyone over the age of 50 about the Pinto, their immediate response will still be "exploding gas tank." It's an important reminder that the consumer is the one who assigns and controls the position, and that the product marketer can only influence that position with messaging that is consistent and hopefully honest, and that matches the consumer's experience.

Our understanding of the brain—including its perceptual filters, its natural resistance to information overload, how it recalls what it knows, and how it applies information to decision-making—leads us to a number of principles about how to create a strong position. These principles are:

- Comparison to similar ideas
- Resonance
- Relevance

Comparison to Similar Ideas

Our brains are stereotyping engines. To make sense of the world, we are constantly trying to group things into categories by their similarities and differences. Strong positioning tells you what category something belongs to and then identifies how it's different from other things in the same category. Underlying the comparisons we make, there are some attributes that we care about more than others:

- **Ranking.** The brain makes lists and tries to sort them. Recall that we can generally only remember up to seven items in a list, and that we are pretty good at identifying the top three items as well as things that are adjacent to other list items. The best rank to be is number 1 (the leadership position), because we can almost always remember the top item in any category that we care about. In fact, a rule of thumb when positioning is that the only position that counts is leadership, and if you aren't or can't be the leader, then you need to "position against" the leader.

- **Being first.** Your first girlfriend. Your first car. Your first apartment. The first concert you attended. We remember firsts long after we've forgotten who or what came second or third. It's a special case of ranking, and it's not based on value, quality, reliability, or other attributes, but on chronology. The first time has special meaning, even if it ranks nowhere near the top on any other quality.

- **Novelty.** While we like the familiar, we also crave newness and notice differences.

Resonance

Simply, there are things that we care about and things that we don't. No amount of advertising and promotion is going to get a male interested in female sanitary products. A young fit person doesn't care about Geritol or adult diapers. A retiree isn't going to get excited about the newest boy band constructed to appeal to tween girls.

The things that resonate the most are those that are in general categories of interest (to the individual) and deliver desired outcomes. Things that aren't one of these two create cognitive dissonance, so that even if one group of people finds a message highly interesting, another group that isn't interested can find it highly annoying.

Want to get a male to turn off the football game? Try a steady stream of advertisements for tampons. On the other hand, there is a reason that beer advertisers do well promoting their products at sports events—when we're together with friends having a good time, beer resonates.

Key resonance factors include:

- **Consistency.** Even with products we care about, inconsistency can lead to cognitive dissonance. When promoting a BMW, the visual imagery, words, showroom, test drive experience, and even the sales personnel all need to be consistent with the message of the "ultimate driving machine." If BMW suddenly started promoting safety, it would be confusing and perhaps even contradictory to the excitement that many expect of an ultimate driving machine. For BMW, safety is an expected hygiene factor, not the raison d'être. Being consistent with yourself and with what your target audience expects of you is a very important part of resonance.

- **Repetition.** Repeating a key message, both literally and in a variety of contexts, is an important tool for breaking through both the selective exposure and selective attention filters. If you are not present in the places that your target chooses to go or during the times when they are predisposed to pay attention, your positioning won't matter because it won't be seen. Repetition aids in awareness, recall, and in creating the initial store in memory.

- **Strong emotional connection.** Even the most boring products benefit from being associated with love, fear, family ties, fun, or any other strong emotions. We may perceive ourselves as rational, cost/benefit oriented creatures, but the reality is that if a spreadsheet allows you to spend more quality time with your kids, you're far more likely to see it as a necessary purchase that resonates.

Relevance

For a product position to earn a permanent place in the mind, it has to be relevant. Relevance means subject matter that interests me, news, associations, and connections to other things that I care about, and most importantly, how well the characteristics of the product satisfy a job that the consumer needs to get done or anticipates needing to get done in the future.

Tip To establish a strong and unique position in the consumer's mind, resonate with the target consumer, be relevant to the consumer's interests and JTBDs, and be the leader in accomplishing the JTBD when compared with all alternative solutions.

Use of Appropriate Keys to Unlock Perceptual Filters

None of these factors—comparisons and relationships to other things, resonance, nor relevance to the consumer—matter if a message fails to get through the perceptual filters. If one of these keys—sex, fear, surprise, shock, humor, strong emotions, connections, or news—can be directly made part of the position then it will have a much easier time breaking through into the recipient's consciousness. Indirect use of these keys is also a useful tactic to package a product message to get through the filters.

The preceding paragraphs are a crash course in positioning. Not intended to be complete, these principles and guidelines offer a general overview of how to effectively position any product. Disruptive positioning is both simpler and more difficult, and we'll come back to the how-to at the end of this chapter after discussing some examples.

Example: Positioning the Apple iPod

At its introduction, the iPod was positioned as the first portable music player that allowed you to carry your music collection in your pocket. The advertising focused on this, plus the unique attributes that enabled it for mainstream consumers (design elegance, simplicity, and small size) with the tagline "1,000 songs in your pocket." (See Figure 6-1.)

Figure 6-1. The introductory ad for the iPod summed up the unique value proposition, JTBD by a digital music player, and the product positioning with a short, snappy, and compelling tagline. This ad simultaneously embodies the message of who the product was designed for with its elegance, simplicity, and fashion-forward design. It was the exact opposite of everything that came before it.

Although there were at least 13 MP3 digital music players that had been released prior to the introduction of the iPod, the iPod immediately established itself as the leader by the simplicity of its design and its focus on the compelling reasons why a consumer would choose to buy a digital music player.

Prior to the iPod, you practically needed to be an engineer to use an MP3 player, and every bit of using it required expertise and/or determination that mainstream users did not possess. It was difficult to rip your music, difficult to get it from a computer to the music player, and difficult to use the player. Worse, the players suffered from insufficient capacity to make it all worthwhile, even after compressing every bit of musical quality from the songs you wanted to load.

The iPod wasn't the first. But it was the first to get it right by properly addressing the JTBD requirements of regular users with a "good enough" solution to create the market. Then, they quickly followed up by addressing additional desired outcomes and improving the functionality, a lot of which was accomplished by iTunes, which made it dead simple for anyone to rip music, organize it, create playlists, and load the iPod simply by plugging it in, and ultimately to legally purchase MP3 music for the first time.

Apple also realized that music was about pop culture and fashion and made cool devices that made a statement about the purchaser. Early users of the iPod were style leaders, and when we started seeing people everywhere with the telltale white ear buds and cable, they were walking advertisements to the rest of the market.

So what if Apple had released the iPod, but focused on its features and presumed benefits? You don't need to look far to see what that kind of poor positioning and messaging does. It's how everyone before Apple did it, and it was also instrumental in the failure of products by heavyweights like Sony and Microsoft.

Take what is considered the first commercially successful MP3 player—the Diamond Rio PMP300 (still not the first, but with sales of 200,000 units, it was the first to sell enough to call it successful and earn a small profit). See Figure 6-2.

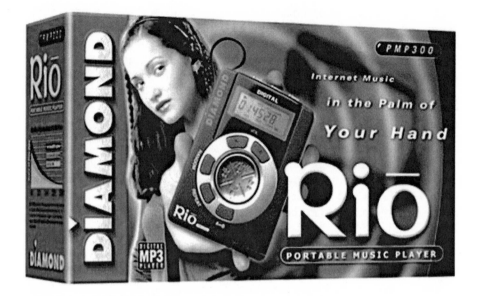

Figure 6-2. While moderately successful in the market, sales of the Diamond Rio PMP300 were insignificant when compared with the music player market as a whole. The advertising, and weak positioning it expresses, is illustrative of mistakes made by most technology-based innovations. At its core, it fails to communicate the reason a consumer would hire this product—the JTBD—and as a result, doesn't connect in any meaningful way with its intended target audience. Until the iPod, all other products in this space did an even poorer job than the Diamond Rio.

Here is how this product was described: "Internet Music in the Palm of Your Hand! Diamond's Rio PMP300 is the first portable MP3 music player for under $200 that stores up to 60 minutes of digital-quality sound. It's smaller than an audio cassette and has no moving parts, so it never skips. Powered by a single AA battery, Rio provides up to 12 hours of continuous music playback."

Positioned completely by its features, there's nothing here that says why I would want one. Ask yourself:

- What is "Internet music"?—remember, this is pre-Spotify and streamed music—and why would I want to carry it in the palm of my hand?

- What is "MP3 music"?—in 1998, mainstream customers familiar with MP3 would have associated it with file-sharing sites for illegal downloads.

- Why would you go through all this trouble to store "up to 60 minutes of sound"? That's about 10 songs, and less than the capacity of a CD, and at high compression rates and low sound quality.

- Does it matter that it's smaller than an audio cassette? I have to think about what that means and why I care.

- Why would I spend around $200 ("for under $200" implies that by the time taxes are added, it's actually over $200) for something that holds the equivalent of one crappy CD's worth of music, when I could buy a high-quality portable CD player for less than $25?

The only important feature that relates to a JTBD is "no moving parts, so it never skips"—presumably useful for joggers or at the gym, and the only application for which this product is marginally "good enough." Unfortunately, the ad makes us figure that out by ourselves. Compared with Apple's JTBD focus on "1,000 songs in your pocket," which is clear, understandable, compelling, and simple, there is no comparison.

Tip Uniquely position yourself by identifying with the customer's JTBD and you will establish yourself as the category leader, forcing everyone else to position against you.

Identifying with the customer's "job to be done" (or the one that you uniquely do best), rather than with a product category, or features/benefits, or price, or any of the other common positioning strategies, tends to uniquely position why you are the only or best solution, which is a critical step to disrupting any market. And, once you've established yourself as the category leader, everyone else needs to position against you.

Choosing Your Competition

In staking out a disruptive market position, you are trying to create an absolute reference point so that in the customer's mind, you are singular, unique, a leader, and the best value (regardless of price). Yet, as noted at the beginning of this chapter, positioning is also about comparison, which means it's also about your relative standing in the market against all other alternatives to solve the same problem.

Absolute, but relative. Positioning is a paradox. The best positioning for a disruptor (certainly for a new-market disruption) is centered on the JTBD that you serve uniquely, but at the same time I'm suggesting that you need to evaluate and communicate how you compare to alternatives. How can that be done if you have no competitors?

It may be true that there are no direct competitors that satisfy the same JTBD, but it is never the case that there are no alternatives to your product. Even in the unlikely event that there is truly no other product that fully or partially accomplishes the same goals and outcomes, there is always the choice of doing the job manually or not doing it. If neither of these alternatives has sufficient pain or cost attached to motivate action, then the need probably isn't as compelling as you think.

Most of the time, there are many alternatives. Take the iPad, for example. When introduced, it was the first "usable" tablet computer—a new category of mobile multi-media Internet-connected appliance. Unique, but not without alternatives. Depending on how it was going to be used, the alternatives included:

- Desktop computer
- Notebook computer
- Netbook
- Handheld computer (iOS, Android, or Blackberry devices)
- TV
- Phone
- Portable DVD player
- Gaming consoles and handhelds
- Camera
- Camcorder
- Pencil and paper

These are the known alternatives out of the box. The iPad has been used for everything from demonstrations to sales presentations to mobile checkout to designing halftime shows for marching bands. For each of the different JTBDs that implies, there are alternatives. So what positioning makes sense? How do you choose what to compare yourself to and where you fit in the market?

This is the most difficult decision you have to make, but also deceptively simple.

Identifying Where You Fit in the Market

The iPad was indeed defining a new category—the tablet computer. Like an iPhone, but big enough to do real work on. Like a notebook computer, but lacking a keyboard and much more portable.

Logically, the right thing to do is to create a new market position in between handheld and notebook computers, which is exactly what Apple did. The name "tablet computer" already existed—several ham-fisted attempts at creating a usable tablet pre-dated the iPad by more than 10 years. However, the category did not exist.

Why? The market failures of previous tablets were so absolute that many speculated there was no need or market for such a device. These failures left the mid-tier position between handhelds and notebook computers wide open for Apple to stake a claim to being first (to deliver on the promise of tablets and satisfy the JTBD).

True mobility required being lightweight, thin, wireless, no extra bulk implied by a keyboard, no CD or DVD drives, and many of the other innovations that the iPad delivered. It required that the device not be a PC-hybrid (which the earliest tablets were). The tablets of the 1990s didn't even look like "'tablets" and were neither as functional as notebooks, nor were they able to do anything better than a notebook that made them suitable for other jobs.

Awkwardly, the early tablets were actually considerably bulkier, heavier, and thicker than notebooks are today, but with crappy small screens. They simply weren't good enough, nor were they priced appropriately to serve a different or under-served market. The iPad was both.

Steve Jobs, a master of disruptive positioning, showed us how a tablet could be more friendly, mobile, and usable as an Internet-connected multi-media appliance than a notebook, which was ill-designed for that purpose and twice the price.

He also managed to convince us that even though it was in many ways a larger iPhone, the iPhone was too small to do the kind of work that a larger (paper-sized) screen afforded, and therefore it was worth approximately twice the price of an iPhone.[5] Thus a new market disruptive innovation and position was established.

As tablets have grown in capability, they are also replacing notebook and desktop computers. It is the "inferiority"—the lack of features such as keyboards, mice, and media drives—and the low price relative to a notebook that has established it as a low-end disruption against those alternatives.

When identifying where you fit in the market, you should always follow this example. Choose to compare yourself favorably with a product or category

---

[5] It is well worth watching exactly how Steve Jobs introduced the iPad and carefully positioned it between the iPhone and notebook computers, as a text-based description simply can't convey how craftily he demonstrated the job to be done, the market need, the capabilities, what it should be compared to (including a smart dismissal of netbook computers as irrelevant), and finally how pricing supported the position and made it seem like a great value. The entire keynote where the iPad was introduced can be watched here: http://www.youtube.com/watch?v=_KN-5zmvjAo#t=4704. Accessed: May 15, 2012. After some general updates, the iPad introduction runs from 5:08 to 12:30 in this clip, and completes with summary and pricing after the demo between 1:14:02 and 1:15:50.

that is more functional and more expensive. (Identify the category you intend to disrupt, without saying that.) In doing so, you position yourself as a substitute that offers a better and different value proposition.

Also anchor yourself to products that are clearly lower in the food chain (not "good enough" for the JTBD). The positioning should communicate, "My product is the first that enables you to do this job you need to get done, and compared with these alternative products I am better at these critical outcomes" (e.g., less expensive, easier to use, more mobile, etc.).

Sustaining, Disruptive, or Both? The Importance of Comparison

It is easy to forget that the notion of a disruptive or sustaining innovation is relative, and not absolute. To be disruptive, there must be a market or industry that is getting disrupted. If an innovation is sustaining, it's because it is along the evolutionary path of innovation that the industry is already following. So, relative to existing products, it offers some performance enhancements, but doesn't change the basis of competition.

Note Surprisingly, products can be disruptive and sustaining at the same time, depending on what you compare them with. In fact, how a product is positioned often determines whether or not it is disruptive.

Is it possible to be both sustaining and disruptive simultaneously, or can you choose to be one or the other? Surprisingly, the answer to both of these questions is "Yes," and the reasons why illustrate how positioning can be critical to disruptive market success.

An easy example is the iPhone. Relative to the market for mobile phones in 2007, the iPhone was the new pinnacle in sustaining innovation. Even when compared to so-called smartphones from Blackberry and Nokia, the iPhone would have been a sustaining innovation. Disruption theory, as we've discussed, predicts that when a new market entrant releases a sustaining innovation, the advantage goes to incumbents, who usually win handily. Clearly though, Apple won and won big. So what happened?

Simply put, the iPhone was never a phone, and despite its name, it wasn't positioned to compete against phones. It was positioned as the first mobile Internet-enabled handheld computer. Positioned as a new market disruption, disruption theory now correctly predicts that the iPhone will win and win big.[6]

In retrospect, the iPhone looks like an obvious call, even though in 2007, it was not. So to really drive home this point, I want to use a much less obvious example—the Gillette Fusion razor—to illustrate how and why positioning is critical to market disruption.

Example: Gillette Fusion—Sustaining, or Maybe Not?

The Gillette Fusion razor was officially launched in 2005. It was introduced broadly and with much fanfare during the 2006 Super Bowl. It was a technological marvel, with a website to match, and the epitome of a sustaining innovation that exceeded the needs of most of the market when it first came out.

The market for razors and blades was already very mature, with multiple tiers ranging from disposable single-blade, single-use at the low-end, to double-bladed and triple-bladed cartridges, each with multiple variations both in the blades and in the handles. It was a classic over-served and over-saturated market.

After all, was a three-bladed razor (prior to the launch of Fusion, the Mach 3 three-bladed razor was Gillette's state-of-the-art safety razor) really even necessary? I still used the Trac 2 at the time. How could you justify the outrageous price for a five-bladed cartridge (not to mention an extra trimmer blade on the back)?

With a launch campaign focused on "technology" and a laundry list of features without meaningful outcomes, Gillette's inauthentic marketing failed to address any compelling reasons (JTBDs) to encourage anyone to upgrade.

---

[6] In 2007, on the eve of the iPhone's release, this article—http://disrpt.me/iPhone_ strategy, Accessed: April 15, 2014—used disruption theory to predict the success and likely trajectory of the iPhone in the market over the next several years, including accurately predicting sales growth rates, the App Store, and the demise of Blackberry and Nokia. It focused specifically on the importance of positioning and compared the iPhone to the right market category in order to determine whether it would be disruptive. At the time, Clayton Christensen and his consulting company, Innosight, went on the record predicting that the iPhone would not likely succeed, again by applying disruption theory. The difference between the two predictions? Christensen compared the iPhone to the existing phone market, not to the mobile computing market.

The evidence for this assessment is strong:

- One year after its big launch with $5M worth of advertising at the 2006 Super Bowl and a $100M marketing budget, Fusion was the first upgrade product in Gillette history not to become the new bestseller.[7]

- Fusion ads made nearly identical claims as previous product generation (Mach 3), except more "technology."

- Incomprehensible website.

- No indication of who the product was for or why they should upgrade.

- Introductory campaign touted:
  - Five blades
  - Comfort guard
  - Extra trimming blade on back
  - Micro-pulse power
  - On-board microchip
  - Low battery indicator light
  - Enhanced indicator lubrastrip
  - Enhanced forward pivot and ergonomically designed handle
  - Spring-mounted blades
  - Progressive blade geometry

---

[7]*BusinessWeek* reported Gillette's disappointment with Fusion sales and signs of price-resistance as early as mid-2006. ("Gillette's Lost Edge," *BusinessWeek*, August 1, 2006, http://www.businessweek.com/stories/2006-08-01/gillettes-lost-edge-businessweek-business-news-stock-market-and-financial-advice. Accessed: June 14, 2014.)

All of this screams "sustaining innovation" to an over-served market—exactly the sort of thing that we know incumbents do.[8] In fact, in the long term it is the kind of activity that increases costs, commoditizes product categories, lowers margins, and creates the opportunity for disruption. But what was Gillette to do?

Mach 3 had been one-upped by the Schick Quattro four-bladed razor in 2003, and the market expected a response from the leader. Gillette razor products have consistently commanded nearly 70% market share globally, and around 80% in the U.S. market, about 5 to 6 times larger than its closest competitor, Schick. In effect, Gillette competes only with itself. Creating a higher-end product sold at an eye-popping price and commanding huge margins seemed like a perfectly logical brand-extension choice.

Disruption Takes a Personal Detour

At this point, I am injecting a personal story to illustrate the importance of JTBD and frame of reference (what you compare yourself to) to positioning, and how it could have resulted in a very different story for Fusion.

At about the time that the Fusion was introduced, I had been considering buying an electric razor for a very specific reason. I can't use shaving cream—it makes my face break out and pimples on a middle-aged guy don't exactly communicate maturity and cleanliness.

I simply used hot water, but I would almost always have a bit of razor burn and would occasionally get nicks and cuts (like most of us, I think). I wondered if an electric would solve these problems while delivering a better shaving experience. I had been thinking about this for a few years, but never acted on my hypothesis because I didn't know for sure, and I couldn't bring myself to spend a couple of hundred dollars for something that might not solve the problem and that I'd end up not using.

---

[8] The Gillette Fusion was so extreme that it seemed a bad case of life imitating parody. Two years before Fusion was introduced, *The Onion* ran a story "announcing" a five-bladed razor from Gillette (http://www.theonion.com/articles/fuck-everything-were-doing-five-blades,11056/. Retrieved: June 6, 2013) that seems to reflect the view of cynical skeptics even today. The razor skeptic/satire meme goes back a long way though, as anyone old enough to remember the very first episode of *Saturday Night Live* in 1975 can recount. On that show, the first of SNL's renowned fake ads premiered for Triple Trac razors (Trac II was still a relatively new innovation), 23 years before Gillette introduced the Mach 3, which was basically what the fake ad forecasted. The ad appeared completely real, right up to the punch line—"The Triple-Trac. Because you'll believe anything." Unfortunately, there is no online video of this primordial episode, but you can read the transcript of the sketch at this link: http://snltranscripts.jt.org/75/75atriple.phtml. Retrieved: June 6, 2013.

One day, as I walked past a Fusion display at the store, it occurred to me that the micro-pulse vibration feature made Fusion essentially a poor man's electric, and that it would potentially solve my problem or tell me whether it was worth going all the way and buying a traditional electric. At that moment I thought, "There are lots of things that I waste $20 on without a second thought. I can afford to throw this away if it doesn't work." So, I made the decision to try it just for that and grabbed one off the display.

My experience using Fusion was revelatory. I haven't cut myself once since switching over. I never get razor burn any more. The shave is smoother. And Gillette probably doesn't want me advertising this, but I get all this without shaving cream.

Considering what I had thought to be a grossly over-engineered razor—a wasteful product that I would never consider buying—I realized that the geometry of the system was the reason why it solved my shaving problem. Five thinner blades did make a difference, as did the vibration. Interestingly, this provided a solution to a JTBD that was different from previous razors, and that Gillette had never promoted, choosing instead to try to persuade skeptical users that all their previous products were now no longer good enough.

It is clear that when compared to disposable safety blades—or Trac II or Sensor or Mach 3, or any of the competing or historical products in the safety razor category—that Fusion was a sustaining innovation and one that over-served the needs of most of the market. However, the point of this story is to highlight how different positioning—comparing the product to a different category and competing on a different set of performance criteria—could change that.

In fact, based on my personal JTBD, the alternatives were don't shave, stick with the status quo, change to an electric razor, or try Fusion. Relative to my desired outcomes, only the Fusion or an electric were viable alternatives, and within that frame of reference, the Fusion razor was disruptive when compared with an electric at 10 times the price. It had a sustainable cost advantage versus the electrics and several important performance attributes that made it superior, although on the single defining attribute of substance/durability it was arguably an inferior product.

In other words, if Fusion had been targeted at the traditional electric shaver market, it had potential to be highly disruptive and would have appeared very inexpensive. Instead, potential switchers like me were left wondering—is it good for this or isn't it?

Fusion did eventually become Gillette's flagship bestseller, but only after several years and a lot of people like me discovered by accident what it was good for, and then spreading the news via word of mouth. Had I relied strictly on the insulting advertising and promotions and not had a specific need that other products in the category did not satisfy, I would never have tried it. I probably would have rejected it permanently as wasteful and unnecessary.

That it became the bestselling flagship product is more attributable to Gillette's status as the incumbent category leader, largely competing only with itself. For the last several years, messaging has focused on how much better Fusion is than Mach 3—on getting its own customers to switch to the higher margin product, rather than on gaining customers from elsewhere (a strategy that would have proved the value to skeptics and that would also have brought their core user base over to Fusion faster, ironically).

Sometimes You Get to Choose

Gillette's total market share for shaving products has remained virtually unchanged (until very recently—see Fusion Epilogue below), but what if Fusion had been introduced to market as a competitor to electrics, with the advantages of 10x lower entry cost, a smoother and closer shave, and a constantly sharp blade (because you replace them when they get dull). A product for people with sensitive skin who have trouble with alternative shaving solutions and especially with shaving cream? A system with extreme control and the ability to be used for whole body shaving and in sensitive areas such as the groin (where a mistake could be very painful).

For each of these jobs, it would have entered the market as a virtually unchallenged competitor, creating new classes of high volume, passionate, and previously underserved users, and would have been a new market disruption—growing the market and market share and rapidly jumping to the traditional markets as a perceived winner.

Instead, we got laughable sports stars' endorsements, as if anyone uses a razor because Tiger Woods does. Given that, historically, most market disruption has occurred by accident, and that Gillette was lucky enough to face no real competition for the first few years after introducing Fusion, one could argue that over time, people began to figure out JTBDs that it was suitable for without being told, and that while not disruptive, this could account for the eventual success of the product in achieving market leadership.

This is exactly why positioning matters: you have a choice, especially if you've followed the strategy outlined regarding JTBD and segmentation. Whether you are a startup or you're simply not Gillette, you probably don't already have the market-leading brand, but if you choose to position against an incumbent industry or category and claim to be better, you've chosen to position as a sustaining innovation and one that is almost certain to never catch the incumbents. If you position as a low-cost alternative to a known JTBD (e.g., against electric razors in this case), or as the perfect solution for an emerging JTBD that no one else adequately serves (e.g., manscaping), you will seize those markets and grow the pie.

Fusion Epilogue: The Dollar Shaving Club Goes Where Gillette Wouldn't or Couldn't

When the Fusion was introduced, the incumbent competitors were locked in a mode where innovation meant coming up with the next blockbuster product with higher-end features and margins to match. The razor and blade business model originally designed by King Gillette a century ago is so engrained it is practically a business case for how to profit by selling or giving away a loss leader that requires a high-margin refill/replacement regularly.

But it's easy to become complacent and forget that moving consistently upmarket has a cost, that high margins are not guaranteed, and that consumers almost always have choices for discretionary products. Gillette has been considered an unassailable brand mostly because no one dared to assail them.

After 100 years of industry dominance, Gillette now faces potentially disruptive competition that Fusion helped to create. Mark Ritson reports in his "Branding Strategy Insider" column[9] that when Fusion was introduced, the price premium over Mach 3 was 40%. Even more stunning is the markup over cost of 3,000%. As Gillette has spent hundreds of millions of dollars convincing its customers to upgrade to this flagship product with extraordinary margins, it has also increased its vulnerability to a different business model that offers a lower total price and competes on different value dimensions.

Enter Dollar Shave Club—a two-year-old startup that recognized several JTBDs that incumbents were not satisfying and decided to rewrite the razor and blade business model. Over-served markets with high-priced products are beckoning for disruption, and that's what the Gillette-dominated shaving marketplace has become.

Dollar Shave Club designed a business model that was the opposite of Gillette's in almost every possible way. They positioned accordingly as irreverent, inexpensive, sensible, and perfectly good enough—equal to the super-expensive blades, but at a fraction of the cost, while also being more convenient because

---

[9]In his blog column, "5 Reasons Gillette is the Best a Brand Can Get" (http://www.brandingstrategyinsider.com/2009/06/5-reasons-gillette-is-the-best-a-brand-can-get.html#.U73MuKhhBFX: retrieved Nov 1, 2012), brand expert Mark Ritson takes the traditional brand-management viewpoint heralding why Gillette's brand strategy of squeezing ever more dollars and margin out of the same users is the best possible example for brand managers to look up to. Especially in this day and age, when innovation on dimensions of both technology and business model is changing the basis of competition in industry after industry, I am inclined to disagree with this point of view. Sustaining a 3,000% margin on any product is an open invitation to competitors, especially startups and new entrants from outside your industry, to think up non-traditional ways to target your customers and challenge you in ways that you are unable to defend against. In other words, this strategy invites disruption, and in the long term, you're far better off if you design your most fearsome competitor yourself and become it.

they were delivered automatically via subscription/membership rather than as a nuisance that you needed to go purchase every month at the pharmacy.

DSC has spawned many low-cost imitators, from Harry's to Dorco (whose blades Dollar Shave Club sells at a significant markup), ShaveMOB, and others. So, will they disrupt the market? It's hard to say whether the end result will be more than establishing a new low-end segment that carves out a sizable share and creates a new market equilibrium.[10]

Ultimately, they have forced Gillette to offer blades on subscription through Amazon, and other online venues, at a discount, but it's more of an incumbent concession than a truly competitive alternative, as the Gillette offerings still price at two to three times Dollar Shave Club.

The problem for Gillette is that they can't effectively position as a low-cost, convenient, and simpler solution to themselves without undermining their incumbent quality leader position and significantly hurting profitability.

Today, these low-priced alternatives are mostly trimming the edges,[11] and doing quite well surviving on the table scraps left by the incumbents.

---

[10]Dollar Shave Club does not have a sustainable cost advantage over other low-end alternatives, nor do they control the means of production of their products, nor is their business model uncopyable. And they have not necessarily priced low enough that switching is an obvious and compelling decision for the majority of mainstream shavers. The only clear advantage they have is brand recognition due to their viral video commercial and first mover status in this new segment, so the answer to disruptive or not probably hangs on business decisions yet to be made over the next few years. In just over two years though, they have shaved a few points of market share from the incumbents and have approximately doubled in size year over year.

[11]*The Economist* wrote in 2013 that both Schick and Gillette reported sales erosion in their razor blade businesses, although they attributed it mostly to trends among men to have more facial hair and shave less. ("Razing Prices," *The Economist,* August 13, 2013, http://online.wsj.com/news/articles/SB100014241278873236819045786404040260 7201338. Accessed: June 15, 2014.) The *Wall Street Journal* also reported the incumbent view that sales declines simply reflect a short-term hirsuteness fad, but also openly questioned the impact of low-end competition, whose sales are rising dramatically even as the majors notch double-digit declines. ("Sales of Razors and Blades are Falling," The *Wall Street Journal,* July 31, 2013, http://online.wsj.com/news/articles/SB10001 42412788732368190457864040402607201338. Accessed: June 15, 2014.) Certainly it has become more acceptable for professionals to wear facial hair in the office, but it is also clear that the rapid sales growth of subscription services and low-end shaving systems has already clipped a few points of market share from the incumbents in just the past couple of years. With current market dynamics, it appears that share for the low-end subscription segment could plateau around 20% within a few years, which would be a significant bite out of incumbent profits, but not disruptive.

In the short term, Gillette will not likely be the brand that is hurt the most[12]—Schick-Wilkinson Sword and Bic are the likely first casualties or acquisition targets for DSC. But, in the long term, the writing is already on the wall.

With minimal marketing dollars spent, Dollar Shave Club has demonstrated that disruption is possible in the razor and blade market (the Gillette market). All it takes is effectively marketing to low-end niches of price-resistant users and satisfying a different JTBD and positioning around that.

In the developing world, these values will be even more compelling, and the low-priced alternatives are far more likely to capture significant global share even faster than in the big markets of the United States and Europe. It also demonstrates that if someone can innovate by solving a truly unique JTBD—for example, eliminate all the disposable waste by creating a biodegradable or recyclable razor cartridge—Gillette is there for the taking.

Perception and Positioning—Why It Matters to a Disruptor

As discussed at the beginning of this chapter, the job of positioning is to build a frame of reference the human brain understands and can remember—to occupy a unique and differentiated space in the consumer's mind that belongs to you and no one else.

The reason we care how the brain works is not to manipulate people (although that is the goal of some marketers), but rather to be able to communicate the value of what we do in ways that will be perceived correctly and remembered.

People are more overloaded with useless data than ever before, and the pace of change means that we must absorb more things in less time than the previous generation, just to keep up. If people don't understand what you do quickly and simply, don't identify your products or services as something relevant to their needs, and don't remember you when it's time to make a decision, you're going to have a very tough time making a sale. If you can't make a sale, you can't disrupt a market.

---

[12]Gillette has, in fact, responded the way that incumbents always do. It is claiming its razors are better and last longer. It has also retreated to the high end, focusing innovation efforts on improving the shaving handle with a Dyson-like pivoting ball—a patentable feature that low-end brands can't match. Also, for the first time, Gillette's new flagship product uses the same Fusion blades, so if you want to try it, no need to wait until you've exhausted your supply of expensive blades. Time will tell whether that matters—it will likely preserve margins on high-end products for a few more years, but in the long run, Gillette will find itself under pressure to simplify and lower prices to retain its market share.

Information overload, a concept introduced by Alvin Toffler in 1970, no longer requires any explanation—we've all experienced it and we've all seen its effects. Too much unstructured, unfiltered, redundant, conflicting, and often irrelevant information means people suffer too many choices and slide into analysis paralysis, or more plainly—the inability to make a decision.

I Don't Hear You; I'm Not Listening

Against that backdrop, your goal is to introduce unfamiliar technologies that do things differently and hope that your value message gets through both the brain filters designed to reject it and our natural resistance to change. The goal is to ultimately have people remember why it matters and choose your product when they're ready.

That's a tall order, and it is why positioning is critical for disruptive innovators. It's also the key to breaking through to becoming the new dominant incumbent, because if you don't establish a unique and clear position you will be yet another "better mousetrap"[13] that no one has ever heard of.

If you want to disrupt a market, you need to create the structure, simplify the data, help it penetrate the filters, lodge it in persistent memory if it's relevant, and have the meaning be readily retrievable for use.

Rules of Disruptive Positioning

Good positioning always speaks a truth that resonates with the consumer. However, when you are a potential disruptor, you have a number of factors working against you to establish a position in the minds of your customers.

- They haven't heard of you and don't know who you are.

- They don't have a frame of reference to compare you to alternative products/solutions.

---

[13]It's a very common misconception that if you build a better mousetrap, the world will beat a path to your door. Ralph Waldo Emerson gave us this aphorism, but consider the facts: Over 6,000 inventors have been issued patents to "build a better mousetrap," but only about 20 of them have ever made money. Deep down, we want to believe that "better" means "disruptive" (it doesn't—often it's the opposite, that is inferior products are the ones that disrupt), and as a result, we don't understand why supposedly great innovations fail in the market—untouched, unloved, and unneeded.

The common "snap trap" has passed the test of time, and is far and away the best-selling type of mousetrap despite many incredibly complex technological marvels that have been introduced to replace it. Market disruption doesn't happen that way, except in very rare instances. When you're ready to go to market with a potential disruption, it's worth remembering that we still catch mice virtually the same way we did 150 years ago.

- Your budget to build awareness is likely smaller than any of your competitors.

- You aren't the incumbent category leader.

Sounds formidable. However, you do have some very important advantages in your favor:

- The best position is first and/or leadership in a category (and if disruptive, you will always be first or a leader at something),

- You have designed your product to be a unique solution to a high-value JTBD (new market disruption), and/or

- You have a sustainable cost advantage relative to all the alternatives that can do the same job (low-end disruption), and have targeted an unserved or under-served niche for market entry.

So, let's take these advantages and what we know about brain science and the general principles of good positioning, and offer a list of guidelines/rules that are specific to creating market disruption by design. This list is a radically condensed and simplified version of positioning strategy creation, but because you are a potentially disruptive innovator, it's easier for you to define a coherent and powerful strategy than it is for much larger companies who choose to compete in crowded marketplaces.

Tip Great positioning describes core truths simply. It resonates with the consumer because it is a job that they need to get done, but you need to communicate that and be the first to own that position in the mind, or it won't matter.

Keep it simple and get these things right now, and you won't need to worry about it again until you're ready to expand your market footprint.

1. If you are establishing a new market, you should always build your positioning strategy around the most important/highest-value unique JTBD for your product. Focus on the desired outcomes enabled by your solution.

   Rationale: One of the key selective perceptual filters is what we choose to pay attention to, and we will tend to pay attention to things that relate to our important personal JTBDs. Since you are designing a new-market disruption, your JTBDs are unique, therefore any position defined around this JTBD will be unique. At the time that either recall or recognition is being called on to identify a solution, the brain ranks alternatives by how closely they match the precise JTBD. The first position in any ranking is always the most memorable, and since your positioning is centered on the JTBD, you will be in the leader position by default.

2. If you are introducing a low-end disruption, always position against the category leader, drawing attention to the differences and your value proposition.

   Rationale: If you are targeting a low-end market disruption, you are aiming for unserved or under-served niches, who are typically excluded from participation in the market by cost or usability constraints. A low-end disruption should be recognized as the price or value leader, and a simpler alternative to incumbent solutions.

3. Your positioning should include memorable keyword and sensory cues to aid recall.

   Rationale: After rank, the next most likely characteristics that stimulate recall are cues related to the JTBD. Cues can be visual, auditory, olfactory (smells), or strong words.

4. You should aim to express the essence of your position in three words, no more than four.

   Rationale: The brain organizes data into lists and can almost always recall the top three items in a list. A three-word position is also a three-word list. Enumerating the essence of your position in the fewest possible words also forces you to focus on the simplest and most powerful emotional and outcome-based cues that are desirable to your target customers. This also enables much stronger consistency through your messaging. Obviously you will have headlines, ads, taglines, elevator speeches, and a variety of other communications tools to express your position that are varying lengths, but it is much easier to ensure that every communication and product decision is focused on the most important elements when you can summarize the core in just a few words. It also has the benefit of enabling employees to have a common understanding of what the company and product stands for and why customers should choose you. Keep it short, simple, and powerful if you want to disrupt.

5. Ensure your positioning tells the market what you want to be compared with.

    Rationale: In order to choose you, customers need to understand where you fit. Your positioning should either define a category, which implicitly compares and differentiates you from alternatives, or position against a category/market leader to establish a low-end disruption. There is always something to compare yourself to, including doing nothing.

6. Resonate and be relevant.

    Rationale: If you are focused on the most important JTBDs, you should automatically inherit relevance (this is a problem they need to solve) to your target audience and a bit of resonance (emotional connection to the pain or benefit). Keeping the essence of the position down to three or four words will increase resonance, because it enhances consistency and repetition in your communications.

Using these guidelines, I have adapted the simple formula described by Geoffrey Moore in his "high-tech marketing bible" *Crossing the Chasm*.[14] Simply fill in the blanks to position your product disruptively:

-   For <the target user>

-   Whose <desired results exactly match the JTBD your product is designed for>

-   The <product name> is a <name of the new category that your solution to the JTBD uniquely defines>

-   That deliver <the top one to three outcomes of accomplishing the JTBD desired by the target user—i.e., the compelling reason to buy>

-   Unlike <the primary alternative solutions the target user might consider>

-   Our product offers <primary differentiation statement>

Doing this, you will have expressed all the salient points necessary to describe your product in one to two sentences, and from this you can distill a position that will enable you to develop taglines, elevator pitches, sales messaging,

---

[14]Geoffrey Moore, *Crossing the Chasm: Marketing and Selling High-Tech Products to Mainstream Customers* (New York, NY: HarperBusiness, 1991).

advertising—basically everything you need to market your product consistently and effectively to your target customers. If you follow these guidelines, your product and company will be better positioned than most of the Fortune 500.

Positioning Is Not . . .

It should be obvious by this point, but it bears repeating that positioning strategy is much more than a marketing tactic, or even a set of tactics. It is an expression of the core truth about what you are, the value you provide, and the job you do for customers.

With that in mind, it's useful before I conclude this chapter to be reminded of what positioning isn't, because like the term "disruptive innovation," positioning is widely misunderstood and you may be tempted to "leave it in the hands of the experts." Don't do that, because positioning isn't:

- Something you do to the product
- Coming up with a tagline
- Your messaging strategy (although it should certainly drive it)
- What you or your product does
- Branding, advertising, or a new slogan
- Promotion
- "Spin"
- Marketing B.S.

Summary

Positioning strategy is really quite a simple thing. What are the alternatives to what you do for customers and how does your solution compare to them? What is your value proposition? What are the most important outcomes that your solution delivers to customers? How do you summarize that in a few concise words perfectly chosen to communicate your values, your ethos, and what the market should expect from you? What piece of real estate do you want to occupy in your customer's mind?

Unfortunately to many, positioning feels like faery dust. Seemingly ethereal, mystical, and ungrounded—it's not like any of the other things you need to worry about to create a successful (disruptive) product. It's not about capturing requirements. It's not about designing a solution. It's not about deciding who the product is for or trying to sell it to them. It's not about setting a price or creating an ecosystem or even designing a business model. Those things all feel more concrete and necessary.

Yet, positioning is no less important than any of these other activities if you want a chance at being disruptive. And, if you are still struggling with this idea, it may help to remember that if you don't create your own positioning strategy, there are many interested parties who will happily fill the vacuum. Imagine what your toughest competitor would say about you if you need motivation, or what message will be communicated by well-meaning employees if the founding team never agrees on what your unique value proposition is and the JTBD you want to be hired for.

Consider also that all the best companies—the ones whose products and market success you admire—have all been where you are, trying to sort this out. They didn't get to be disruptive without a solid positioning strategy, and neither will you.

Consistent. Resonant. Relevant. Simple. Follow the guidelines in this chapter and achieve these qualities.

Key Takeaways

- Positioning is something that happens in the customer's mind. Your job is to define the pigeonhole you want to own there.

- The most important unique outcomes you provide and how you compare with the alternatives are the key inputs to your positioning strategy.

- To be considered as a solution for the JTBD, you must first break through a number of barriers (selective perceptual filters) that actively prevent your message from reaching the customers.

- Leadership is the best position in any category. As a potential disruptor, make sure you define the category around the core JTBD that you uniquely serve and/or do better than anyone else.

- Positioning is relative and so is disruptive innovation. In many cases, the difference between being disruptive or not is what you choose to position against.

- Every position is unique and can be occupied by only one product/company at a time. Dislodging a product from a position is almost impossible if it is successfully delivering on its brand promise. That includes your products, so make sure you choose your position well.

Positioning strategy is medium to long term. It should evolve as the market does, but the core should largely remain the same if you got it right. In fact, if you succeed in creating a strong position, there's a good chance it will outlast you in the company (if your product category lasts that long).

Next, Chapter 7 discusses pricing strategy, which is about the "now." It's also one of the most powerful levers impacting market disruption that you control.

Pricing Strategy

Simplicity and sexiness, that's what people want. At a price that's not outrageous.

—Diane von Furstenberg

People want economy, and they will pay any price to get it.

—Lee Iacocca

Outside of providing a unique solution to a job that consumers want to hire a product or service to accomplish, no other lever within your control is as important as pricing strategy to achieving market disruption. The reason is quite simple when you think about it.

As I discussed in the first chapter, innovations become disruptive when they provide a solution to a market scarcity that dramatically shifts the equilibrium to abundance. Disruption is caused by the distortions of the supply and demand curve that this extreme shift creates—distortions with the apparent power of a black hole to suck light into the grasp of its gravitational vortex. But nothing can be supplied in abundance if it is priced above what the market is willing to pay.

Although theoretically any price or pricing model that delivers better value to the user than the current set of alternatives could potentially enable disruption, in practice, being disruptive by design necessarily limits the good choices for pricing strategy. Market disruptions most often begin with underserved customers at the low end of the market (which frequently implies a lower price), and even when you are creating a new market disruption, its effect is amplified when it is simultaneously a low-end alternative.

When you are thinking about buying something, price seems like an absolute, give or take a small discount if you can negotiate one. As a seller, however, price may seem infinitely elastic, which makes choosing the "right" price—a price that will maximize signups, customers, active users, market share, speed of adoption, revenues, profits, or whichever is your primary goal—exceedingly difficult. You can set your price and price model to be whatever you want—except you can't really.

The difficulty in setting the "correct" price is that any price is arbitrary, but once set, it impacts:

- Perceived value
- Who is a member of your target segments
- Total market size
- Volume sold
- Total revenues and profitability
- What alternatives you will be compared to
- Whether competitors will enter the market
- Sales velocity
- Channels available to sell through
- Promotional strategy
- How much you can spend to build your product
- Product design

Indeed the impact reaches beyond even these critical strategic factors, and is the single most important decision you will make about any product. So, as a wanna-be disruptor, how should you approach pricing?

Just as product positioning is about telling the market who you want to be compared with, your price will be compared to all perceived alternatives, and more than that, it's used by customers as a signal for what you think you should be compared with.

Get it wrong and you can forget about maximizing anything. The wrong price strategy can create more sales friction than almost any other decision you make. It can slow down decisions, cost you sales, or worse, get you lots of demanding users who are mismatched to your offering and who are costly or impossible to support.

On the other hand, despite volumes of marketing texts focusing entirely on price strategy, there simply aren't any good rules to follow when setting prices, and each situation will be determined by context and judgment. This chapter looks at the factors that you need to consider when setting your prices, including:

- What the market compares you to
- Cost versus value
- Size of your market
- Whether you are targeting businesses or consumers
- How you sell
- The nature of your product (tangible, intangible, or digital)
- Multi-sided markets and network effects

I'll try to distill these factors down into some general principles to follow that will maximize your probability of being disruptive. The first subject is how price dictates what the market compares you to and vice versa.

Reference Price and Price Anchoring

Most people who are tasked with setting a price or pricing strategy start by asking what their product is worth, how much value the customer receives, and what it costs to build. These are interesting questions, but mostly irrelevant to setting the right price for your product. The right place to start is with target customers and how they view the market and their available alternatives.

The first question you need to ask is how the customer perceives value and judges a fair price that they're willing to pay to get a job done. In an established category, the answer is reasonably straightforward—consumers compare you to what they perceive as equivalent products, and then with related alternatives.

Note The "reference price" is loosely defined as what the customer expects to pay. Customers assess "value" by comparing your price to the reference price that they have saved in their mind.

Every solution category has a "reference price," which can be loosely defined as what the consumer expects to pay. It is determined by the following factors:

- **Memory of what they've paid in the past.** Simply, if I paid $4/gallon for gasoline last week, I don't expect to pay $10 this week. For a fungible product like gasoline where most brands are perceived to be more or less equivalent, the reference price will be approximately the average price that I see as I drive past service stations, with a bias toward the lowest.

- **Price charged by a dominant market leader.** The reference price for a fast food "value meal" (hamburger, fries, and a soft drink), for example, is the price that McDonalds charges. In fact, the Big Mac value meal (priced at approximately $5 in the United States) is so strong a reference price that it is used by *The Economist* magazine in its famous "hamburger index"[1] to show the relative buying power of different currencies around the world.

- **Context.** The consumer adjusts their reference price by various contextual factors such as location (I expect to pay more for gasoline in California and even more in Europe), convenience (a can of soda purchased at a service station convenience store will cost considerably more than the same can of soda purchased at a grocery store), volume (usually I expect to pay less per can of soda when I buy a case of them than when I purchase them one at a time), and other situations.

- **Other similar categories or product lines.** The reference price, especially for niche products, is often set by the mainstream category, so for example, a basic refrigerator will serve as the reference for a bar fridge, a high-end built-in integrated fridge with custom cabinet covering, and a wine fridge with zoned temperature and humidity controls.

---

[1]The Big Mac index began as a comical way to compare the relative buying power of different currencies, but resonated so strongly (and has proved to be fairly accurate as a predictor of purchasing parity) that it is often quoted in financial journals and economics texts as a very real indicator of the strength of national economies around the world. This page describes how the index works and shows its value in the various regions on the global map (see http://www.economist.com/content/big-mac-index, Retrieved July 31, 2014).

There are some categories of products for which the consumer has a harder time judging what fair value is, either because it's something they purchase infrequently, or because there is a high design component factored in to the price. This can be a problem for sellers, because if the consumer lacks sufficient knowledge they will resist making a decision until they have fixed a reference price in their mind.

Tip When customers lack knowledge of the reference price, they will resist making buying decisions until they've gathered enough data to make an educated guess and have created a reference price in their mind.

In retail fashion, where this problem is quite common, you will often see a top or a skirt, for example, with a "retail price" crossed out, followed by a 50%-off sale price. Often with shady retailers, the product has never actually been sold at the full retail price before being offered at the 50% "discount" (a practice that's generally illegal, but persists nonetheless).[2]

This is done to register the list price as the reference price in the consumer's mind and to make the sale price look like a great deal (which enables the customer to make a decision). This sale price is actually the real price, since it's what most people pay, but the consumer is encouraged to compare it to the original price tag or MSRP, so in effect they are trying to establish a reference price that is twice the real price to reduce buying resistance.

More commonly (and legally), retailers will stock three alternatives—a high-priced or luxury version that they expect few people to buy, an inexpensive and low-quality product, and an option in between the two that they expect to be the mainstream choice and that offers better value than either the low-end or high-end offerings. Averaging the three price levels (or taking the median) establishes the mid-level option as the reference (expected) price and helps the consumer arrive at a decision.[3]

---

[2]The slightly more ethical version of this happens at stores where everything seems to be perpetually on sale but in reality what they've done is introduce the product without fanfare for a high price simply to establish a reference price. After a couple of weeks, the new 50% off price tags are added with loud promotion.

[3]Interestingly, it doesn't matter which of the three options is chosen—the presence of options helps the consumer feel confident in making a decision. Having established a reference price allows them to choose the low price to save money, the high price because they desire quality, exclusivity, or "the best," or the mid-tier mainstream choice that the retailer prefers and that appears to offer the best value.

So, what happens when the consumer has no knowledge at all, or if as a disruptor, you are attempting to create a new market for something that has never existed before? That is a problem, because if the consumers have no reference to go by, they will either defer a decision until they have one or create their own reference price based on questionable data and potentially inappropriate comparisons.

The need for a frame of reference is so strong that in the absence of a reference price, the customer will use whatever hooks and connections their mind can find to compare you to the alternatives—even using data points that are completely irrelevant or made up. If you want control of your pricing strategy, you need to provide these hooks yourself. This more general case of a reference price is referred to as the "anchoring effect" (or anchor price).

The anchoring effect was first described by Kahneman and Tversky[4] in a study of how people made decisions when there was a high degree of uncertainty or ambiguity. What they found was that any initial value will bias an outcome in its direction, often quite dramatically.

For example, imagine that I conducted a survey where I told half of the participants that 90% of a group is made up of lawyers and the rest are accountants, and then asked them to estimate the probability that a randomly selected member of the group is wearing a blue suit. Then, just for fun, imagine that I repeated the experiment with the other half of my sample, but I told them that 10% of a group is accountants and the rest are lawyers. (In other words, it is the identical survey question, just phrased differently.)

Anchoring theory predicts that those who were told the percentage of lawyers would give a much higher estimate of the probability of a blue suit—in fact, a number close to 90—than those who were told that 10% of the group was accountants. And, not only would the estimate by the second group be a lower number, it would be a number close to 10. Strangely, it wouldn't matter if they were told what percentage of the overall group was actually wearing a blue suit (which would be the correct answer, regardless of the distribution of lawyers and accountants)—they would still bias their answer in the direction of the first number they were provided.

Caution The need for a reference price is so strong that consumers will often anchor to completely arbitrary numbers that have no relationship to your target price or value. If you inadvertently set a low anchor price, you will have great difficulty raising it.

---

[4]Tversky, A. & Kahneman, D., (1974). Judgment Under Uncertainty: Heuristics and Biases. *Science,* Vol. 185, No. 4157, 1124–1131.

Dan Ariely has studied the irrational arbitrariness of anchors on consumer perceptions of value (that is, willingness to pay a price), describing in his book *Predictably Irrational* how something as irrelevant as your personal Social Security number can be used as an anchor that significantly alters willingness to pay for a variety of consumer goods. He demonstrated that by creating a price anchor tied to the last two digits of an individual's Social Security number, the amount they were willing to pay was on average 346% higher for people in the highest bracket (last two digits ranging from 80 to 99) than those in the lowest bracket (00 to 19).[5]

In the previous chapter, I discussed how Steve Jobs used iPhones, netbooks, and notebook computers to position the iPad. In his introduction he talked about how "if you listened to the pundits, such a device should cost $999,"[6] and left this number on the screen for a couple of minutes while he talked about how hard Apple had worked to meet its cost goals for the product.

Then as he described how this number would be a great value if the iPad could do everything he was claiming, both from a productivity perspective and because it was unique in its ability to handle a number of jobs the consumer wanted done, he let the actual introductory price of $499 drop to gasps and cheers from the audience. Since there was no existing reference price for the iPad, Jobs positioned it against notebook computers, which were more expensive, and used pundit estimates to provide the audience with a solid anchor that made the actual announcement price of $499 for the base model feel very inexpensive.

As with most elements of psychology, it's possible to use anchor pricing dishonestly or with intent to take advantage of the consumer, but that's not why I present it here. Eventually, and especially if you expect to have a long market run and relationship with customers, you need to price your product appropriately. However, it's important to recognize that when you launch your product, you will create an anchor that can bite you badly if you aren't aware of it.

For example, if you offer an MVP (Minimum Viable Product) for free, hoping to entice early users, it will be very difficult to change the anchor from zero later. On the other hand, anchoring gives you an important tool to introduce novel products that don't have direct competition and demonstrate their great value by comparing them to other categories of products that have high prices. The anchor is your reference price when one doesn't exist.

---

[5]Ariely, D., *Predictably Irrational: The Hidden Forces That Shape Our Decisions* (New York, NY: HarperCollins Publishers, 2008).
[6]The entire iPad keynote can be seen here: http://www.youtube.com/watch?v=_KN-5zmvjAo#t=4704. Accessed May 15, 2012. The summary and pricing discussion begins after the demo and runs from 1:14:02 to 1:15:50.

In general, you want the reference price or price anchor to be as realistically high as you can present it, and your price to be a minimum of twice as good (lower is better) when targeting market disruption.

Cost-Based versus Value-Based Pricing

If you assume that the primary goal of a pricing strategy is to maximize either profitability or revenues, as most marketing and sales texts do, then the discussion of whether to base price on your costs or on value is obvious. If you have strong differentiation, you would choose to capture the maximum "economic surplus"[7] based on the value created for customers. This implies the highest price that a sizable and high-value target market will bear. On the other hand, many products and services opt to base pricing on their costs plus an acceptable margin, assuming this will mean a lower price and faster growth.

In general, neither of these approaches is right for a disruptor who wishes to remain on top.

Let's start with cost-based pricing. To begin with, your costs have nothing to do with the market reference price, and could well be above average, especially if you are offering features that no one else does. A well-differentiated and unique product can price above the market, but doing so relegates you to a specialized niche and usually means slower growth, not faster. If your costs are below average, you may be able to price below market incumbents, but a cost-plus margin basis means two things. First, unless you have a large and sustainable cost advantage, it is easy (and rational) for incumbents to lower their prices to prevent you from gaining share. Secondly, your price advantage needs to be very large to persuade incumbent customers to switch.

On the other hand, value-based pricing usually seeks out the customers with the greatest ("must have") needs who are willing to pay the most for a solution and then sets the price to balance demand at the point that realizes the largest total profit. The problem with this approach for disruptors is that while it captures high-margin customers, it also attracts competition who see a greenfields high-margin opportunity. In doing so, it limits your ability to grow

---

[7]*Economic surplus* is defined as the sum of consumer surplus and producer surplus. The *consumer surplus* is the monetary gain (or savings) captured by consumers when they can purchase a product for less than the maximum they are willing to pay. The *producer surplus* is the monetary gain captured by a producer when they sell for greater than the least that they would accept. Usually, the goal of both the consumer and the producer is to reduce the surplus of the other party to zero to capture the maximum economic surplus for themselves. In general, disruptive strategies attempt to minimize the total economic surplus to deny competitors opportunities to take market share and, in the long run, keep the majority of the market surplus. This is exactly the opposite of a value-based pricing approach.

and to target unserved or underserved markets and to gain a strong beach-head from which to expand your footprint. In other words, most of the time, it will prevent you from disrupting the market to become the new dominant player.

So, if neither cost-based nor value-based pricing is right for a disruptor, what is?

The best approach if you have disruptive potential is to start with the customer and the market reference price. If you are targeting a new market, there will still be alternatives, as previously discussed, even if the alternative is doing nothing.

■ **Tip**   Set your price target before creating your product, by evaluating the price of alternative solutions available to your target customer. Assume that the lowest-priced alternative is the reference price and beat it by at least two times. Then design your product to meet that price for maximum disruptive impact.

Collect price data for the alternatives, including assigning an aversion-to-pain cost to manual labor if that's what you're competing with. Then set your price target to be a minimum of two times better than the lowest-priced alternative (50% lower).

Now price becomes a critical point in designing your MVP—even if the best you can do is design a product that you initially sell at cost. If technology prices are falling, you can project a future profit based on winning the early adopters, growing into adjacent market spaces, and—when costs catch up to where you are—controlling the market. Ideally, you will try to design the MVP to have some profit, but in the early days that is not the goal of a growth company. The idea is to ensure that your product design embeds the price you need to meet to achieve disruptive lift off.

It's only a little different when targeting a low-end disruption. If there is an unserved or underserved market space at the low end, it's usually because either incumbent products are too expensive or require too high a level of expertise (they aren't easy enough to use).

First, determine a target price that's low enough to capture users who don't participate in the existing market. Then look at the incumbent cost structure (not their price—they may have set prices high to capture "economic surplus" value, but actually have a low-cost basis). Then determine whether you can design a product that has a low enough price to reach the low end and a sustainable cost advantage over incumbents.

Your goal is to make it highly undesirable for incumbents to compete with you at the low end. If you have an ease-of-use advantage, you still want to target the lowest price you can manage for the under-served market following these same principles.

If you are unable to accomplish price targets as described here, you probably don't have disruptive potential anyway and more likely are designing a specialized niche product.[8] Remember that disruptive innovations always address a market scarcity and replace it with abundance.

Scarcity can manifest in many ways—from shortage of skilled labor, to real or artificially-created shortages of supply, to high prices supported by lack of competition or old technology, to monopoly/oligopoly market scenarios, to poor service, and so on. When you factor in the JTBD and divide the value created by the price, the ratio should be increasing by at least three times (which can be accomplished by highly productive technology that dramatically increases supply, new processes, lower costs, lower labor requirements, and so on).

In all cases, it should translate into a significantly lower cost to get the job done.

Free

As in, there is no such thing as a free lunch.

Giving away products to gain share and control markets is not a new idea, although it has gained new prominence as the Internet has grown to become a principal engine of commerce, thereby dis-intermediating middlemen and lowering the costs of promotion and distribution.

---

[8]Are there exceptions to this rule? Of course. Certainly before we started to understand the dynamics of disruptive innovation, most disruptions that occurred historically were accidental, and accidental disruption still occurs because not everyone plans for it or understands how it works—that's the reason for this book. There are also companies like Apple that have serially disrupted several markets while targeting to keep the maximum economic surplus for themselves. Accomplishing this is very difficult and rare, however, as it requires consistently innovating ahead of the market, delivering a nearly whole product and ecosystem on the first release that is easy to use and obviously better on several outcomes desired by customers. In other words, it requires exceptional understanding of the JTBD and exceptional execution on delivering to that, as well as visionary leadership. Since Steve Jobs' passing, it appears that Apple has lost that edge. While it's still innovative, it's not the company that created the iPod, iTunes, iPad, and App Store.

As one of the goals of a disruptor is to minimize the total economic surplus, "free" has also gained prominence as an approach to building user bases quickly and figuring out how to monetize later.[9] Free is an option that you should consider if it makes sense for your market, but there are times when it is completely the wrong approach, as I'll discuss later. In the following paragraphs, I discuss some of the most common flavors of free and how they support disruption.

Freemium

Freemium is the concatenation of "free" and "premium," and is pretty self-explanatory as Internet-age words go. Free is used as an enticement to sign up users quickly for a basic service, with the hope/expectation that a percentage of them will convert to paying users of a premium version.

Freemium is most appropriate for software and cloud services products, especially those with network effects and viral spread potential, and when the cost of manufacture and distribution is near zero. The design of the product should naturally lend itself to a break level where the user feels not obliged, but glad, to pay for the premium enhancements, and where upgrading to paying is both fair and reasonable. (Note: This may mean giving away a more complete product than you, as the developer, feel is reasonable.)

Tip   When using a freemium price strategy, make sure that you don't treat users of the free version as second-class citizens by crippling your software or withholding essential capability, or you may lose the benefits you hoped to gain from the free offering. Users who need the premium services will be glad to pay for them when it feels both fair and reasonable to upgrade to a paid subscription.

It is a mistake to try to force users to upgrade by withholding some essential capability of what would otherwise be a complete logical unit of functionality. This creates a feeling of resentment and a segment of users who try to "game" the system to get what they feel they were rightly denied, rather than supportive users who help spread your technology. Withholding essential capability largely negates the benefit that freemium provides to a disruptor; disaffected and/or angry users will jump to the next wanna-be disruptor who doesn't try to force the issue and drag lots of other users with them.

---

[9]Chris Andersen explored how and why "free" has grown as an approach in his book, *Free: How Today's Smartest Businesses Profit by Giving Something For Nothing* (New York, NY: Hyperion, 2009). If you are considering offering all or some of your product for free, I encourage you to read this book for more ideas and insights.

Similarly, it doesn't help to nag or to remind someone who doesn't have the budget or doesn't really want to pay—they aren't going to upgrade, and nagging them is simply an annoyance that prevents them from acting as a viral agent. If you feel inclined to build these types of "features" into a freemium offering, you probably shouldn't be using the freemium model.

Freemium works well with consumer-oriented products and with tools that are very easy to learn and use. It can also work well with inexpensive business-oriented utilities that don't require senior buying approval to bring into an organization or permission from IT to use. It is highly recommended for social networking or communications tools (where sharing is a natural part of using the product), products that sit on top of social networking platforms, metrics tools that might create a badge showing rank or some other positive numbers that users will want to post on their websites, or other products where sharing is part of the reason that you do it (such as photography). These sorts of products all have strong potential to benefit from network effects and viral spread.

Freemium doesn't work, or is much less appropriate, with enterprise software tools, non-digital products, tools with a high degree of complexity or that require support to be used, or when the likelihood of sharing is low (such as with accounting software). If there are already competitive alternatives that use freemium, you may feel you have no choice. However, avoid the "me-too" temptation. If you don't differentiate and there's no reason to switch, freemium won't work for you.

Finally, it's tremendously important that freemium products just work. No bugs, no difficult installation and configuration, no need for help or handholding. If your product isn't good enough to meet this standard, don't offer it as a freemium option. You will have a high degree of abandonment and bad-mouthing from users—exactly the opposite effect of the reason you want to use freemium.

Cross-Subsidization

Cross-subsidization occurs when one group of customers pays more than another or when the purchase of one product pays for the cost of another. Freemium is really just a special case of cross-subsidization, whereby a small piece of the same product is given away for free in the hope that users will want to pay for the more advanced functionality. There are many other kinds of cross-subsidies.

The term free lunch (as in, there's no such thing) actually arose from a cross-subsidy provided by tavern owners before prohibition, who offered a free lunch to anyone who purchased at least one drink. Aside from the negative externalities of too many men returning to work after several drinks, and encouraging people to drink alcohol who might otherwise not have done so, the free lunch worked marvelously well to fill the pubs. Even today, alcoholic beverages still cross-subsidize restaurant meals with much higher markups applied to drinks than to food, although you can't usually get a free lunch anymore.

In the modern world, an example that almost everyone is familiar with is Adobe's free distribution of Acrobat Reader, which was cross-subsidized by business users of Acrobat's document-creation capabilities. Another example is open source software, such as Linux, where companies such as Red Hat cross-subsidize distribution of the software with their support and training services.

Cross-subsidization works well when the product or service you are trying to sell is closely linked to the JTBD of the free (or subsidized) product. Cross-subsidization is a useful tool for disruptors when it reduces the market friction and perceived cost of acquisition of their product.

For example, an obvious objection of business users of Acrobat would have been the requirement by document readers to pay for and/or register Acrobat Reader—if the reader was not a free and unrestricted download, the likelihood that Acrobat would have taken off as the standard way to package documents for distribution is near zero.

Cross-subsidies don't have to result in a free price (loss leaders at the grocery store are a cross-subsidy), but they work best as a tool for disruptors when they do.

Razor and Blades Model

Again, the razor-and-blades model is a type of cross-subsidization, but one where the thing that is perceived to be valuable (the razor) is given away or heavily discounted, and a necessary recurring item to make use of it (the blades) are strongly marked up. The razor-and-blades model was highly disruptive when introduced nearly 100 years ago, and may still offer opportunities when the "blades" (not necessarily blades, but whatever the required recurring add-on is) are reasonably priced.

As discussed in Chapter 6, razor-and-blades price models are susceptible to disruption when a market becomes over-served and the incumbent uses its market power to extract the maximum economic surplus. This leaves considerable room below for a low-end disruption from an alternative business model, whether it's subscription/membership-based, as in Gillette versus

Dollar Shave Club, or other types of hidden cross-subsidy. Cellular carriers, for example, use the razor-and-blades model, giving away or heavily discounting premium "smartphones," in exchange for locked-in and extraordinarily expensive service and data plans.[10]

Market Size

Market size has an impact on pricing in that if a market is too small, development and operating costs must be amortized across too few users, forcing prices to be higher. One of the significant impacts of e-commerce, besides reducing distribution, selling, and marketing costs dramatically, is that it has also broadened the market for many products to a global audience, especially if the product or service can be offered digitally, and made it possible to reach them quickly.

Market size will obviously vary by type of product and whether it is intended for business or consumer use; however, there are still some guidelines to keep in mind. If you are targeting a consumer or digital product, 100,000 users is a small market today, and a business product needs to have at least 5,000 target users to be a viable launch pad for your innovation.

Price Impact on Market Size

Given the need to have a large enough total market to be viable, your biggest strategic concern related to price is whether what you envision building burdens you with a cost structure or price model that limits the market size. A smaller market size not only means costs will be spread across fewer potential users, but it also means that your sales velocity will be slower.

These two factors can stop you from gaining the necessary beachhead to get over the hump and build a profitable company. If the price you need to sell for reduces the market size substantially, consider simplifying the product (taking out features), trying a different price model, finding a way to cross-subsidize or

---

[10]The limited number of alternatives for carrier services has resulted in monopoly or oligopoly conditions in most markets that has been exploited to raise prices far beyond what a free market would support. In fact, as carriers have switched from 3G to faster 4G services, they have benefited from higher efficiency, which has reduced costs. Yet they are raising prices by as much as 50% and claiming a better service, according to technology news site ReadWrite.com. "Why Your Cell-Phone Bill Should Be Going Down—But Isn't," ReadWrite.com, May 9, 2014, http://readwrite.com/2014/05/09/4g-3g-smartphone-data-price-difference. Accessed June 5, 2014. This incumbent-style market exploitation has left the door wide open for disruptive outsiders such as Google to offer free WiFi services that will likely put a major disruptive dent in carrier revenues wherever they are available.

offer something for free, or rethinking your core JTBD and value proposition. If you are successful in disrupting the market, there will be plenty of time later to add specialized features needed by smaller niche segments, which they will happily pay more for.

Product/Market Characteristics

The nature of your product often has an impact on your options for price strategy and the best alternatives for a disruptive innovation. The biggest factors you need to consider are these:

B2B or B2C. Consumer markets are much better suited to some version of free (ad-supported, cross-subsidization) for a few reasons. An individual is much more likely to accept the trade-offs that come with free, such as embedded ads or limited/restricted use agreements, and to take the risk that the product may fail in the market and be unsupported.

Business markets are motivated by price, but they also want to know that the organization has the financial strength to provide various levels of support, including compatibility and security updates, and are more likely to view a paid product/service as a positive for this reason. As well, many if not most corporate users are behind much stricter firewalls, so they will find it difficult to use your product if it embeds things (such as ads) that are blocked by the firewall.

Business users are more likely to sign up for subscription services and expect guaranteed levels of service (and will be willing to pay for it), whereas in many cases requiring these things for consumers are barriers to rapid adoption, which makes disruption more difficult (but not impossible).

Freemium works well for many B2B products, where it serves the purpose of a no-commitment free trial and allows end-users to bypass IT department controls to sample something before engaging in a formal justification and purchase process.

Tangible, Intangible, Digital. Tangible products (physical goods) have implicit distribution costs (logistics, shipping, returns, damages, and inventory) that have to be embedded in the product and usually prevent "free" from being an option. Services (intangible products) and digital products are much easier to offer inexpensively over the Internet, which makes some version of free, or low-priced subscription model possible.

Many service-based businesses are ripe for disruptive innovations that use the Internet, from accounting, to legal, to medical, and even personal trainer services—we've only begun to scratch the surface with services such as AirBnB, Uber, Netflix, car sharing, and travel booking—and what will drive these new services is creative pricing and business models that reduce the friction in engaging with the service provider.

Multi-Sided Markets. Multi-sided platforms create value by creating focal points that enable two or more types of participants to transact business or exchanges more easily, creating a multi-sided market. Multi-sided platforms are not new—shopping malls attract shoppers to a central place and shared facilities that house many different retailers; newspapers and magazines sell space to advertisers who want to reach their readers; and auction houses help to get the highest (fair) market price for unique items consigned to them by getting those interested to bid against each other.

Note   The near-zero transaction costs of operating a global network via the Internet has enabled the formation of many of today's fastest-growing and most highly disruptive companies that operate multi-sided platforms.

Though these business types have been around for a long time and are employed by conventional (and non-disruptive) businesses, many recent market disruptions have been triggered by a business model that employs an online multi-sided platform. The reason for this is that the Internet reduces transaction costs to near zero while facilitating formation of global networks and point-to-point connections that would have been prohibitively expensive before the existence of an open platform such as the Internet.

Thus we have companies like eBay, Google, AirBnB, Uber, Facebook, Amazon, and Match.com, and many of the largest, fastest growing, and most disruptive startups of the Internet era basing their business model on multi-sided markets.

A property of most multi-sided markets is that, as the number of participants of one type grows, it adds value to the other types of participants, so there is an indirect network effect. However, in most cases, multi-sided markets function because one side values access to the network, data, or user base more than the other(s)—in economic terms, they get more utility from the existence of the market—and is willing to subsidize the market's operating cost.

In fact, it is usually the case that the marketplace or network couldn't get off the ground unless one side is motivated to subsidize it, but by doing so, they create greater economic surplus for everyone.[11] Examples include free use of web search engines with advertisers paying to display ads based on keywords used in the search query, to auction sites like eBay, to recruiters and business advertisers paying for access to the LinkedIn social business network while users get a free ride.

In complex markets with more than two sides, the value proposition for each to participate can be very different from the other parties, and sometimes even conflicting, and this complexity makes pricing a very difficult exercise.

Most importantly, long-term success of a platform often depends on balancing the needs of the different participants—for example, early search engines made a strategic error in biasing their search results to give higher placement to paying advertisers and, in the process, annoying users who learned not to trust the results. This created the opportunity for Google to take the leadership mantle by forgoing ad revenues in its early days and focusing simply on building the fastest, most accurate, and most complete search capability. This caused users to abandon other search tools and flock to Google. Content creators then focused their optimization efforts on Google, which reinforced its leadership position.

Later, Google was able to introduce advertising without damaging its reputation for accuracy (because the results didn't change and ads were kept in the sidebar and out of the inline results). Even though advertisers pay for the platform, it was critical to Google's success (and therefore to the advertisers as well) to ensure that the search results were relevant, accurate, and untainted. Even as Google has recently begun to include more ads and make them more prominent, they have retained their reputation for best search results, although we would caution that the direction Google is going may well kill the goose that laid the golden egg (making them vulnerable to a disruptor with a different value proposition) if it begins to alienate users.

---

[11]This "launch" problem (often described as the "chicken and egg" problem) is the biggest issue multi-sided platforms usually face, since there is no value until the network exists. Although all participants benefit when the market is functioning, there isn't sufficient motivation or incentive for one side to fully engage, or for the market to scale quickly, unless there is a subsidy. The example of Ethoca discussed in Chapter 4 is a multi-sided market that provides different benefits to different members of the network and strongly exhibited this "chicken and egg" syndrome until a few visionary card-issuing banks helped kick-start participation by providing data (a form of subsidy). Once off the ground, such markets tend to grow virally as the benefit increases as the number of participants grows, and often result in a single company "owning" the market (especially if the value decreases when there is more than one provider of the service).

Similarly a site with too many display ads or intrusive pop-ups will turn off users and send them elsewhere, thereby destroying the value in the platform for everyone. Failing to appreciate which group of users is the most important to attract and keep, and understanding what their core value proposition is for joining and using a multi-sided platform, has led to the toppling of many early market leaders.

David Evans proposes a useful way to categorize multi-sided platforms into three types (see Figure 7-1), which can help you determine how to balance the pricing model[12]:

Price Balancing in Multi-Sided Markets

Platform Category	Participants	Who Is Most Subsidized	Examples
Market Makers	Brokers, Buyers, Sellers	Buyers	Amazon.com, eBay, dating services, shopping malls
Audience Makers	Content Providers, Content Consumers, Advertisers	Content Consumers	Google, Facebook, media, bloggers
Demand Coordinators	Application Providers, Users, Data Consumers	It depends	App Store, payment networks, iOS/Android, gaming consoles

Figure 7-1. To build a functioning multi-sided market, it is usually necessary to bias prices so that one side—typically the side that values access to the other more—pays a higher share of the fees. Without such price balancing, most multi-sided platforms will never successfully launch or remain self-sustaining. Disruptive innovations often fully subsidize at least one side of a multi-sided market (i.e., make it free to users), experiencing rapid, viral growth as a result.

Market Makers. Market makers connect two or more distinct groups—often buyers and sellers—thereby improving their efficiency of finding each other, lowering transaction costs, and improving the likelihood that the right connection will be made. Examples include eBay, which exposes goods (especially rarities and collectables) via auction to a global audience that has historically been excluded from market participation, ensuring the best price to sellers within a relatively short period of time; Match.com, which helps

---

[12]Evans, David S., *Some Empirical Aspects of Multi-Sided Platform Industries.* Review of Network Economics, Vol. 2, Issue 3, 191–209 (September 2003).

singles find compatible dating partners; stock exchanges, which provide market liquidity enabling those who want to buy equities to find those who are interested in selling them; and real estate brokers whose agents help buyers find homes that suit their needs while helping sellers get the best price for their homes. In most cases, the seller pays the majority of fees.

Audience Makers. Audience makers attract groups interested in similar things and monetize their "audience" (primarily) through selling advertising. Examples include media (newspapers, TV, radio, and magazines), online search engines, social networking sites, bloggers, trade fairs, and directories. Audience makers create messages, themes, or content that audiences assemble around, or identify actions that signify intent; advertisers pay to reach these audiences and the intending purchasers.

Demand Coordinators. Demand coordinators provide goods and services that create indirect network effects between different groups. Examples include operating systems, browsers, social networks, and game consoles. Ethoca, the case example covered in Chapter 4, is a special case where participants pool data to create insights about fraudulent transactions that wouldn't be visible any other way, and that no member of the network could determine without the participation of other members of the network. Demand coordinators are like the hub airports that everyone passes through on the way to somewhere else.

Generalizing, there are three principles to follow if you are a potential disruptor trying to create a multi-sided market:

- If one side is more sensitive to price than the other, they should be subsidized with a lower price and, if possible, offered use of product or network data for free to accelerate adoption and build value for all network participants.

  On LinkedIn, for example, users posting a profile or commenting on discussions would be far less likely to participate if there was a charge, while advertisers and recruiters are happy to pay to reach network users and to search/browse the database. Users actively seeking a new job, on the other hand, have lowered price sensitivity and are often willing to pay for access to executive recruiters and corporate HR executives who aren't "in their network."

- Assess the highest fees to the side that benefits most from the participation of the other side(s) to address the "chicken-and-egg" problem.

Sellers tend to benefit more than buyers, businesses more than consumers, and data seekers more than data providers. As well, in B2C markets, consumers will always default to choices that are free, while in B2B markets, businesses will consider what provides the best value, de facto standards, and stability, and are willing to pay something for that (and value the network more if they do) even when the other side is subsidizing the market.

- As a potential market disruptor, it is better for a platform provider to act as a "benevolent dictator" and leave money on the table to ensure widest participation and forestall competition. If a competitor sees excessive economic surplus, they will design a price structure that undermines yours and win by growing a larger market.

  Google has employed this principle very well by offering Android and Chrome and other applications for free to ensure the widest use of their search tools to drive advertising revenues. Although contrary to most advice given for "optimizing" revenue from multi-sided platforms, it is rent-seeking behavior by short-sighted platform owners that most often creates the opportunity for the next generation of disruptive innovators.[13]

---

[13]Contrast Google's approach of offering most of their software free, including the Android operating system on mobile devices, with the history of the payment card industry. Evans (*Ibid.*) provides a case study describing how Diner's Club created the modern credit card industry when it provided a single card that diners could use to buy meals on credit at a number of restaurants in New York. They charged 7% of the restaurant tab to restaurant owners and, after a short time offering free cards to users to get them on board, raised fees from cardholders in a series of steps up to $26/yr by the late 1950s. American Express saw an opportunity to leverage its travel industry reputation and experience to broaden the utility of a general-purpose credit card and quickly launched and grew a competitive service to Diner's Club by charging lower fees to merchants (thus growing the number of places that accepted cards making them more attractive to consumers), while positioning as a more exclusive product with a higher membership fee to users. Later banking cooperatives such as Visa and MasterCard were able to enter the market by lowering merchant fees significantly and reducing cardholder fees to zero but introducing the idea of revolving credit at much higher interest rates than a traditional bank loan. Today, we have PayPal reducing the transaction cost to merchants and consumers even more for online payments. None of these subsequent market disruptions could have occurred without excessive economic surpluses that new competitors could attack with a different business model. Google's market approach is better for consumers and better for Google in the long run.

Network Effects

There are two types of network effects that matter—direct and indirect. Indirect network effects are most often present in multi-sided markets, where the presence of one type of platform participant creates value for another type. The second type is a direct network effect, whose largest and most obvious examples are telephones and the Internet.

Networks have the interesting property of being useless if no one participates, but increasingly valuable as more people join the network. After a point, it becomes nearly impossible to create a competitive network based on the same technology because if the majority of users is already on another platform, switching to another that has no possible connections has limited to no value. Direct networks often support true monopolies and/or a single de facto standard (such as use of telephone numbers to call other telephone owners, IP addresses on the Internet) and are virtually impossible to displace until and unless the core technology becomes obsolete and is superseded by a new platform that accomplishes a different JTBD.

When you can leverage a strong network effect, there is a very high probability of market disruption, as it likely means that you have tapped into a core social need to connect and communicate with others in a way not previously possible or affordable, and that you have a natural "viral" property that ensures rapid spread at low cost. The key to pricing is to be as low as possible so that you eliminate friction in the joining process. Remember that all networks have a chicken-and-egg problem, as described previously.

As the network effect is well known, I mention it mostly for completeness; however, it's important to note that pure network effects are rare. It pays to be sure that the potential is really there and that your business model decisions aren't an impediment to formation and stability of the network. Even when there is early evidence of viral tendencies for your product, sometimes it is just a passing fad (platforms like MySpace, Digg, and Flickr come to mind—although these are all still used by many people, they have all proven to be less universal than originally thought or lost leadership to better designed networks).

Particularly if switching costs are low, or if someone else comes along and performs the JTBD better, you may find that the network effect is weaker than expected. Any barriers to entry, restrictions on usage, or product decisions that act as an incentive to leave can undermine the network—all of these can be thought of as a network tax that increases the price.

Price Model

Other than freemium, or completely free to one-side in a multi-sided market, there is little evidence for a general rule about the price model's impact on disruption. Whether you charge a one-time fee, impose a subscription, or charge recurring fees is more related to the nature of the product and the intended customer.

If there is no benefit to an ongoing relationship, a one-time price is the most common model. In the case where usage is continuous or ongoing, and the customer benefits from support services, a subscription model tends to make more sense. End consumers are more likely to opt for lower payments over time, even if the net present value (NPV) of those payments exceeds what they'd be willing to pay as a one-time cost. Businesses are more likely to opt for a lease, either for the purpose of expensing usage or when they desire flexibility to terminate, upgrade, or downgrade the contract, and they expect that may happen in the short term.

From a disruption perspective, the important point to consider is—again—what the customer's JTBD is. If you think of price as a product feature, then the more closely aligned your price model is with how the customer is likely to use your product and their desired outcomes, the better your probability of achieving disruptive potential and minimizing price as an objection.

Assessing the Price Curve Over Time

Often, the price of important components of your product will rapidly decline over time, especially when your innovation depends on the Internet and/or computing technology and/or miniaturization.

In particular, a number of "laws" predict exponential rates of decline in cost for processing, storage, and connection speed:

- **Moore's Law** projects that the number of transistors that can be squeezed onto a chip roughly doubles every two years.

- **Kryder's Law** estimates that storage density roughly doubles every 18 months (faster than processing power).

- **Nielsen's Law** forecasts that connectivity bandwidth available to high-end users will grow by 50% per year.

Each of these implies that whatever the price is today, it will be half as much for the same capability in two years or less. What this further suggests is that many disruptive opportunities will continue to open up as new lower price thresholds enable applications to address market scarcities.

More importantly, when the rate of price decline follows such a steep grade, it should be taken into consideration when creating and pricing products and services now. Price your product at the minimum margin you can afford or even lower when you can reliably project a date by which the cost will catch up with the price.

Note "Deflationary economics" can drive disruptive opportunities as falling prices for core technologies continuously create opportunities to target new low-end and under-served markets profitably and thereby create abundance from scarcity.

For example, when Google introduced Gmail it offered free storage capacity for email of 1GB—200 to 500 times more than competing services. By projecting forward the rate at which their storage costs would fall and assuming that the real cost was near zero per user (both because of how much average users would store as well as how long it would take them to use up their allocation), it was able to price it at zero and steal significant numbers of users from Hotmail and Yahoo!.

Even after the competing free services bumped their allocation of free storage by 10 to 100 times, they were still only offering 20-25% of what Google did in their initial release. Every time storage costs have declined, Google has increased how much space free accounts are allocated, staying ahead of all competitive services.

Amazon has followed similar price-leading strategies, both in the early days of building out their online shopping emporium, by eating shipping costs, and leveraging the projected future cost in current pricing, and cross-subsidizing of Kindle readers and Fire phones that are tied to their shopping services. This effect has been described by prominent venture capitalist Mark Suster as "deflationary economics," and it is a strong indicator of businesses with disruptive potential.[14]

---

[14]Mark wrote powerfully about this effect in his blog Both Sides of the Table, discussing why he likes to invest in companies that are able to leverage deflationary economics and how this notion has driven many of the greatest Internet companies' growth. This highly recommended article reviews the types of companies it applies to, explains how you can apply it if it's right for you, and provides examples of how a number of disruptors actually did it. Mark Suster, "The Amazing Power of Deflationary Economics for Startups," December 22, 2011, http://www.bothsidesofthetable.com/2011/12/22/the-amazing-power-of-deflationary-economics-for-startups/ Accessed August 22, 2012.

Can You Sell for Less?

In Chapter 3, I discussed the factors that enable you to predict whether an innovation has disruptive potential and how likely it is to disrupt markets. Price is one of the critical factors and one of the easiest to measure and control for. As a general rule, an innovation needs to be below the market reference price to be disruptive. In practice, a disruptor needs to have a sustainable cost of production advantage that is at least two to three times better than incumbents to have a high probability of market disruption and to be able to compete on price and not face incumbents head-on for the same customers (initially).

Another assumption that you can usually make is that if technology is enabling a cost advantage for you over incumbents, it is also enabling it for other innovators (unless you have a patented/proprietary advantage). An important question to ask after you've done the analysis and come up with a price model is whether there is any way you could sell your product for less, and what assumptions would have to be different for that to happen. If it's possible, you have to assume that someone will (another would-be disruptor).

It's counter-intuitive, probably contradicts what you learned in business school, is likely to drive your finance guys mad, and will be strongly advised against by most price theorists who are focused on setting the "optimal price" (the price that generates highest profit). But you are playing the long game, targeting market ownership and leadership. Disruptive innovation is not about maximizing profits in the short run, and especially not during the rapid growth phase of your business.

This is how deflationary economics works, and if the total market is potentially very large (and if it isn't, why are you investing so much time in targeting disruption?), the lowest viable price will eventually be hit. You want to be the one who hits it, is recognized as setting the new reference price, and eventually becomes the new incumbent.

What About Apple?

Much of this chapter has discussed how the best strategy for introducing a disruptive innovation generally targets a sustainable lowest price, which has the effect of deliberately reducing the economic surplus and discouraging competition. For companies like Google and Amazon, that has been a highly effective approach to continuously expanding their market footprint and erecting ever-higher barriers to entry into their core businesses where the majority of profits are made. It is the surest way to defend your market position in the long term.

I could not end this chapter, however, without discussing the one glaring exception—namely Apple. Since 1997, Apple has consistently been able to charge above-market prices and sustain the highest margins of any of the competitors in its many businesses. As described in earlier chapters, it has effectively disrupted market after market, growing to become the world's largest company by market capitalization, passing Exxon Mobil for the first time in 2012. After a see-saw pattern for the top position, Apple surged ahead in August 2013 and the gap has widened to approximately $180B in valuation by August 2014.

How is this explained and is this sustainable? Does this demonstrate that low price is not the right approach?

Early on in the second "Steve Jobs era," Apple created a series of new-market disruptions that changed the landscape for mobile computing, rewrote the rules for the music industry, redesigned how offline retail should work, and created the idea of an App Store that feeds the growth of its entire ecosystem. Though disruptive, Apple always priced for and maintained superior margins.

There was a key difference in Apple's approach that enabled this price strategy. Focused on enabling a digital lifestyle, Apple presented a coherent product line-up from top to bottom that represented this brand ideal, that had elegant design and simplicity, was aspirational, and that invited consumers to join an elite avant garde who enjoyed technology as part of their daily lives. Importantly, this positioning resonated very strongly because the products were ahead of the market and delivered with pinpoint, almost intuitive, accuracy on the JTBD in a way that no prior attempts at similar products ever had. Apple's CEO and chief spokesman was the living embodiment of this ethos.

This strategy was possible because Apple was a consistent groundbreaker. They showed the industry what user interfaces should look like and how they should feel and how products should work. They delivered products that didn't just live up to, but exceeded, expectations. The problem is that to sustain this approach and the high pricing that goes with it over time requires a continuous stream of market-leading products that take people in the direction they want to go before they even realize that's what they want. That requires a very special kind of leadership and intuitive understanding of the market.

To answer the open question, "Does this demonstrate that low price is not the right approach?," the simple answer is, "No, it does not."

▨ **Tip** It is possible but rare to disrupt markets with premium pricing. It requires a constant stream of intuitive market-leading innovation that understands the jobs customers need done, even before they do. Before trying it, look in the mirror and ask whether you are the next Steve Jobs.

Apple has now become an incumbent, and despite its market leadership during the Jobs era, has not done anything disruptive for at least five years—an eternity in technology development. They are reaping the cash rewards today of earlier successes but will find it increasingly hard for future results to match the present reality. On the other hand, iOS has already been disrupted by Google's Android, which has approached the market with a low price and open systems strategy.

The result of Google's disruptive (low-price) strategy is that as of the second quarter 2014, Android phones have nearly 85% market share to just below 12% for iOS.[15] iOS is still on top in tablets, but that share is declining rapidly as well, and sales of tablets are slowing while phones are not. While the consensus is that Apple's products and ecosystems are still superior, a familiar pattern is playing out where the disruptor's products catch up and amortize costs over a much larger user base, and eventually the only thing that matters to the majority of the global market is that the average price of one product set (Apple) is three times greater than the other (Google). Over time, this will erode Apple's ability to generate profits, growth, and new innovations.

Had Apple been willing to give up some margin in the short term, it is conceivable that their market share could be 30 to 40% higher, and there would be a persistent duopoly in mobile operating systems, but that opportunity has already passed.

So once again, Apple is the exception that proves the rule. Without Steve's leadership, the company appears to have lost the ability to do what is necessary to disrupt via JTBD leadership and has been unwilling to offer products at prices below the premium level, while the low-price strategy of Google is winning the battle in the long run.

On the other hand, if you are the next Steve Jobs, perhaps you'll be able to disrupt with a premium price strategy. It's possible, just not very likely.

Summary

Market disruptions most often begin with underserved customers at the low end of the market who can't afford (or choose not to afford) any currently available alternatives to address their needs, thus pricing strategy is critical to creating disruption. In this chapter, I attempted to review the range

---

[15]Figures come from IDC Research, reported in *The Next Web* (http://thenextweb.com/mobile/2014/08/14/idc-global-smartphone-shipments-pass-300m-q2-2014-android-84-7-ios-11-7-windows-phone-2-5/, Accessed August 18, 2014) and *Business Insider* (http://www.businessinsider.com/iphone-v-android-market-share-2014-5, Accessed August 18, 2014).

of potentially disruptive pricing strategies, provide some rules of thumb for determining the right price model, and offer guidance about how customers perceive price and how to use psychology and price anchoring to establish a price that customers perceive as good value.

How you price your product determines which products you will be directly compared with and the range of alternatives for which you could be considered. It directly affects your total available and total served market, total profitability, potential growth rate, and how large your market share will be.

Price your product incorrectly and nothing else will matter—you won't have a chance to be disruptive. Get it right and you'll have the opportunity to own the market for generations. It's as simple, and as difficult, as that.

Key Takeaways

- A sustainable cost of production advantage of two to three times (driven by patentable technology or a unique process) is usually sufficient to enable disruption, regardless of other factors. An order-of-magnitude (10x) cost advantage almost guarantees it.

- Understand what the market will compare you to and what the market reference price is for your solution space, and aim to be below it while providing significantly better value than alternatives. If possible, tell the market where you fit and use anchoring to establish your value proposition.

- If freemium or cross-subsidization is possible for your product, these strategies are among the most effective for viral spread and rapid growth of market share. There is a huge difference in impact between low cost and no cost, but if you choose "free" as a product price, there is a much higher burden to get the user experience right from the start.

- Price your product as low as you can go, considering whether you can ride the downward slope of "deflationary economics" to market dominance. Squeezing out excess margin will not only help you win the market today, but hold it against future would-be disruptors.

While I've offered guidelines to determine what the right price should be for your product, much is predicated on anticipating how large the eventual (disrupted) market will be, and successful execution in taking the lion's share of that opportunity. In the long term, the companies that succeed are those that never lose sight of the low end of the market and shortages (scarcity) that can be mitigated and eliminated with more innovation and "deflationary economics." In the last century, Kodak was the pre-eminent master of this approach, before it failed to capitalize on digital photography. Today, Google and Amazon exemplify this approach.

The final point to make is that if your intent is to be disruptive, pricing is not something you set once and forget. The history of innovation (in both product and business model) tells us that today's low prices are tomorrow's high prices, and that there's always another disruptor out there hoping to eat your lunch. Price accordingly.

In Chapter 8, I move on to a much less controversial topic (I hope) to discuss disruptive messaging.

Messaging

...the medium is the message. This is merely to say that the personal and social consequences of any medium—that is, of any extension of ourselves—result from the new scale that is introduced into our affairs by each extension of ourselves, or by any new technology.

—Marshall McLuhan

This much used, but little understood, introduction to McLuhan's most influential work, *Understanding Media*, is very apropos for a discussion of disruptive messaging (or messaging that positively impacts the probability of achieving a disruptive innovation). Because of McLuhan's title, and the rising awareness in that time that modern media was changing society as much as it was reflecting it, many have misinterpreted "the medium is the message" as being a statement about modern media, and television specifically.

But if you look beyond that initial catchphrase, you see that the real idea is that we often, if not usually, miss the context of change and see only the obvious. In other words, we see the television—but not how we interact with it, how it organized people and our time around mass cultural events, and so on. We see the foreground, but miss the background.

In the context of disruptive innovation, which is precisely an "extension of ourselves, or . . . any new technology," we see the technology—the shiny new object or cool software—but have a tendency to miss how it changes our behaviors and why. For example, we know how addicted we've become to the search engine and we recognize what it does, but we ignore how it has changed our relationship with technology, the Internet, communications, shopping, information, research, argument, and our expectations of privacy. Or we see the cool new smartphone, but miss how it changes how we talk to each other and how it begins to run our lives, rather than the other way around.

The average person on the street who is simply consuming the technology is blissfully unaware most of the time, but as product developers, we are blindly unaware much of the time. We can't see the forest for the trees.

When it comes specifically to messaging, we see the technology we're so proud of—its features and what it does—and become so enamored of it, that we forget the reason it exists—the job to be done. The "personal and social consequences of the new medium" are exactly the JTBD of a disruptive innovation, which result from this new "extension of ourselves."

Literally, McLuhan's meaning in his most famous statement is that we can know what an object is by its impact and by the change it causes, and it's that change that we need to care about, not the object that creates it.

A hammer drives a nail to fasten things together. A person's shoe leaves a footprint that identifies the weight, size, stride, and gait of the person who left it. Every disruptive innovation we create extends our capabilities and changes what we are able to accomplish.

When creating messaging for things that are disruptive, it's this change that is important, not the product itself.

Remember the Job To Be Done (JTBD)

Messaging is about empathy, and nowhere is this more important than when describing the value of a disruptive innovation. Buyers usually don't have a framework to understand something that is fundamentally new, but they do understand the things they need to accomplish and things that cause them heartache.

In Chapter 4, we discussed how you know what your product should do and how to elicit the jobs that your intended customers need to get done. Then, in each of the strategic decisions you need to take regarding getting your product to market—segmentation, positioning, pricing, ecosystem, business model, and more—I've reiterated the importance of the JTBD.

As a marketing or product leader, or perhaps as the CEO of a startup, you are the chief communicator. This brief chapter is specifically for you.

One of the reasons that communication about your product can be difficult is that you understand the reason for its existence implicitly. It's easy to forget that what's obvious to you can be completely opaque to your intended customers, and they've never heard of you so why should they care?

Worse, by the time you're ready to talk about your product, what it does has started to bore you. You were talking about that six months or a year ago. You're ready to move on to v2.0, because that's where the excitement is.

Tip What you can do right now is exciting. Don't get bored with it and start talking about futures if you want customers to buy what you have now.

Unfortunately, if you want to succeed at market disruption, you must sell what you have, not futures, and you need to develop a consistent, simple message that is repeated over and over again.

What you say and do is what the market understands about your product (if they are listening). And it's painfully simple if you remember this. All the traditional marketing texts will tell you to focus on customer needs and benefits and pain points, but none of that is relevant if the customer has no frame of reference for what you do.

Your product category is probably meaningless gibberish if you are a new market disruptor,[1] and if you are a low-end disruptor aiming at segments that have traditionally been excluded from participation, they won't understand that your messaging is for them unless you say so.

This is why the work you've done up to this point on segmentation, positioning, and pricing is so critically important. You know who your target audience is; you know their most important outcomes (which should align precisely with what you've built for v1.0); you know what your market position should be relative to the alternatives; and you know that you've designed a price model that is palatable and friendly to your intended buyers.

---

[1] Once people have integrated change into their lives and routines, it's very difficult to go back and recall how outlandish the new idea seemed before anyone had heard of it. It's worth remembering that Alexander Graham Bell thought of the telephone as a way to enhance telegraph communications, and that he believed the primary users would be telegraph operators. No one could imagine a telephone in every home and office, let alone as a device we'd all carry around everywhere. Or consider this: Ken Olsen, the co-founder and CEO of Digital Equipment Corporation, said in a talk delivered to the World Future Society in Boston in 1977, "There is no reason for any individual to have a computer in his home." Not only does this statement seem incredulous given that it was made one year after Apple Computer was founded, but it's hard to imagine that the head of one of the most successful computer companies of its time couldn't envision how computers could become personal. The notion that we'd all have a computer (that we call a smartphone) in our pockets, more powerful than the guidance systems used to send Apollo missions to the moon, would have seemed truly preposterous even in 2006—the year before the introduction of the iPhone. Your product is no different. Without context, your intended customers cannot and will not understand why your product is significant and how their lives will be different after your disruption becomes commonplace. (For more on the Apollo/iPhone comparison, see http://www.thedailycrate.com/2014/02/01/geek-tech-apollo-guidance-computer-vs-iphone-5s/. Accessed May 24, 2014.)

All of this is to say, don't hand the "create messaging" task to marketing people who haven't been involved in designing the product and in determining who it's for and what it's intended to accomplish. Don't hire an agency to come up with a positioning and messaging strategy. Don't hire consultants to do market research on what the buyer wants and how your product delivers it. Any of these will be costly and will leave you in a worse place than you are right now.

Tip Don't hand the "create messaging" task to marketing or creative agencies who weren't involved in capturing the JTBD and defining your target users micro-segments. It's your responsibility to get this right. Then you can let communication professionals wordsmith, polish, and figure out how to distribute your message to the market.

You need to create the raw materials yourself (see "A Simple Guide to Strong Messaging" later in this chapter). Give this raw material to marketers for wordsmithing and for determining the best promotion methods to carry the message, not for strategizing the actual message.

Benefits, Features, and Advantages

In most established markets, products are promoted using benefits desirable to different targeted segments, supported by the product features and advantages that confer them.

For example, you might describe a vehicle as being extremely safe on the highway because it offers confident acceleration to merge into traffic and provides traction control and a heads-up display for high maneuverability without needing to take your eyes off the road. In a segment more interested in performance, you might describe the same car as offering aggressive handling and road feel, with 0-60 mph in 3.4 seconds for the most pleasurable driving experience you can have when you aren't on the track.

When your product has disruptive potential and is targeting a new market, the features, advantages, and benefits are largely meaningless because there is no context or frame of reference within which to evaluate such benefits.

Consider that when cars first hit the roads, there were no roads and cars weren't even called cars. They were "horseless carriages."[2] Would it have made any sense to discuss safety or performance or family-oriented benefits?

Yet it is extremely common with new products, especially with technology-oriented companies, to want to promote features before potential customers even know enough about the category to understand which features are important. Recall the example of the Diamond Rio PMP300 discussed in Chapter 6. The advertised product description was:

> Diamond's Rio PMP300 is the first portable MP3 music player for under $200 that stores up to 60 minutes of digital-quality sound. It's smaller than an audio cassette and has no moving parts, so it never skips. Powered by a single AA battery, Rio provides up to 12 hours of continuous music playback.

Now imagine that you have never heard of an MP3 player, which is the state of the market in 1998. Your introduction to this new product category is a list of features, none of which matter because you have no way to attach meaning to any of them.

I picked on the Rio because it contrasts so starkly with Apple's "1,000 songs in your pocket" message for the iPod, but I could have used advertising from almost any new technology product. It is a consistently repeated pattern—the message is a laundry list of features with no context for understanding why they matter.

---

[2]Imagine the context for promoting cars when horses were the incumbent form of transportation. People didn't commute to work; they largely walked. We didn't live in suburbs (in fact, most people didn't live in cities, but on farms). Average people couldn't afford cars—they were toys for the rich. The best clues we have about the cultural disconnect and what that might have meant to messaging may come from laws left over from the late 1800s and early 1900s. For example, in Pennsylvania, a "motorist who sights a team of horses coming toward him must pull well off the road, cover his car with a blanket or canvas that blends with the countryside, and let the horses pass. If the horses appear skittish, the motorist must take his car apart, piece by piece, and hide it under the nearest bushes." In South Carolina, male drivers are permitted by law to "discharge firearms when approaching an intersection in a non-horse vehicle to warn oncoming horse traffic." In Denmark, there must be a person at the front of the car waving a flag so that carriages with horses coming from the opposite direction know that there's an engined car coming. And again, in Pennsylvania, "automobiles travelling on country roads at night must send up a rocket every mile, then wait ten minutes for the road to be cleared of livestock" before continuing. Talking about safety, how fast your car can accelerate to highway speed, fuel economy, or almost any of the benefits that are now used to sell cars would have resulted in blank stares and created unnecessary fears and questions that would have more likely cost sales than helped.

Don't do this.

You aren't introducing a product into a known category in an existing market. You need to first educate the market, provide context, and talk about outcomes that matter to your prospective customers.

Put Yourself in Your Target Buyer's Shoes

Your intended customers are busy people, bombarded at work and at home with myriad messages and overloaded with new technologies to understand and learn.

In today's world, things are changing faster than ever before. Compounding this accelerated pace, new product releases are increasingly being distributed in the cloud and updated automatically for everyone, whether they want the changes or not. The result: users have less feeling of control.

Psychologically, that translates into less confidence, more frustration, and more feelings of helplessness. And, you want them to pay attention to your new product?

It doesn't matter whether you are selling to a B2B or B2C market. Emotionally, most of us have a need to feel in control. We prefer to assert our choices rather than have things done to us, and to feel confident, secure, and successful. It's one of the reasons Apple was so successful. The simplicity and elegance of their design makes users feel in control and smart. Empathy in your messaging is absolutely essential.

Your Customers Don't Want to Be Disrupted

One of the biggest mistakes that companies who believe they have a disruptive innovation on their hands make is describing their product as disruptive. Don't do it. Whether you are or aren't, it's irrelevant to your prospective customers.

■ **Tip** Strike the word *disruptive* from your marketing vocabulary. No one wants to be disrupted; it's not a customer benefit and has nothing to do with the reason the customer is hiring your product to get their job done.

There's an even bigger problem with describing yourself as disruptive. If your target customers do understand what a disruptive innovation is, saying that you are one provides no clue about what they'll be able to accomplish with your product that they couldn't do before. If they don't understand what disruption theory is about, saying you're disruptive sounds like a big negative. Either way, you're hurting yourself.

Empty gratuitous hype always weakens your message. That's what describing yourself as disruptive is to a customer. It's no different than other useless hyperboles such as *advanced, high tech, sophisticated, next generation, paradigm-shifting,* and other adjectives of similar ilk. They add no value.

The ultimate irony is that companies who describe themselves as disruptive in their marketing messages almost certainly aren't. That's because one of the key predictors of disruption is execution, and focusing on descriptors that say nothing, instead of using the JTBD and your customer's desired outcomes to tell your story, is poor execution.

Your excitement at having a potential market disruption on your hands is understandable. But the place to talk about it is in the boardroom as it relates to business strategy; with your investors as it relates to growth potential, needed investment to carry out your strategy, and valuation; and perhaps with outside consultants who need to understand why you are following the approach you are. Don't let it creep into your marketing, your elevator pitch, your tagline, or your core messaging. You'll regret it.

Disruption is not a customer benefit, and users don't want it as an outcome.

On the other hand, customers do like novel ways to solve their problems that make their lives easier, cost less, save time, do a better job of preserving and conserving the environment, help them spend more quality time with loved ones, earn more, upgrade their standard of living, increase their profits—you get the idea.

The buyers who are ready and willing to go first want authenticity and integrity. They want to feel that they are not just doing things faster and cheaper, but in some small way, contributing to a better world. Early adopters and visionaries, and even the early majority, are aspirational.

A Simple Guide to Strong Messaging

Most of what I've said here focuses on common mistakes and things you want to avoid. For the most part, your job in developing a disruptive messaging strategy is to not over think it, nor do things the way an incumbent would at this stage. Keep it simple.

Your primary goal for a messaging strategy is consistency. You want to make it easy when talking inside the company, as well as to journalists, analysts, or investors, to prospective customers or to new employees, for everyone to "sing from the same songbook." It's noticeable when a company does this well—there are no mixed or confusing messages, and not only will your audiences understand what you do more quickly, but they'll view you as more professional and as a company that's going places.

An advantage that you have in the early days is that you are more focused than incumbents on a core JTBD that alternatives do not satisfy. Your messaging benefits from this as you will automatically be more consistent (and valuable to your core target audience) if you stick with the most important things that make your solution unique.

As you draft and use your core messages, use these tips to create resonance in your market:

1. Write down the positioning you developed in Chapter 6 using the JTBDs for your core target audience(s) at the top of a page.

2. Write down the top 3-4 results (the ones that are most important to the customers and unsatisfied by alternatives) that you deliver based on the core JTBD.

3. For each outcome, document how it is achieved and the value (metrics used by the customers) of getting it done.

4. Identify the top three competitive alternatives you are likely to be compared to (it doesn't matter whether the alternatives are in the same product category or completely different approaches, or are accomplishing the task manually or doing nothing). Write at least one "unlike" statement for each alternative. (Unlike product x, <name of your product> enables you to <key outcome> <key value metric>.)[3]

You're done. Everything you create to market your solution will rely on this single page outline of what makes you important, credible, and unique to your target audience. Hand this page to your marketing agency and let them improve on how the message is conveyed, test alternative ways of saying it, and help you build the key vehicles that will deliver your messaging strategy, including the elevator speech, website, product brief, sales presentations, advertising, promotions, and inbound marketing campaigns, as needed. Judge everything by conformance to this document.

As you expand your market audience, you will repeat this process for each target, but the core of what you do should remain the same but become more generalized.

---

[3]An example for Zipcar when they first came to market might have read, "unlike traditional car rental companies, Zipcar's car sharing approach gives you the spontaneity of car ownership without the expense, and the flexibility of accessing a car when you need one without the hassle of signing contracts and having to get to a rental lot to pick up a car."

Summary

When introducing a potentially disruptive innovation to market, the rules are different. You do not have an established market to sell into, and therefore your intended audience does not have a frame of reference to understand the value that your product offers. Whether your product is a low-end innovation targeting a segment that's been excluded from participation historically, or a new-market innovation that introduces novel capabilities and benefits, your focus must first be on market creation. This means explaining the JTBD and how you accomplish it, not the features, advantages, and benefits messaging that most marketing programs are designed to communicate.

Resist the temptation to be conventional; many marketing consultants and strategists don't know any better and will try to convince you to waste money and time on studies and positioning and message development that don't matter. Do the hard work of message development yourself, and then hand off the wordsmithing, not the other way around.

Your medium is your message. The job you uniquely accomplish is news, and the outcomes you enable that couldn't be done before are what matters. Messaging for disruptive innovations is deceptively simple. Keep it that way.

Key Takeaways

- Disruptive messaging must communicate the change you deliver to the world in a way that is credible (provable and/or believable). It must show how your product is important (accomplishes a JTBD) and unique.

- Being disruptive is NOT your message. Being disruptive doesn't tell your customers what you enable or how or why. And, if you fail to communicate that, you won't disrupt anything.

- Think about the vision, but stay grounded in what you deliver today. Outcomes (desired results) are what matter to your customers and to your messaging strategy.

- Keep it simple. If you can't summarize your core message and positioning in a two-sentence (maximum) elevator speech that your intended audience immediately understands, it's too complicated.

In the next chapter, I conclude the second section of this book, which has focused on implementing a disruptive strategy. The next chapter ties the product, marketing, and business strategy elements together into a business model framework for disruptive innovation.

CHAPTER

9

A Disruptive Business Model

The competitor to be feared is one who never bothers about you at all, but goes on making his own business better all the time.

—Henry Ford

The golden rule for every businessman is this: "Put yourself in your customer's place."

—Orison Swett Marden

Every successful business operates a bit differently from every other. Businesses need to be conscious of what competitors are doing (and especially what they aren't doing). But as Henry Ford suggested, the most important factor in moving forward is focusing on what makes your own business better, rather than trying to copy your competitors' strengths. Easier said than done, right?

Disruptors are less worried about making their business better, at least not initially, but they share a common sentiment. Incumbents are incumbents because they rely on old business models, old value chains, and old ecosystems, all of which can be made vulnerable by new technology and methods. Therefore, if you hope to disrupt a market the best course is to completely ignore those who will be competitors; rather, disruptors succeed when they put themselves in the shoes of their target users and help them accomplish the things they need to get done that no alternative accomplishes adequately today.

Much of this book has been about how to do exactly that. But as yet, we haven't put it all together into a big picture that describes how the business will operate, make money, serve customers, and reach the first milestones in becoming a success.

Historically, entrepreneurs have used business plans to document how they intended to build a company, even though experience told us business plans were woefully inadequate and rarely survived the first encounter with a customer. Having largely abandoned traditional business plans as an antiquated idea, thanks in large part to the work and insights of Steve Blank,[1] we now recognize that startup business plans are flawed because they attempt to articulate unknowable facts. More importantly, a startup's job is not execution of a business plan, but experimentation with a goal of discovering the right set of repeatable processes that enable the business to survive and thrive. Until that occurs, every assumption is an untested hypothesis.

While the formality of a business plan is unnecessary, you still need a model of the business that outlines the intentions, assumptions, and expectations of how your business will be built. Short and succinct, a business model implicitly acknowledges the fluidity and uncertainty of your hypotheses. Yet it still provides the means for everyone (including investors) to be on the same page as the assumptions evolve and are tuned to reality.

Thanks to the efforts of Alex Osterwalder and Yves Pigneur,[2] the tool most commonly used to document the business model is a Business Model Canvas—a single page that brings together the most important elements of how you intend the business to work and what you know about customer needs, how they are served, cost structure, and how the company makes money. For an existing business, the Business Model Canvas is a documentation of facts (even if the reason it is recorded is to determine which elements of a company's business model need to be changed). For a startup, a business model is intent and hypotheses.

The original business model template by Osterwalder & Pigneur is a good general map that can accommodate any business. However, there are some factors that are significantly more important to a potential disruptor and to a startup than to a large company. In fact, a few alternative business model templates have already been adapted from the original to better handle the specific needs of startups.[3]

---

[1] As Steve states unequivocally, "a startup is not a small version of a big company … [but a] temporary organization designed to search for a scalable and repeatable business model." http://www.slideshare.net/sblank/lean-startup-conference-moneyball. (Start-up definition from 2:01-3:35.) Accessed August 15, 2014.

[2] Alex Osterwalder and Yves Pigneur, *Business Model Generation: A Handbook for Visionaries, Game Changers, and Challengers* (Hoboken, NJ: John Wiley & Sons, 2010).

[3] Rob Fitzpatrick published an online Startup Canvas alternative to the original Business Model Canvas at http://thestartuptoolkit.com/x90D51oKLcAJ/ (accessed May 30, 2012), based on Steve Blank's worksheets outlined in *Four Steps to the Epiphany: Successful Strategies for Products that Win* (Pescadero, CA: K&S Ranch, 2007). Ash Maurya describes how and why to use his Lean Canvas alternative in his blog post, "Why Lean Canvas vs Business Model Canvas." (http://practicetrumpstheory.com/why-lean-canvas/. Accessed May 30, 2012.)

Disruption by Design Canvas

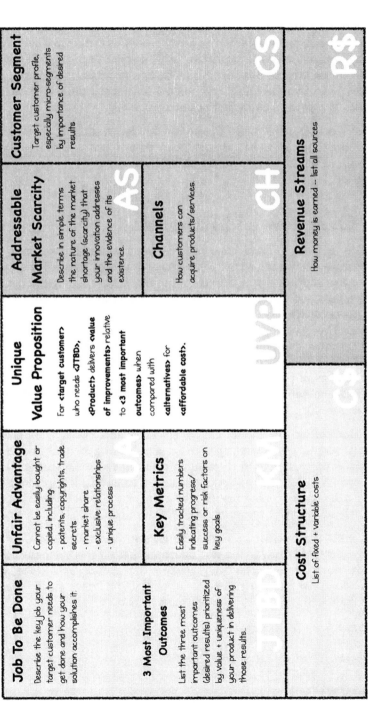

Figure 9-1. Disruption by Design Canvas is an adapted work copyrighted under the Creative Commons Attribution-Share Alike 3.0 Unported License. To view a copy of this license, visit http://creativecommons.org/licenses/by-sa/3.0/ or send a letter to Creative Commons, 171 Second Street, Suite 300, San Francisco, California, 94105, USA. The Disruption by Design Canvas is attributed to the Business Model Canvas, created by Alex Osterwalder and Yves Pigneur, which can be found here: http://businessmodelgeneration.com/canvas/bmc. It is also attributed to Ash Maurya's Lean Canvas, which can be found here: http://practicetrumpstheory.com/business-model/.

In this chapter, I present a variation that I've labeled the Disruption by Design Canvas. It is shown in Figure 9-1. The balance of this chapter focuses on how to use it and the reasons it is different from others already published. The Disruption by Design Canvas is closest to Ash Maurya's Lean Canvas, which he adapted from the original Business Model Canvas to focus on the key risks a startup faces. Disruption by Design targets the unique attributes that distinguish potential disruptors from ordinary startups.

If you've been working through the Disruption by Design process, then much of what goes on your canvas has already been determined and at least partially, if not fully, validated. I will describe each box in the order I recommend their completion.

Canvas Overview and Rationale

The Disruption by Design Canvas captures a business model focused on what makes a disruptive innovator unique, while recognizing that most of the time disruptors are also startups with a different set of risk factors and milestones to success than established companies. Consequently, some of the standard business model canvas building blocks are irrelevant or very low priority to a disruptive startup. These include Key Partnerships (usually a startup doesn't have partnerships, so rather than waste real estate, add any partnerships to Channels); Key Activities (there are only two key activities for a disruptive startup—building a product and getting customers); Key Resources (resources are important, but also obvious and not a key risk factor in getting a solution to market); and Customer Relationships (there are no customer relationships to manage).

Thus, when comparing this model to Osterwalder and Pigneur's Business Model Canvas, several boxes are replaced or modified to focus on product and marketing strategy, simplified to reflect a reduced set of choices and the narrower focus required of a disruptor, or added to highlight the risks that could derail a potential disruptor before they even get a product to market or during the early stages of customer and market development.

Rather than start from scratch, I have adapted Ash Maurya's Lean Canvas, which already addresses many of the startup issues that a disruptor also needs to care about. However, even Maurya's canvas is too general, as it makes no assumptions about disruptive intentions or potential, and hence takes a more broad-brush approach to market discovery and validation.

Like the Lean Canvas, product issues are recorded on the left half of the canvas and market issues are on the right. The Unique Value Proposition binds product and market together, which is why it straddles the middle. Unlike the Lean Canvas, the Disruption by Design Canvas has less risk and fewer unknowns if you have started with analysis of the JTBD, as described in Chapter 4, so some of its features are collapsed to make room for documentation of an Addressable Market Scarcity.

Let's get started.

1) Addressable Market Scarcity

Addressable Market Scarcity

Describe in simple terms the nature of the market shortage (scarcity) that your innovation addresses and the evidence of its existence.

In Chapter 1, I showed how alleviating a condition of market scarcity is the root cause of all market disruption because the shift to abundance causes a radical deformation of the supply and demand curve. Of course, what this means is that if there is no addressable market scarcity, there can be no disruptive innovation. Therefore, it is the most important factor to validate, understand, and know how your innovation mitigates the shortage.

The first step in understanding and validating the scarcity is to write it down. Define why it's a problem and how the shortage manifests in behaviors of people, other companies, the market, and workarounds that are used because of the lack of supply. Are prices too high, leaving out a large percentage of would-be users? Is there a monopoly or oligopoly market condition that creates artificial shortages, price gouging, or poor service? Would people make different choices about how to get their job done if they could?

Both your description of the scarcity and evidence should be testable and verifiable by talking to people and observing macro behaviors and trends. Look especially for contrary evidence, and if you find any, try to explain whether it invalidates your hypothesis or is simply a false indicator or an anomaly.

It is obviously important that the scarcity is addressable, either with a new technology or new process that creates more of the desired result at the same or lower cost. While opportunities for disruption exist only where there is a scarcity condition, if you can't do anything about it, it's best to wait until you have a better idea or technology catches up, enabling a better solution to the problem.

2) Job To Be Done (JTBD)

Job To Be Done

Describe the key job your target customer needs to get done and how your solution accomplishes it.

3 Most Important Outcomes

List the three most important outcomes (desired results) prioritized by value + uniqueness of your product in delivering those results.

In Chapter 4, I reviewed how to capture and evaluate the importance of the results that your target users desire and group them into JTBDs.

Your list of desired outcomes likely numbered in the dozens, and resulted in several JTBDs. The hard part now is selecting just one, two, or three jobs that are high value and "underserved," that is, not adequately addressed by available alternatives.

This process results in pre-validation of the opportunity, which is important when contrasting the Disruption by Design Canvas with the Lean Canvas. There will likely be tweaks when you show prototypes to target users and discover that the importance of some results is over-stated, or that the job could be described better, but in general, the work you did to establish jobs and prioritize them means you should already have a high degree of certainty about product/market fit and that your job description is at least 90% correct.

This is why I don't allocate space on the canvas for a set of problems and solutions as the Lean Canvas does—both of these are encapsulated in the JTBD box. You are much more interested (as potential disruptors) in how getting this job done for the user addresses a market scarcity, and does so in a way that is clearly unique when compared with alternatives.

Remember that being unique doesn't mean no one else is trying to address this scarcity—there were many search engines before Google, for example— but that your solution addresses the real JTBD uniquely.

To clarify the difference, let's dig a little deeper into why Google became the dominant search player and a massive disruptive innovator despite coming late to the party. All the search tools before Google compromised the perception that they were providing accurate and unbiased results with the priority they gave to selling ads and how they designed their solutions to accommodate that. We used those tools because there was nothing better available, but none dominated the market or were perceived to be head and shoulders above the rest because none of them served the right JTBD.

By comparison, when Google was introduced, it appeared to generate better and unbiased results, so in short order we all changed horses from whatever we used previously to make Google the preferred choice for search, which made it the most desirable platform for advertisers. When Google did eventually place ads on their results pages, they had already established themselves as accurate, trustable, and as having the most complete results. And, when ads were placed, they were not given priority over organic search results, nor did they directly impact the rank order of the results.

Even though advertisers were eventually part of Google's solution and are the primary payers, if users had not trusted the tool to deliver the right results, Google would have been one of many failed attempts to emerge from the pack with a (disruptive) viable solution.

So, in this example, the uniqueness of Google was relative to accomplishing the job of accurate, trusted, and the most complete results for users. There are many instances, especially in multi-sided markets, where it's easy to prioritize the wrong needs and harm everyone's interest—most often this occurs when solution builders put top priority on how to generate revenue, placing it ahead of satisfying the most important JTBD.

You don't have to be first. Just the first to get it right. This is also why Apple was able to introduce such hugely successful disruptive products in several markets that already had numerous competitive alternatives.

Note   Never forget—you don't need to be first to market with an innovation. You simply need to be the first to get it right. Apple and Google have proven themselves masters at this.

---

3) Customer Segment

Customer Segment

Target customer profile, especially micro-segments by importance of desired results

CS

Note that the Disruption by Design Canvas says "Customer Segment," not "Customer Segments." As you read in Chapter 5, the key in the early stages is to be laser focused on the JTBD that exactly matches the required results for a single segment, or better yet, a single micro-segment that values the outcomes you're providing in exactly the rank order that you have prioritized them.

Consequently, whatever you entered in the JTBD box will dictate the target users you enter for the Customer Segment box and should be exactly the same as the work you did in Chapter 5 to define your segmentation strategy. Your goal is that no other solution can better satisfy the JTBD, and therefore you will always be the preferred solution for this segment.

When you are ready to target additional segments or micro-segments, you should complete a new canvas so that everything is in sync (your Unique Value Proposition is also likely to be different, and this may affect entries in other parts of the canvas).

4) Cost Structure

> **Cost Structure**
> List of fixed + variable costs
>
> C$

Use the cost structure box to list your fixed costs (such as leases, computing resources, and so on) and variable costs (such as people, travel, and so on). At this stage, profitability is less important than the speed of cash burn. You need to be sure that you know how much time you have to establish a profitable model or when you will need additional financing to continue. Keep it simple, but make sure there aren't any major omissions.

5) Revenue Streams

> **Revenue Streams**
> How money is earned -- list all sources
>
> R$

Record the sources from which you expect to earn revenues. If you are building a multi-sided platform, you can record each type of participant on a single canvas, although I prefer to have a separate canvas for each (different user types will often have different value propositions for participation, and revenue contributions are usually unequal). Remember, a disruptive pricing strategy needs to offer significantly better value than incumbent alternatives (sometimes the value differential will come from other factors than simply price, such as miniaturization, mobility, convenience, usability, and so on), usually at least two-three times better.

6) Unique Value Proposition

Unique Value Proposition

For <target customer> who needs <JTBD>, <Product> delivers <value of improvements> relative to <3 most important outcomes> when compared with <alternatives> for <affordable cost>.

UVP

The Business Model Canvas asks you to provide one or more value propositions. As a disruptor, that isn't good enough. It's not focused enough for success, and it diminishes your potential for disrupting markets.

Your value proposition must be unique relative to the JTBD and deliver significant improvements for the results that are most important to your target users. For that reason, I recommend that you use the generic formula in the Disruption by Design Canvas, filling in the blanks as appropriate.

Replace <target customer> with the value(s) you entered in the Customer Segment box. Replace <JTBD> with the job from the JTBD box. Replace <product> with the name of your solution. Replace <value of improvements> with metrics that relate directly to the top three outcomes you listed in the JTBD box, and define each by specifically naming the outcome that it improves. Lastly, name the alternatives that you are comparing your solution to and identify why your solution is a better value specifically in terms of benefit/cost.

This statement might not be usable as is, but it will express exactly why there is no better solution for your target customer at any cost, and should serve as the basis for all communications about your product, from your elevator speech to your website.

7) Channels

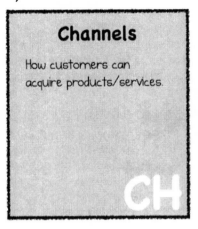

Channels

How customers can acquire products/services.

How does a prospective customer acquire your solution? Is it sold in stores? From your website? Via direct sales? List the ways that you intend to sell your product or accept orders. The Disruption by Design Canvas has eliminated Partners as a cell since most startups don't have or depend on partners. If you do depend on a third party for access to customers, list that partner as a channel.

8) Key Metrics

Key Metrics

Easily tracked numbers indicating progress/ success or risk factors on key goals

I have borrowed the Key Metrics cell directly from the Lean Canvas because it is critically important for any startup to track a small number of indicators that measure risk and/ or show progress toward your ultimate goal.

Examples include percentage of signed up users that convert to sales, growth rate (by week or by month; choose the smallest time period that makes sense for your business), cash burn rate, retention or churn rates, and so on. It is best to track easy-to-understand numbers that are actionable, avoiding vanity metrics (such as site visitors, number of keyword searches that result in your product on the first results page, downloads of literature, and so on).

9) Unfair Advantage

Unfair Advantage

Cannot be easily bought or copied, including

- patents, copyrights, trade secrets
- market share
- exclusive relationships
- unique process

The Unfair Advantage cell is also borrowed from the Lean Canvas, but applies even more to potential disruptors, because every disruptive innovator has an "unfair advantage."

Consider that you are offering a Unique Value Proposition for an unmet need for a target user who is an exact match for the JTBD you are offering a solution for and directly addressing a market scarcity with your solution. From a marketing perspective, this is a powerfully unfair advantage.

Additionally, disruptors tend to hold patents (or patents pending or other intellectual property) on unique technologies or have developed processes that radically reduce cost, improve productivity, increase quality, or improve usability. And after you've succeeded in disrupting a market, you should have dominant market share or be the preferred choice among all the alternatives, and customers always prefer to buy from market leaders.

Unfair advantages are unfair because they can't be easily bought or copied by competitors. You may not have any unfair advantages if you are just starting up, but being disruptive implies that you have or will have at least one. When you have established one, it should be guarded and leveraged for rapid growth, best profit margins, exclusive access to customers—whatever your unfair advantage confers as a benefit to your company.

Summary

As a potential disruptor, your business model will usually be very different from that of large incumbents. The Disruption by Design Canvas is designed to capture what's different and help you focus on your key success and risk factors.

As with any business model canvas, it is most useful when it can be seen by everyone and is an active document that you keep updating with yellow stickies when you have new or modified hypotheses about your business. Especially while you are in the process of creating a repeatable and scalable set of processes to sell your product(s), things will be changing rapidly, and you'll want everyone to be on the same page. My recommendation is that you have a poster-sized version of your business model in a prominent place in your office, and that you use it whenever you discover new information that changes (or may change) your thinking.

To get started, there is a free online version of the Disruption by Design Canvas available at https://canvanizer.com/new/disruption-by-design-canvas. It's great for collaborating, especially when collaborators are in different locations, and it can be used in meetings with a projector to discuss the current version or make live updates.

Keep in mind that over time, your business and your business model will evolve. You will establish Key Activities, Key Resources, Key Partnerships—all of which are recorded in the standard Business Model Canvas, but not the Disruption by Design Canvas. My recommendation is that you stick with the Disruption by Design Canvas, creating a new one for each of the first few JTBDs you tackle and their associated target segments. As you grow, you will likely target segments more broadly and expand into adjacent market opportunities. That's when you should consider adopting the standard Business Model Canvas, but not before.

We have now completed our review of the key strategic elements involved in creating a business that is designed to disrupt, including product and marketing strategy, and we tied it all together into a coherent business model. Having read the first two sections of this book, you should now have a good understanding of what makes an innovation disruptive, including the dynamics of how market disruption happens and why, how to identify disruptive opportunities, why product and marketing strategies must align, and the critical nature of your business model in executing a disruptive strategy.

The last section of this book assumes that you've established a profitable and sustaining business model, and that your disruptive business strategy is working. Where do you go from here? How do you cement your position and stay on top? What will prevent you from being disrupted by the next upstart? How do you avoid becoming enamored of your disruptive success and becoming the next Blackberry?

In Chapter 10, I discuss some practical tactical tips for implementing your disruptive strategy, before concluding the book in Chapter 11 with a discussion of your future.

The Last Mile

CHAPTER

10

End Game

The revolution is not an apple that falls when it is ripe. You have to make it fall.

—Che Guevara

You have created the perfect strategy to disrupt by design. There is a real, addressable market scarcity that you have uncovered. You identified the most important JTBDs that your product can serve, and the results that the market desires from your solution. You have a killer price strategy. You even have the potential for a strong network effect and viral growth. Your marketing strategy is flawless.

On paper.

Unfortunately, your target customers haven't seen the paper, and they don't know who you are. They don't understand what your product does, that it was designed for them, or that none of the alternatives are as good.

The apple isn't going to fall just because it's ready to be eaten. You have to make it fall. Execution and tactics are important, and there are still many things you need to do well, even with the right framework in place to disrupt a market.

I can't give you a cookbook recipe for all those things, but in this chapter I quickly touch on some of the important tactical elements you should worry about, some practical advice about how to approach them, and advantages and issues you'll have as a potential disruptor.

Establishing Thought Leadership

Entrepreneurs tend to see themselves as thought leaders, but unless the market, the pundits, the analysts, the media, and your peers see you that way, it doesn't matter what you think. Most entrepreneurs have the potential to be thought leaders, but it takes work—a lot of work at a high level.

Given all the places you need to be spending your time, it's reasonable to ask the question: What exactly do I mean by thought leadership? And why does it matter? Thought leaders are individuals or sometimes companies who are broadly recognized by prospects, partners, industry influencers, the media, and even competitors as a foremost authority in a discipline or specialized area of knowledge. They are the ones seen as visionaries—the ones you go to when you require specific expertise and insight about their field of specialization.

Note Thought leadership usually leads to or correlates with market leadership and trust, and to winning more than your "fair share" of business.

Attaining this status is valuable because it usually leads to or correlates with market leadership. Thought leaders are the first ones you add to your list when you have question or a problem to solve, need to get a job done, or need the best thinking available in that particular area. Being perceived as a thought leader means you are sought out for your services and win more than your "fair share" of business. Thought leaders tend to set or bless industry directions, which is a very powerful position to be in when you have products in that space.

It's certainly possible to disrupt a market without being perceived as a thought leader, but this tactic is a potent weapon in the disruptor's arsenal because if you have figured out a way to provide a unique value proposition based on a JTBD that others haven't recognized or understood, you have unique data and a unique point of view that easily lends itself to a thought leadership position.

The time to begin the process of establishing thought leadership is well before you have a product, ideally before you even start a company. Certainly you should be thinking about it from day one, because it can strongly influence your likelihood of success, help get meetings with the right people, and begin to establish a baseline of market education that is often necessary to introduce disruptive products, because the activities you do to establish thought leadership help create the frame of reference that people will need to understand your solution.

Social media is a great place to begin establishing thought leadership, partly because distribution is free and it has exponential growth of reach and viral potential. You can also begin to establish a body of work that uses the keywords that people will eventually use to search for solutions after they've been educated about the opportunity, which is critically important to inbound marketing and getting found later.

Thought leadership is not the fast, easy way to the top of your field—it's more like the diet and exercise plan to good health. But it is something that any original thinker with unique knowledge can achieve with discipline, hard work, and a plan. Following are a few of the key elements that should be part of your plan to become a thought leader.

Subject matter matters. Don't just talk about your product or what's going on in the company. In fact, you should avoid these things, unless you can relate them to industry trends or present them in the context of a job that customers need done. Blog about the market scarcity you address (in general terms—don't talk about specifics of a product until you have one) and all its manifestations. Do compare the strengths, advantages, weaknesses, and differences between alternative technologies available to solve problems. Talk about results that people desire and about problems they have accomplishing the JTBD that you address.

Put it in the context of big trends, particularly social ones. Discuss all the things that are impacted by your core subject matter/area of expertise and use relevant articles published in the media as springboards to offer a unique point of view or alternative way of looking at the problem. Do not publish the typically empty generic prose of average consultants, which speaks volumes about how little they actually know—be specific, use original insights, and speak your own mind.

Create your own data. Use numbers you've researched or uncovered that illustrate the magnitude of the problem. Numbers add credibility and authority, and get the attention of media and industry pundits who are always looking to quantify a problem or write interesting stories. If you are the go-to source for numbers that express the size or nature of a problem, you are automatically seen as understanding the JTBD better. It enhances the perception of your expertise and knowledge, which gives your statements more of an aura of authority, if not prescience.

Tip Numbers add credibility and authority to everything you say, enhancing the perception of your expertise and knowledge. If you don't have numbers, figure out how to get them by measuring, monitoring, and tracking, and then creating the ratios, graphs, and insights that others will want to quote (and attribute to you).

If you don't have this data, create it. Conduct surveys, gather metrics, monitor and measure trends, and report it impartially.

Creating your own data is tremendously important because there is a scarcity of quality information and authoritative numbers, and it is therefore extremely attractive for others to quote and use in their own communications. It will generate links, trackbacks, and references, and will result in your name and original sources being quoted in journals, in the news, and by other bloggers. The data will get retweeted and reposted to a far broader audience than you could ever reach on your own. Most importantly, it is yours, which makes you the thought leader smart enough to gather it, synthesize it, and position its importance.

People like data because it allows their rational and rationalizing selves to judge the veracity of your claims and build trust in you. It allows them to believe, even when there's little to believe in. Unique data, statistics, ratios, graphs, and trend lines that define the problem's scope and position a solution are the things you most need to get free coverage, persuade the analyst community, blog, and "cross the chasm"[1] from early adopters to early mainstream customers.

Persist. Unless you are a skilled writer who finds this kind of communication natural, you may find this to be some of the hardest work you do, and early days, you will see little obvious payback, especially if you don't yet have a product or way for site visitors to engage and convert to (qualified) leads.

It takes time to build followers, engage readers in commenting and discussing the issues you talk about, and get people to retweet your tweets, articles, and news. Achieving this level of engagement means using the tools at your disposal to participate in conversations and find interesting things that others have said to comment on and share, rather than simply broadcasting your thoughts in a monologue.

And it takes consistency and personal engagement. You need to be posting at least two to three times a week (daily is ideal), and responding when people comment or tweet you back. And in any case, your goal is not to generate leads or offer generic content that could come from anywhere, but to educate the market and establish a unique voice with a different viewpoint from everyone else.

---

[1] Geoffrey Moore, *Crossing the Chasm* (New York, NY: HarperBusiness, 1991). The main thesis in Moore's "Bible for the tech industry" is that every new technology-based product faces a major barrier in adoption between the stages of early adopters and early majority, as defined in Everett Rogers' Diffusion of Innovations model, because these groups are so different from each other in their expectations of new products, and that it takes an extraordinary and focused effort to jump the gap ("cross the chasm").

In the long term, this will yield fantastic results and magnify the payback of everything else you do or spend time and money on. It will easily double the productivity of your PR programs. It will attract exponentially larger volumes of natural search traffic to your site, and the people who follow you before you have a product are those most likely to buy or subscribe as users (because they have self-identified as having an interest in the things you talk about). They are the early adopters, visionaries, and pundits.

It will enhance your credibility over competitive alternatives. It will help secure speaking engagements at trade conferences and unsolicited interviews with magazine editors who need quotes to flesh out a story. It will demonstrate clearly your focus and commitment to the industry.

Be where your target audience is. In addition to a personal/corporate blog, create or participate in LinkedIn groups if your product is a B2B solution. Consumer-oriented products and solutions are more suited to Facebook, but Facebook can also be useful for business-oriented communications, depending on who your target audience is. But remember, you don't have time to do everything, and where you participate is part of your message.

Pinterest might the be right place, or more specialized sites like Hacker News, or Fred Wilson's AVC blog might yield better results. Look around—where is the greatest traffic, the most intelligent discussion, the most relevant subject matter, and where are the people most likely to become your natural audience and followers hanging out? Tweet your own data and news as well as curated content (articles by others, including traditional media) that is related to your area of expertise and engage others in conversation about it.

Don't just be a member of your community—be its natural leader, push the envelope, be controversial—you will inherit the mantle of thought leader.

The CEO Is the CSO (Chief Sales Officer)

If you are the CEO of a startup, you are more than the top decision maker, custodian of the culture, and chief visionary. The CEO must assume the role of CSO—Chief Sales Officer—and keep it until you have developed a repeatable sales process and business model that works. In fact, all the founders should have sales or customer service/support roles in the early days, no matter how uncomfortable it is for you.

This is so important that if you feel unable to act as the CSO, you shouldn't be the CEO.

There are several reasons why this is absolutely critical:

Credibility. When a company is just beginning, the product may or may not exist, but will almost certainly be incomplete or flawed. If you are selling to businesses, you aren't really selling a product. You are selling yourself, your vision, and your commitment to make the product and the relationship work.

Businesses that invest in you are taking calculated risks—risks that you will survive to be able to support them in the medium to long term, and that the time they invest in learning your solution and shaking out the bugs won't be wasted. No one but the CEO or founder can make credible commitments about the future and stand behind the handshakes and promises. Customers at this stage aren't judging the product or the company. They are judging you and whether they believe you have what it takes to deliver.

▓ **Note** When your business is just getting started, you aren't selling a product so much as yourself, your vision, and your commitment to your customer's success and to making your product work. Only a CEO or founder can credibly do this.

If you are selling a consumer product, this is less important. Customers don't necessarily expect to hear from the CEO, but they do appreciate it and are far more likely to believe in your future and tell others about you if you directly communicate with them about the product, even when you don't think it's necessary. Remember, Steve Jobs was known to take calls from customers and personally respond to emails to stay in touch with how people felt about Apple and its products—if he had time, you certainly do too when you have just a handful of customers.

Validation. If you've followed the process for defining the right JTBDs, you should have high confidence that you're solving the right problems. However, that doesn't mean that you're solving these problems the right way, that you've prioritized the desired results accurately, that the user interface is appealing and easy to use, that you've got the right pricing strategy, or that there aren't show-stopping problems that prevent customers from getting the benefits they're expecting.

You need to be validating all these, as well as confirming that you are still the only and/or best solution for the JTBD and that there aren't new alternatives showing up in the market that could derail your plans. At this stage, anything that isn't working the way you expect needs immediate attention—from the reaction you receive to your messaging, to the way the product works, to the enthusiasm you see from target customers.

As CEO, you need to internalize these customer reactions and ensure the market reality is fed back into the company in real time and then tweak whatever needs changing. You can't afford a filter between you and the customers; it will slow your reaction time, which means you can't respond in real time to needed changes and opportunities. Filters also increase the likelihood of "playing telephone," resulting in incorrect interpretations of what is seen and heard and lost data.

Repeatable sales process doesn't exist. One of the things that you need to experiment with and validate is a sales process that works and that you can scale. Until you know the necessary steps, whether your message is correct, how to qualify leads, which tools you need to close and support business, that the price model is correct, whether you need a trial period or a lease offering or a money back guarantee or another inducement, you aren't ready to hire a sales specialist or outside CSO.

Worse, in the early days, you won't have reference customers yet, and the only people who have a chance of closing business before you have references are the founders, who can make implicit promises on behalf of the company that a salesperson can't.

Why can't a professional sales VP (who isn't you) do the validation, create a sales process, and document and gather this feedback and data for you? Are you going to believe their conclusions when they tell you:

- Prospects are complaining that the price is too high

- Feature "x" doesn't work, and everyone they have spoken to says it is a requirement

- People are saying this isn't a problem they need solved—there are lots of alternatives to choose from

- You should see their eyes glaze over when we demonstrate the product—nobody understands it and they can't see how it will fit into their business

Or, are you going to say, "You're wrong. You don't know how to sell."?

I've seen this kind of takedown happen in many companies where the sales VP has been successful at company after company, but suddenly has become an incompetent idiot after joining yours. What's more, they truly lack the ability to ask the kind of probing questions that might identify what the real issues are, or even to know if they are talking to the right target prospects, because their job is to execute the repeatable, scalable, proven process that you haven't yet created.

This is true even with consumer products. Trying to push product through channels before you know what the right channels are, before you have an educated and receptive market to sell to, and before you have validated the whole business model, can be disastrous. You need to be directly in contact with the lead channel opportunities, providing guidance and support, fixing issues before they become intractable problems, and experiment with selling direct so you know what it takes.

A professional sales team's job is to execute a defined and repeatable sales process, and the sales VP's job is to operationalize and manage that process. When that process doesn't exist, salespeople and/or channels will be expensive failures. They will inevitably chase unqualified opportunities, promote inconsistent product stories, complain that management "doesn't get it," and generally cause a lot of turmoil. When this happens, know that it's probably not their fault, and even if it is, you'll have no way of knowing, because you didn't first create a repeatable process to measure against.

▓ **Note**   Never forget that the sales VP's job is to operationalize and manage a repeatable and scalable sales process. Until you have one, you, the founder or CEO, are the Chief Sales Officer.

Competitive Analysis

In an established market, competitive analysis normally consists of looking at product categories across narrow industry definitions and compiling comprehensive data about features, capabilities, and marketing strategy for the list of a company's most "direct" competitors. The analysis focuses on what is being sold (product attributes and competitive behaviors) rather than what and why customers are buying.

If you have disruptive potential, you should not have any direct competitors at this point. You should be "competing against non-consumption"—targeting a new market or a niche for whom existing alternatives to get the job done are too complex, inaccessible, poorly designed, or just too expensive. In this context, traditional competitive analysis is unnecessary and may even distract you from your unique value proposition and how you are the best solution to the customer's JTBD.

What you do need to do instead is identify the most likely substitutes in the market that you will be compared to, based on your positioning, messaging, pricing, and the jobs you accomplish for a user, or more specifically, the desired results that will motivate them to buy your solution. Because you are focused on a very narrow target customer range, the alternatives are likely only a handful—perhaps three to five possible solutions (including performing the job manually, without any products).

For each of these, look at the top three desired results that you deliver and how they are accomplished with each competitive alternative. If the possible substitute solution has no capability to deliver on a critical outcome, this is ideal for you. However, assuming that each alternative provides at least partial benefit, the critical thing you need to do is quantify the performance difference objectively and translate that into dollar or time savings, quality improvements, or other metrics the customer uses to define successful completion of their job.

If your sales message to the target market is focused on these key metrics and comparisons, you will find yourself easily talking about the customer's JTBD and what is important to them, and if you are truly disruptive, you shouldn't lose to a substitute solution for the simple reason that they fail to deliver on the most important qualities that the customer desires.

By contrast, this type of competitive analysis is not only directly actionable, but it's faster, more useful, and keeps you focused on the customers and what they're trying to get done, in contrast to worrying about competitors.

Market Education

The biggest difficulty you may have if you are creating a new market or product category is when the prospective users don't understand what the opportunity is to get their jobs done better and why.

Consider the category of word processing, for example. Today, we take for granted the ability to edit text electronically, format it with a variety of fonts and graphic design choices, and output it with a button push or attach it to an email to send to someone. It's so much part of what we do that it just makes sense; if you're under the age of 30, you probably can't even imagine all the difficulties an older generation endured using typewriters.

Consider how foreign the idea of word processing would have seemed to a student drafting an essay or an author writing a book in the early 1980s—applications that are simply impossible to imagine doing things the old way today. I recall watching someone struggling to use word processing software for the first time. They had spent two hours trying to write their first sentence, and when I asked if I could help, I realized just how difficult it was to someone unfamiliar with computers. (I know, that too is hard to imagine.) In those days, the spaces between words showed up as little dots on the CRT screen, and my friend had spent two hours trying to delete the dots.

Typewriters were still more common than word processors at that time, even in office environments. Ideas like reusing documents, cutting and pasting text across documents, dragging a paragraph or sentence to another place in the document, having automated assistance to check spelling and suggest fixes, changing fonts, bolding headlines, searching for text strings and globally replacing them with something else, and ultimately not even bothering to print many documents, but simply sending them to recipients electronically would not only have seemed futuristic, but entirely unnecessary—outside of double-line spacing of manuscripts, people just didn't care what documents looked like. And, that's just scratching the surface of the new capability that word processing offered.

In the beginning, the idea that every home would have the ability to do this (and that kids would be expected to do their schoolwork this way) was almost unimaginable.

Today, 3D printing is at a similar stage. Inexpensive machines like those made by MakerBot[2] are starting to stimulate early visionaries to think about how these devices will eventually be like inkjet printers, what things we'll be able to create with them, and the implications for IP protection of physical goods when a home user can simply replicate whatever they want. For many, this possibility still seems far-fetched, as it will require major developments in materials science and engineering.

Although engineers and early adopters have recognized the potential, most of the public has no conception of what is possible or why they would want a 3D printer, or the new opportunities that they will create, even though there are many JTBDs that this new class of machine is ideal for.

As with word processing, spreadsheets, and inkjet printing in the 1980s, the disruptors creating this new opportunity must first educate the market about what can be done, explain why we'll all want one, the simple things that can already be done that are really cool and useful, and get people exposed to them so they can start to imagine for themselves why they would want to own one.

Note   Every pioneer needs to consider market education as an essential element of their go-to-market planning.

For every product, this market-education process is going to be different. It begins with thought leadership activities, but that's just the door opener. Product demonstrations, viral videos, blog articles, getting on the right TV program, writing whitepapers and e-books, running webinars, and running contests with early users are just a few possible ideas. The focus needs to be on getting potential users to imagine possibilities and to want to learn more and/or try it themselves.

---

[2]http://www.makerbot.com/

The one thing you cannot do is assume that just because you understand the jobs that your product accomplishes and how and why it is the best way to get them done that anyone else will. If a market doesn't yet exist, it is because people don't understand the new technology and the connection to a job they need to get done. You need to make that connection for them and show how your solution is an essential tool.

In 10 years, if you've been successful at disrupting the market, education will no longer be necessary, but every pioneer needs to consider market education an essential element of their go-to-market planning.

Metrics

There are many common metrics used by startups, and for the most part, the same set of metrics apply to disruptive innovators. Measuring progress is an essential task, so for convenience I have listed a set of some of the best measurement tools in a variety of categories you should consider using as indicators.

Marketing and Sales Metrics

Customer Acquisition Cost (CAC). Take the total spent from all channels (sales, distributors, search engine marketing, PR, and all other marketing and sales programs) over a period of time (month, quarter, or year) and divide by the number of new users signed in that same period. If you can isolate new users by channel, you can also calculate the cost of acquiring a customer via that channel, which helps with budget allocation. (Some customers need to see you in multiple places before making a decision, so this is only an approximation.)

CAC tends to be higher with high-cost products with long decision cycles, so it's also important to know the payback, average revenue per user, churn/retention rates, and lifetime customer value before making decisions solely on CAC. Sales and marketing efficiency is often expressed by CAC/Total Revenues, with a lower percentage being better than a higher one almost all the time.

The cost of acquiring customers is frequently underestimated, even in businesses that don't require a direct sales force and can attract and convert users into paying customers using web techniques. CAC must be lower than LTV (see below) to build a successful business, and usually a ratio of three to five times CAC is ideal.

Payback. Either the amount of time or the number of orders from a customer to cover the CAC. A good payback target for most businesses is less than one year.

Magic Number. The Magic Number[3] is an indicator of sales and marketing efficiency for subscription-based (SaaS) or leased products. The idea is that spending in the previous quarter most directly influences new contracts in the current quarter, whereas revenues are not realized at signing, but spread out over the life of the contract.

The Magic Number is calculated by taking the increase in revenues between two quarters (such as Q2–Q1), multiplying by four to annualize the number, and then dividing by the total sales and marketing expense in the earlier quarter (Q1 in this example).

A Magic Number of 1 implies that spending an extra dollar in this quarter will result in an extra dollar of revenue this year (without factoring for churn, gross margins, or add-on sales to existing customers), so a number of 1 or better suggests that more profitable growth is possible with increased spending, while a number less than 1 may indicate much slower growth ahead.

Sales Cycle. The sales cycle is a simple average calculated by measuring the time between initial contact and closing a sale and dividing by the number of customers. High-priced and enterprise products tend to have longer sales cycles of up to 12–18 months (six months is very good for this type of product), while cycles for inexpensive and subscription products tend to be extremely short. Sales cycles for governments and educational institutions can be twice as long, or even lengthier depending on the nature of the product.

Lifetime Value (LTV). The Lifetime Value of a customer is just that—the total revenues from all sources that you will receive from a customer while they continue in a relationship with you.

In practice, and especially in the early days, this can be very hard if not impossible to know, but it's still important to have an estimate and refine it over time as you get more data. Average the total revenue of a period (month or year are most common) and multiply by the average length of time that you retain a customer to get the LTV.

Since it is usually easier to determine churn, you can use your churn rate (see below) to estimate your retention rate. In other words, if you have a 20% churn per year, the average expected retention is five years. LTV needs to be three to five times greater than CAC in order to build a successful (profitable) business.

---

[3]The rationale behind the Magic Number is described in detail by Rory O'Driscoll of Scale Venture Partners in a couple of excellent blog articles—"Magic Number Math" (http://www.scalevp.com/magic-number-math, Accessed January 20, 2014) and "Magic Number Facts" (http://www.scalevp.com/magic-number-facts, Accessed January 20, 2014).

Net Promoter Score (NPS). The Net Promoter Score purports to be a measure of how fervently customers support you and their overall level of satisfaction, based on a single survey question (how likely on a scale of 1–10 are you to recommend product "x"?). Those who answer with 9 or 10 are considered "promoters," and those who answer with 1 or 2 are "detractors." Subtract the total number of detractors from the total number of promoters and divide by the total sample size to get your NPS.

Though many companies believe this is the single most important number to track, I am highly skeptical. For one, the score is highly culturally dependent— Americans are much more likely to respond enthusiastically with a 9 or 10 even if they don't really feel that way (it seems to go with the self-esteem trends of grade inflation, and giving every kid a trophy just for participating), whereas in other parts of the world, almost no one answers with a value that high, because recommendations are context dependent and because they would feel it more honest to answer with a 7 or 8 if they are satisfied and likely to recommend. Americans are also much less likely to choose 1 or 2 unless extremely dissatisfied, even if they would say negative things about you to others.

Still, if you view it as an abstraction, rather than an accurate number, it can be useful to compare against other companies and against yourself over time. True disruptors are likely to have the highest NPS when focused on the target segments that are a perfect match for their key JTBDs, and should be able to approach 80 to 90% ratings when focused on these niches. If you are below a 50% score at this stage (that is, the stage of selling to "must-have" users), you have a problem that needs addressing urgently. In later stages of market development and expansion, a score of 40 to 50% is pretty good.

User Metrics

Churn. Churn measures the rate that users or customers stop using (or paying) for your product. Every product has some churn, if only because customers go bankrupt, die, sell the business to a company using something else, and so on. A low churn rate (0–3%) is likely made of mostly of these kinds of users who stick with you as long as they are viable (i.e. it's extremely good).

High churn rates may indicate problems with value received, training, customer service, or a new (often disruptive) competitor who addresses the JTBD with a better unique value proposition. Enterprise software products tend to have lower churn because of the long decision cycle, switching costs, and higher product cost, implying more upfront commitment to using the product. Freemium solutions can have very high churn rates, especially when people expect something else or don't engage immediately and start using the product regularly.

Take the number of users who leave during a period (week, month, or year) and divide by the total users. The Churn Rate directly impacts the LTV of a customer, so it's important to realize that it is often easier to focus on improving retention or lowering churn (through better service or training, for example) than on reducing CAC.

Cohort Analysis. A cohort is any group with a common characteristic or set of characteristics, used to compare one group to another. Useful cohorts to analyze include customers who signed up during a fixed period, users who joined in response to a specific promotion, users who were referred by other users, customers who invested in training versus those who have not, customers who have used the product for at least six months, and so on.

The trick is defining a cohort that allows you to compare one to another and create actionable insights (for example, customers who take training may have 50% lower churn rates). Churn is a specific type of cohort analysis that measures decay rates in engagement/use of a product.

Comparing customers who signed up at different times allows you to see the impact of all the contact points of one group versus another and see anomalies (for example, customers who signed up in January received a special offer, which increased conversion rates by 40% over customers who signed up in February). Cohorts can be used to study engagement, revenues, satisfaction levels, marketing programs, lifetime customer value, customer acquisition costs, referrals, and more. This information can be used to identify problems and spot opportunities.

K-Factor. K-Factor measures *virality* (borrowed from epidemiology, it is basically a measure of how fast a disease spreads through a population while it is infectious).

Pick a constant timeframe—a week or month usually. For virality, you care specifically about users who sign up because other users referred them (such as via an "Invite your friends" link). Take the existing users and new users via referral at the end of the period and divide by the total users at the beginning of the period. So, if you started with 10,000 users at the beginning of the week and added 1,500 users via referrals, you would have 11,500/10,000, for a K-Factor of 1.15.

The K-Factor is powerful because it measures exponential growth. So a factor of 1.15 may sound like a small number, but if it continued at this rate, the initial 10,000 users will grow to more than 60,000 in one quarter, and to 15 million within a year—clearly at some point this kind of growth becomes unsustainable and the K-Factor declines when there is no one new to "infect." It couldn't even continue another year at this pace, because it would require three times the world population to be signed up.

Few products are truly viral in this way. The original free email tools (Hotmail and Gmail in particular) and social network platforms like Facebook, Snapchat, and Pinterest come to mind. Still, if you have viral potential, the longer you can keep the K-Factor greater than 1, the faster you'll grow and the bigger you'll get.

Financial Metrics

Run Rate. The revenue run rate is the current monthly revenue, annualized (multiply by 12, assuming revenue is constant). This number is useful for projecting ahead (we're at a $5M run rate today, targeting a $12M run rate by year end, and we need to spend "x" dollars to get there).

Since early-stage companies are generally growing much faster than established companies, the run rate provides a normalized basis for comparing different companies at their current stage and valuing the expected growth. It tends to take much larger amounts of capital to fund this growth, so it also highlights risk and helps explain your budgeted CAC.

Gross Margin. The gross margin is the percentage that revenues are above variable costs (cost of goods sold). Early-stage companies in particular have a much higher percentage of fixed costs for office overhead and administration, so gross margin is more commonly used than net margin because it shows how efficiently capital can be used to grow the business to generate return.

Take total revenue, subtract COGS, and then divide by revenue. Net margin is basically the same as profit before taxes, and includes rent, lease costs, and other expenses not related to sales, marketing, or product development. Subtract all expenses from revenues and divide by revenues to calculate the net margin.

For margins, you need to care both about the absolute level as well as the trends (are they increasing, decreasing, or staying the same, and why). Often the presence of a new competitive alternative will compress margins, so if your business model assumptions are based on a certain margin level, you need to watch this very closely.

Burn Rate. Since startups are usually not immediately profitable, a very important financial metric to track is how fast you are spending your capital. Usually expressed as a monthly number, burn rate is the total expenses minus revenue. The burn rate tells you how long you have before you either need to be profitable or seek another infusion of cash (this period of time, often referred to as "runway," is equal to cash in the bank divided by the burn rate). So, if you have $1.8M in the bank and monthly burn rate of $150,000, you have a runway of 12 months.

Average Revenue Per User (ARPU). A simple but important measure, ARPU is total revenue divided by users. Together with CAC, LTV, and Churn Rate, you'll have a good understanding of the opportunity to grow the business profitably, the most you can spend to acquire a customer, and what things you can do to earn more revenues by creating more value.

About the Metrics

You need to have metrics that help guide and correct your business; however, there are three things to keep in mind:

- The tools you use are highly dependent on your type of business (for example, the lifetime value of a customer is highly relevant if you expect repeat purchases or sell via subscription, but is largely meaningless if your sales are one-time purchases).

- Different metrics will apply at different stages of your growth.

- Any metrics you use to guide your company from inception to a repeatable and scalable set of business processes should be actionable—that is, any measured numbers should give you a clear indication that you are on the right track and should stay the course, or that something is wrong and needs to be fixed.

For these reasons, most startup metrics should provide indicators that help you manage the most important risk factors at each stage. This implies that if your greatest risk is unique to you, your most important metric should also be something unique that you design yourself. Steer clear of so-called "vanity metrics"; for example, the absolute number of visitors to your website is meaningless, whereas growth rate in sales conversions is highly useful and actionable.

■ **Tip** Startup metrics need to be actionable and highlight key risk factors in your business. Ratios, growth rates, churn, and conversion rates to sales are examples of good startup metrics. Avoid vanity metrics—such as the number of website visitors—which give no guidance for acting or making decisions.

In the very earliest stages before you have a product, it is often harder to know what to measure. Your primary goals at this stage are to identify an addressable market scarcity, validate the boundaries of your JTBD and the top three results your target customers desire, and then design a solution that implements the JTBD and addresses the scarcity. The last thing, of course, is to build your MVP and get customers for it.

Even though you can't measure sales, users, or website conversions, there are still vital objectives that encapsulate both the risk and the milestone(s) that you need to hit to progress through these stages.

My recommendation is to create a single Vitally Important Metric (VIM) that encapsulates the risk and the milestone that you need to hit. It should be published to everyone in the company and be the major topic at your team meetings until you're ready to replace it with the next VIM.

For example, you may decide that you need to conduct 20 onsite behavioral interviews to understand the JTBD and the most important unmet needs. If that's true, you can't effectively move to the next stage of designing a solution until you've collected this key data. Therefore, the fastest rate at which you can set up and conduct these interviews is your single vitally important metric. There may be (and probably are) other things that also need to get done, but since this is a gating factor, everyone needs to understand that nothing is more important. If they can help or are asked for assistance, achieving the current VIM is their number one priority.

Creating VIMs not only ensures that everyone is on the same page, but it also focuses the team on whatever the most important thing is right now and speeds the process of driving to your ultimate objective of helping customers solve problems with your product. The right VIM will provide you with lots of vigor.

That said, there are two specific metrics that I recommend to all disruptors.

Constant Revenue Growth Rate. After you begin generating revenues, nothing is more important than growing quickly so that you own the market space before an alternative comes along (and alternatives will come if you demonstrate the viability of the market for your solution). The best metric for focusing the company at this stage is the constant revenue growth rate, because it forces you to fix whatever stands in the way of maintaining growth.

Choose the shortest practical period—usually a week or a month, but as long as one quarter. To get your actual revenue growth rate, divide the revenue in the most recent period by the period immediately preceding it. For example, this month's revenue might be $10,000 and last month's was $9,000. That's a revenue growth rate of 11% per month. Now, decide whether this is an anomaly or whether you can achieve that rate in every month for the foreseeable future. At this stage, it's often better to be a little conservative. Is 8% per month a more reasonable target, or 5%? You can always adjust your target later, but you want to come up with a reasonable best guess to start.

Let's say you settle on 8% per month as a CRGR target. In the next month, that makes your target revenues $10,800, and the month after that $11,660. Your overriding goal is to continue at this pace until it is no longer reasonable. If you miss it (or are in danger of missing it), the entire company needs to focus on what has to happen to hit that growth.

Targeting a CRGR will force you to confront questions like these and address them immediately:

- Are we getting enough referrals?

- Does marketing need to generate more leads or traffic to the site?

- Is there a problem with conversions, and if so, what experiments do we need to try to increase the conversion rate?

- Is the target micro-segment we started with becoming exhausted and do we need to refocus on an adjacent segment with a different primary JTBD?

- Is the churn rate too high, and what can be done to increase retention?

- Is the onboarding process too slow or does it require too much handholding before users can get started?

- Is usage growing within existing customers or stalling after the initial signup?

- What compelling upgrade would increase the number of freemium users who convert to paying and shorten the time it takes to convert from free to paid?

- Should we divert development resources to get a new feature tested and in production faster?

In other words, by using CRGR as your VIM metric once you have worked out your business model and are generating revenue, it automatically prioritizes whatever stands in the way of continuing to achieve that growth rate and quickly gets you back on track when you fail to hit it in any period. A constant revenue growth rate also has the benefit of giving you immediate short-run targets that make achieving ambitious run rates feel more attainable. For example, if your target CRGR is 8% per month, your run rate will increase by 250% within a year.

Obviously, higher percentage CRGRs are likely to be maintainable for no more than a year or two, but even a CRGR of 3% per month results in an annualized growth rate of 43%, which isn't too shabby once you've achieved scale.

Disruption Grade. The disruption grade (described in Chapter 3) is not critical in the same way some of the previous metrics are for business success, but it is a worthwhile signpost to add to the dashboard of things you monitor as a company with disruptive potential. Run the Disruption Grader[4] tool every one to three months to update your grade. It will help ensure that you aren't making choices that reduce your chances of being a market disruptor and may give you guidance in what to do to course-correct.

Marketing Tactics

This is a set of odds and sods—rules of thumb for early-stage startups that are trying to become disruptive innovators. In the beginning, the biggest risk you face in marketing is getting ahead of yourself and spending money or time on things that you may believe you need to do, but that won't make any difference in the long run. Later, once you have customers and have established a working business model, the biggest risk is going too slow.

The tough thing is knowing when you've hit the inflection point where you need to step on the marketing accelerator and make that shift from slow to fast.

Industry Analysts. Ignore them in the early days. They can't help you until you have customers, and you are of no help to them either. In fact, without market data, success stories, and a compelling vision of the JTBD and validated unique value proposition, you are wasting their time, and the impression you create when you do so will be lasting.

Showing off a product or outlining a product vision that you have no proof points for is just frustrating for everyone involved—the analysts will feel compelled to give you some feedback that, unless you are lucky, will be no better than your own internal navel gazing, and you will feel compelled to argue or disagree if you think they're wrong, or worse, take their advice, which hasn't been validated by the market.

If they call you, don't be coy. Be polite and answer their questions—it likely means that one of their customers has made an inquiry about you (a good thing), or that they've read something that has piqued their interest. Remain passively connected by following them on Twitter, but that is the extent of what you should be worrying about until you have something relevant to their need to analyze the market for their clients.

---

[4]Visit `http://www.innovativedisruption.com/disruption-grader/` to run Disruption Grader. It is a free tool, but requires a valid email address to receive a full report.

Advertising. Advertising is an extremely inefficient use of marketing resources for 99.9% of startups, and certainly has no place in your budget until you already have a finished product and customers. Awareness and branding simply doesn't matter until you are ready and able to scale.

■ **Caution** The biggest risk, and a common mistake that many startups make, is spending large sums on marketing before they are in a position to benefit from it, and then later, taking too long to ramp up spending to fully capitalize on growth potential.

Even keyword advertising (for example, AdWords), which is more of a precision instrument, is a short-term accelerant, not a lot different from taking drugs. It gives you a boost that ends abruptly if you don't continue to feed the addiction with a new fix. I do recommend keyword advertising for very specific purposes—A/B testing of messages and testing the relevance and priority of certain keywords for your product—but only after you have something that you can fulfill the expressed interest with.

Once you have established which keywords and messages get the best reaction, you are far better off to stop and invest in creating content for your website that will attract organic interest (search results) via blogging, landing pages, offers, and page optimization efforts using what you've learned. Organic interest doesn't end, but rather builds over time as more and more visitors land at your site based on relevance and quality of what they see there (which has the effect of raising your organic ranking with search engines).

Advertising does make sense when you are ready to start rapid expansion and have built your content and fulfillment library to handle the interest it will generate, but is almost always a waste of money before that.

Public Relations (PR). Until you have customer stories to tell (and customers willing to tell them), a formal PR program is also an extremely inefficient use of marketing resources.

Yes, you should issue press releases, but as much as possible do it yourself, or hire an independent consultant to write them and publish on sites like prweb.com. You should view releases like this as part of your content strategy, however, not explicitly as news that you expect journals to pick up and cover. Some will, and some will republish your announcement, but this isn't your primary objective.

SEO optimized releases will attract attention, and often will get you ranked near the top of search results for certain keywords within a couple of days, so use them to point back to your website at sources of relevant data and fulfillment offers that convert visitors to leads. Use Twitter to publish news and follow editors, bloggers, and influencers who are most likely to be interested in what you have to say. But do not pester them, believing that whatever you have to say in the early days constitutes news of interest to their readers. It doesn't (and, if by some chance it does, they will reach out to you).

If you do capture their interest, they will follow and track what you are doing, and later this will result in coverage. In the early days, any PR you do should be passive, content-oriented, and done internally. Don't bother hiring an agency to help tell your story until there is a story (preferably many stories) to tell, and that means until you have a product in use by customers with documented results specifically addressing a unique JTBD.

For B2B products to reach this stage, you need at least 10 happy and successful customers who are achieving results they will talk about. For B2C products, you need to have spoken with and validated use by at least 100 customers, or done a survey with a 90% positive rating minimum). PR should be one of the first marketing programs that you invest heavily in. Stories published in media outlets will reach many more eyeballs than you can on your own, and they will help to build credibility and may even directly result in sales—especially from visionaries and early adopters.

You must be ready to feed the beast—media outlets have an insatiable appetite for "news" and interesting stories that haven't been told before. If you can help them tell these stories and be a trusted resource for knowledge and data (see "Thought Leadership," earlier in this chapter), you will get your share of publicity. If all you have are press releases announcing new products, you will rapidly wear out your welcome and you'll become unhappy with your agency, blaming them for not getting you enough ink for what you're spending. PR is a power tool—make sure you know how to use it so you don't cut off your hand while you're learning the ropes.

Content Marketing. Content marketing basically means writing relevant and useful material that you publish to the Internet. It can be on your website, on a blog, or to Twitter, Facebook, and LinkedIn (and other social media outlets as appropriate), or posting comments on other people's blogs and news outlets. You will also want to create downloadable e-books, guides, data sources, and so on.

The primary goal is to engage with the marketplace and drive inbound marketing[5] programs to create qualified leads. You should begin creating relevant content from day one, and even before you have founded a company if possible (see "Thought Leadership" earlier in this chapter). Keep in mind

---

[5]Visit http://en.wikipedia.org/wiki/Inbound_marketing (Accessed September 24, 2014) for the definition of inbound marketing. For a more thorough and product-oriented description of the concept, visit http://www.hubspot.com/inbound-marketing (Accessed September 24, 2014).

that good quality, relevant content not only helps others relate to you, it helps you clarify your thinking and work out the best ways to communicate your story, so the payback is immediate, even when you have nothing to sell.

LinkedIn Group. For B2B disruptive innovators, hosting a discussion group on LinkedIn is a very powerful way to get people engaged and talking about the JTBD and concepts behind your technology in a non-sales context. An open group will attract users, non-users, and likely even users of competitive alternatives. Using LinkedIn requires a commitment to moderate the group to keep spam out and quality content and discussion in, as well as to participate actively in many if not all the discussions. If a group becomes popular enough, this can even become a full-time job. The group you create should not be specifically about your product or solution, but rather the job that it helps users accomplish. An example of a very effective and popular group is the one hosted by HubSpot, creators of software for inbound marketing.[6]

Summary

Although this chapter is titled "End Game," it's really just the beginning. You've laid the foundation and are getting started with the real work of building a successful company. Unlike the rest of this book, the tips and ideas in this chapter are much more focused on tactical implementation of a disruptive strategy, although many of these concepts apply to any startup.

The key difference that a disruptive innovator has is the unique solution to an addressable market scarcity and the priority outcomes of the JTBD that the solution provides. Without these, you can't be disruptive. Having something that no one else has also gives you distinct advantages that make some parts of your job easier if you leverage them.

Taken out of context, this could be misleading. The tips in this chapter are certainly not a comprehensive how-to guide for building a startup; there are lots of other texts that do a perfectly good job of that. It's not even a complete compendium of tactics that a disruptor might use. What I've tried to do here is direct you to a few things that, in my experience, work especially well for disruptive innovators because of their focus, and the things that make them unique.

Remember, this is not prescriptive, and not necessary to achieve market disruption, but based on my experience, a selection of these tactics will prove helpful in getting where you want to be faster, while avoiding some of the pitfalls that could sideline you.

---

[6]Inbound Marketers - For Marketing Professionals is a LinkedIn group hosted by HubSpot, a provider of a SaaS software solution for inbound marketing. (See https://www.linkedin.com/groups?home=&gid=21005, Accessed September 24, 2014.)

Key Takeaways

- Leverage the things that make you unique as a disruptive innovator—the market scarcity that your product addresses and the unique results relative to the JTBD—as shortcuts to competitive analysis, for establishing thought leadership, and for developing marketing tactics. This saves resources while increasing your chances of success.

- Avoid most of the traditional metrics of an established business. They won't help you measure progress against your goals or mitigate the unique risks you have. Instead, choose the smallest set of critical metrics appropriate to your stage of development and the risks you face getting to the next stage.

- All founders need to have direct responsibility for selling or working with customers while they are working out the business model.

- Marketing tactics should be heavily biased toward content in the early stages.

Your journey to building a company that is disruptive by design is largely complete. I've discussed the things that make you disruptive, including how to predict disruption, create a disruptive business strategy and business model, and use tactics that will help you along the way.

You will spend the next several years building your solution, expanding your market footprint into adjacent spaces, and dealing with the transition from a startup searching for a working business model to an established and profitable company executing proven processes. But the question remains—how do you stay on top? How do you defend against the next generation of disruptors? How do you succeed where once powerhouse companies like Blockbuster, Kodak, RIM/Blackberry, Borders, Tower Records, Digital Equipment, Polaroid, and many others have failed?

In Chapter 11, we will conclude with a discussion of how companies in general, but especially recent disruptors, need to behave differently to remain relevant and on top of their game.

Staying on Top

You go to any MBA program, and you will be taught the theory of the firm, that the purpose of the firm is the maximization of return on invested capital. I always thought this was a kind of lunacy. A well-managed business will have a high return on invested capital. But that's a consequence. It's not a way to manage a business.

—Peter Senge

Profit is like oxygen, food, water, and blood for the body. They are not the point of life, but without them, there is no life.

—Jim Collins

Success is a lousy teacher. It seduces smart people into thinking they can't lose.

—Bill Gates

It's now three or four years later, maybe longer. You had a great vision, addressed a critical market scarcity with a brilliantly disruptive business strategy and business model, had a great product idea, and executed it well enough that you succeeded in disrupting a market.

Or perhaps you aren't quite there yet—you've captured an important niche or two, and you're growing rapidly. The early startup risks are mostly in the rear view mirror—disruption looks inevitable, but may take a few more years to completely play out. After all, even the biggest hit products of our time—such as the iPod and iPhone—took a few years to firmly establish their market dominance.

So now what?

Is this the time to streamline operations to maximize efficiency and profitability? Do you continue adding extensions, new features, and new markets to grow the business? Build out your ecosystem? Start acquiring other companies? Is it time to milk the cash cow? Conventional management theory would suggest that at least one of these, if not all, is exactly what you should do.

I'm not going to answer these questions directly. Context matters, so there may not be one right answer. To complicate things, these are usually the wrong questions to ask.

To get to the right questions, I've chosen to end this book with a discussion of why firms exist and how business schools, led by the much-vaunted Harvard MBA program, have misdirected at least two generations of professional managers. This is all to the detriment of American businesses and increasingly to corporations worldwide. The chapter also contains some general thoughts and recommendations about what you can do differently to sustain your position of market leadership.

Christensen and The Innovator's Dilemma

When Clayton Christensen first described the pattern of disruptive innovation,[1] his purpose was not to promote innovation by startups and guide them in the process of becoming disruptive. Rather, his research and writing was motivated by the desire to help executives "do what is right for the near term health of their established businesses, while focusing adequate resources on the disruptive technologies that ultimately could lead to their downfall," as he wrote in the introduction to *The Innovator's Dilemma*.[2] In other words, his goal was to help industry incumbents avoid disruption.

From that perspective, and a Harvard Business School frame of reference, he viewed the companies he was helping as being "as well-run as one could expect a firm managed by mortals to be"—again from the introduction to *The Innovator's Dilemma*. The companies he was referring to included IBM, Digital Equipment Corporation, Sears, and Xerox and other similar Fortune

---

[1] In the first paper describing disruption (Bower, J. & Christensen, C., *Disruptive Technologies: Catching the Wave*, Harvard Business Review, January, 1995), Christensen and Bower identify technology as being the means by which small upstarts disrupt large incumbent companies that dominate their industries. This thinking continued in Christensen's first book, *The Innovator's Dilemma* (Boston, MA: Harvard Business School Press, 1997). The term was soon updated from *disruptive technology* to *disruptive innovation*, as Christensen realized that technology by itself was insufficient to disrupt a market, but rather required innovation to the business model, often if not usually supported by technology.
[2] Ibid.

500 firms—companies that in his view, had been disrupted through no fault of their own, but rather had done everything right. Indeed, these organizations, as well as most other large companies, were led by senior executives from the nation's premier MBA programs, all educated in the same theories of the firm and management processes.

Question If businesses and industries are being consistently and predictably disrupted even when "they did everything right" and "followed best practices," shouldn't we reconsider what it means to "do things right"?

It seems odd to insist that these companies were being managed as well as humanly possible while at the same time so easily disrupted by under-capitalized, under-resourced, under-staffed, and unknown companies as if they were being struck unexpectedly by random lightning bolts from a calm sky. The fact that they were all so consistently disrupted suggests exactly the opposite—that their management practices and their ideas about what they ought to be doing were wrong. Of course, that would be difficult for a Harvard MBA professor to admit since they were using the processes taught (some might say designed and promoted) by Harvard and every other progressive business school.

My purpose here is not to criticize Christensen's work. Far from it. His observations and brilliant synthesis of disruption theory have led me to this point, to the work that I do, and to this book.

Nevertheless, I think we have to question whether there is a blind spot—an unwillingness to question whether the opposite conclusion is more probable. Not only were these companies not behaving consistently with a goal of long-term success and sustainability, but the systemic failures of managers to avoid being disrupted across almost all industries, even in technology-oriented firms that were recent disruptors themselves, might be traced back to how they were taught to view the firm's purpose and their role in it.

Theory of the Firm

A reasonable question to ask is, "why do companies exist?" The answer isn't as obvious as it might seem. After all, in theory we could all act as independent (free) agents in an open market system and build the same products and satisfy the same needs as we do in companies. That we don't implies that there are structural, cost, and/or efficiency advantages to organizing as firms. In fact, this notion was first raised by Ronald Coase in 1937.[3] His key insight was that organizing as a firm dramatically reduces the transaction costs of constantly bargaining for labor and creating legal and governance systems and creates the minimum overhead for efficiently delivering products and services.

The problem with Coase's notion is that it essentially removes people from the equation, treating everything as a cost or input or output. His theory doesn't speak to the motivations of people who desire to do intelligent or gratifying work, or to the needs of customers and why they choose to buy from one firm over another. But it does help us to see that a firm might have goals that differ from the individuals who collectively create the products. This also led Coase (an avowed socialist) to believe that a centrally planned economy could do a better job of producing the goods people needed by lowering the transaction costs of a pure market-based system.

This view of the firm also led many socialist economists to talk about social responsibility as a key purpose, which created a forceful pendulum swing in the opposite direction, culminating in the modern view of the firm best expressed by Milton Friedman. In a famous article in *The New York Times* in 1970, he declared that the sole purpose of the firm is to maximize profits and thereby maximize shareholder value.[4]

Unfortunately, what was lost in Friedman's article and the modern "Theory of the Firm" is nuance. His article was a polemic against socialism more than an absolute prescription for how to achieve these goals and has resulted in many of today's worst practices by large public companies, including:

- Focusing on short-term (quarterly) results

- Gaming the system with financial tricks to boost stock price

- Targeting stock price as the goal rather than delighting customers or longevity/survival of the firm

- Implementing overly generous executive stock compensation schemes, resulting in the opposite of what is good for shareholders

---

[3] Coase, R.H., "The Nature of the Firm," *Economica*, Volume 4, Issue 16, 386-405 (November, 1937). http://onlinelibrary.wiley.com/doi/10.1111/j.1468-0335.1937.tb00002.x/full. Accessed July 20, 2013.
[4] "The Social Responsibility of Business Is to Increase its Profits," *The New York Times*, September 13, 1970, http://www.colorado.edu/studentgroups/libertarians/issues/friedman-soc-resp-business.html. Accessed July 18, 2013.

Importantly, it also contributes to, or is directly responsible for, the ease with which established incumbents can be disrupted by upstarts—because disruptive innovation doesn't fit within a corporate context focused on the short term, and even when an incumbent sees disruption coming, the artificial constraints the firm has placed on itself prevent it from acting or creating the disruption first.

In other words, the modern and prevailing theory of the firm taught by economists and business schools is at best incomplete, and at worst wrong (because it leads to outcomes that are bad for the business), and it is responsible for the shortsightedness of professional managers and bad corporate planning and decision-making concerning innovation. It has undermined the strength and competitiveness of firms that employ this philosophy.

Customers at the Core

A better view of the purpose of the firm is that espoused by Peter Drucker, who said plainly, "There is only one valid definition of business purpose: to create a customer." Expounding on that, he continued "Because it is the purpose to create a customer, any business enterprise has two—and only two—basic functions: marketing and innovation."[5]

Intuitively, we recognize that this is mostly true. Without customers, it is impossible to have revenues or profits or shareholder value. If you aren't serving your customers, you aren't doing something that needs to be done and for which the creation of a firm to organize capital and labor is necessary.

In order to get customers, you need to do something differently from other companies that customers desire (innovate) and market the products you create. Drucker's view of marketing was "to know and understand the customer so well the product or service fits him and sells itself." This notion is consistent with the methods I've described in this book to uncover jobs to be done, and to create segmentation and positioning strategies.

As central as the customer is to a business however, there are important elements still missing. Many businesses that have adopted profit maximization and shareholder value as central tenets would also agree that creating a customer is the core purpose, and that to create a customer, the key functions must be marketing and innovation.

---

[5]Peter F. Drucker, *The Practice of Management* (New York, NY: Harper & Row Publishers, 1954).

As a purpose, this is still short-term and tactical. There is no implication of growth, adaptation, what or how to innovate, and other key functions or overriding purposes that shareholders would want for their firm to ensure its long-term health.

Sustainability

A corporation is an entity that at least in theory has the ability to live forever. But ultimately, most businesses do die, and implicit in the death of a business is failure. Failure to make things that customers want; failure to operate ethically, efficiently, or profitably, and within the bounds of the law; failure to sell what it makes; failure to keep up with competition; failure to adapt to a changing world; failure to create new products; or, failure to grow.

Some business failures are due to incompetence, fraud, or other structural issues, such as running out of capital. Although these failures are painful for all involved, we accept these as a necessary cost of capitalism. They clean out what doesn't work or is inefficient, making that which survives stronger. Virtually all of the rest represent failures to innovate and to continuously get better at delivering what customers want. These are the failures wrought when profit maximization and shareholder value are viewed as the core purposes of the firm.

Clearly, shareholders would prefer that the businesses they own not die. This implies that sustainability of the business is a core purpose—what I like to call "securing the future."

From this perspective, the purpose of the firm is to create, serve, and support customers by providing the best possible solution to jobs that the customers need to get done, and to secure the future, ensuring its own continuing viability by balancing current operational excellence with continuing search for new disruptive opportunities.

What Is Different About Managing to Secure the Future?

In addition to the standard modus operandi of operational efficiency, reducing costs, expanding to new markets, and sustaining innovation, businesses need to be balanced and continue to think and behave like disruptive innovators forever. But what does this mean in practice?

Don't focus on "needs" but on JTBDs and on delighting customers. Customer focus should drive you to aim for continuous improvement in serving the jobs that customers want to get done. Sustaining innovations, quality improvements, cost reduction, performance improvements, and better design are all part of this. But so is service. Don't make customers wait needlessly. Treat them like people, not seats filled, items sold, or costs to be minimized. Make the experience of using the product more enjoyable, easier, or accessible. This also means continually re-evaluating whether there are better ways to accomplish the JTBD by employing new technology or changing the business model.

Growth is essential. The standard view of growth is selling more of what you have to a defined total available market, or capturing share from competitors. There's nothing wrong with pursuing these. However, for virtually every job that your product can satisfy, there are more people who don't participate in the market than who do. Ask yourself which performance attributes make the product not good enough for those non-users, and whether it's possible to create or fine-tune special versions of the product to target their desired outcomes. Figuring out how to attract non-users is many times more efficient as a growth strategy than trying to steal share from competitors.

Think like a VC and allow for messy experimentation. Venture capitalists don't use IRR (internal rate of return) as a metric to decide whether projects or startups are fundable. They do look at broad market trends, usually have an "investment thesis," and then place bets on a number of ideas that have potential to turn into big market opportunities. They don't usually turn down an idea because the size of the potential market isn't provable, but rather give the startup team enough funds to prove the viability of the idea and access to their networks of connections to help find initial customers and conduct targeted research. They expect messy experimentation, with many failures leading to eventual successes (failures both in implementation of the JTBD in a product and in the business model). Except they don't view them as failures, but as lessons learned. (It's only truly a failure if nothing was learned.) The C-suite of every established firm should view this as part of its job and be measured on how well they bring a percentage of experiments to market.

Tip Companies that want to succeed in the long term will learn to think like venture capitalists, conducting purposeful experiments to discover better ways to help customers get jobs done. Experiments are designed to test hypotheses, and a certain rate of failure is expected and tolerated. Enlightened companies measure how much was learned and view failed experiments as steps toward success, not as something to be punished.

Don't fear disrupting yourself. If you discover a new way to accomplish a JTBD and it has potential to undermine existing product(s), don't fear it. Assume that if you don't commercialize the new platform, technology, or business model that your competitors or a startup you don't know about yet are not far behind. If you don't bring the solution to market, they will, and you'll lose twice. Your existing product lines will still be disrupted and/ or undermined, and your competition will grab the early lead in targeting the highest value JTBDs. Kodak made this fatal error when it shelved the digital camera that it had invented. Apple did the opposite—bringing out the iPad even though they knew it would undermine both desktop and notebook computer sales for which Apple had grown to be the largest provider. Even though the size of new markets can't always be reliably predicted, the size of obsolete markets can be predicted quite accurately.

Lead on lowering price. If you are fortunate enough to be innovating in a space where Moore's Law, Kryder's Law, or Nielsen's Law apply, you can count on the price of critical components of your solution falling in price exponentially. It isn't just computing where there are exponentially falling costs—the human genome, nanotech, 3D printing, and others all offer the opportunity to design solutions that leverage deflationary economics. Design business models for where the price is likely to be a year or two from now, not what it is today. Regardless of the market space you compete in and the technologies you employ, you are always better aiming for the lowest profitable margins rather than trying to milk the cash cow for short-term profits. High-margin markets attract more competitors, reducing returns for everyone. Companies targeting low price and low margin will grow the market faster, make the pie bigger, and be in a stronger position to hold mainstream customers. They will also attract more non-consumers while making the market unattractive to new competitors.

Reward executives based on new markets established, not on stock price. In the long run, the stock price will be much higher when you bring more successful innovations, especially disruptive ones, to market. Ironically, providing fatter stock option packages to executives results in more explicit gaming of the system to inflate the stock price in the short term, and it discourages investments that don't pay off immediately. Yes, it's beneficial for executives (and all employees) to feel what's happening in the market based on growth in capitalization and share price, but that does not require that the majority of their compensation be derived from stock. Short-term incentives should be more focused on things that can grow the long-term return and help to secure the firm's future, such as establishing new markets, introducing new disruptive innovations, growing market share profitably, reducing customer churn, and so on.

Design your fiercest competitor. If you aren't sure where to expand next or where future competitive disruption might come from, imagine the qualities of a competitive alternative that would be the most damaging to your market position. Think about price, distribution, ways to better satisfy the job to be done, ecosystem, synergies with other industries, bundling, complexity vs. simplicity, modularity vs. integration, ease of use, and adaptability—anything that would create difficulty for you in selling your product. Now ask what it would take for you to become that company and do it.

Avoid thinking like an incumbent and adopt the mentality of a serial disruptor. You may not have a wealth of potentially disruptive ideas in the pipeline, but it is important to always be thinking like a disruptor. Create and maintain the conditions necessary for disruptive innovation and look for signs of and opportunities for disruption. Whether you have the resources or choose to go after each opportunity is irrelevant, but in order to capitalize on your fair share, you must be able to take advantage of opportunities that present themselves and recognize them in the marketplace or in your own portfolio. This is the opposite of how most incumbents are structured—in general, their processes and cultures actively squelch disruption rather than viewing it as a huge growth opportunity.

In general, long-term sustainability and renewal can't happen unless you remain open to creating disruption. It is inevitable that over time, some products and product lines will become obsolete. The only opportunities big enough to replace them and create new opportunities for significant growth are the potentially disruptive ones. Sometimes, embracing those disruptive opportunities will mean acquiring startups with great ideas—whether to operate as new business units or integrate into existing operations—and/or cannibalizing or killing off your own existing products or business lines even when it feels premature.

Prominent venture capitalist Fred Wilson captured the essence of this idea in a blog article at AVC.com titled simply "Sustainability," most of which is quoted here:

> When I was in business school 25 years ago, I don't recall the term sustainability used. Maybe it was, but it certainly didn't register in my brain. The mantras that I recall were return on investment, shareholder value, revenue growth, and driving efficiencies in the business.
>
> But as I look at many of the challenges facing businesses today, it seems to me that the focus on performance and efficiency often comes at the cost of sustainability. ... The recent history of the steel industry in the US is a case study in managers doing everything they were taught in business school and in the end they bankrupt the business.

Going back to business school, they teach you the value of a business is equal to the present value of future cash flows. If the company is likely to stay in business forever, then the value is most likely way higher than a business that is going to be out of business in a decade. The present value of a hundred years of cash flow is likely to be larger than the present value of ten years of cash flow.

And sustainability is all about figuring out how to be in business forever. It is about business models that are win/win and lead to happy long-term customer and supplier relationships. It is about avoiding the temptation to overreach. It is about avoiding the temptation to maximize near-term profits at the expense of long-term health. It is about adapting the business to changing market dynamics. It is about building a team and a culture that can survive the loss of the leader and keep going. And it is about many more things like this.[6]

In most cases, this kind of sustainability requires the CEO to be a visionary marketer or product innovator, and rarely someone from finance, sales, service, manufacturing, or any other department. There is only a handful of examples of this attitude toward innovation in the world, but they are some of the most successful companies. Google, Amazon, Procter & Gamble, and 3M stand out. The most important example was Apple after Steve Jobs returned to the helm in 1997,[7] taking them from the edge of bankruptcy to the most valuable company in the world, although it is rapidly becoming apparent that they look more and more like a typical incumbent since Jobs's untimely death.

Summary

If you've done everything well enough to succeed at market disruption, you now have an even bigger challenge to face—you must avoid complacency and simply becoming "the incumbent." It's easy to start believing your own PR and allow your success to become a predictor of your failure. Many have fallen victim to this sort of hubris.

As Andy Grove proclaimed, "only the paranoid survive," and you need to be paranoid not just about the competitive marketplace and new disruptors on the horizon, but also about your own overconfidence.

---

[6]Fred Wilson, "Sustainability," AVC blog, November 21, 2011, http://avc.com/2011/11/sustainability/ (used by permission) Accessed October 1, 2012.
[7]Apple was the quintessential, fearless serial disruptor for 15 years after Steve Jobs returned initially as interim CEO, and later dropping the "interim" from his title. The rise of Apple, and Jobs's efforts to leave behind a company with a sustainable business model, are documented in Chapter 1 of this book. Since Jobs's death, the signs indicate that, although it's still a great company, Apple is unlikely to have the sort of continuing streak of disruptive innovations that established it as the world's most valuable company.

There is always someone else looking for a way to solve the problem better, reduce costs, and make it easier and more convenient for customers. Just as you came out of nowhere to win the market, the next disruptor who attacks you is going to likely come from a place that you least expect. *The way to avoid being disrupted is to build a sustainable business that is always on the lookout for disruptive opportunities, both inside and outside the walls of your firm.*

Key Takeaways

- Pursuit of profit maximization and shareholder value as the "sole purpose of the firm" encourages short-term thinking that makes companies vulnerable to disruption.

- Securing the future is equal in importance to operational efficiency and excellence in serving customers. Firms that do not take steps to secure the future are setting themselves up to be disrupted.

- Design your business to be sustainable by focusing on the jobs your customers need to get done, continually improving on the metrics that customers care about and lowering cost, while always searching for new disruptive opportunities.

- To stay on top, never stop thinking and acting disruptively.

My goal in this book has been to offer a general guide and set of principles to build disruptive products and companies by design, and I hope that the advice and methods I've presented help you do just that. Disruption is a process, however, not an event, and it's not quite like baking a batch of cookies. There will be hiccups and unanticipated hurdles all along the way.

With that in mind, my last bit of help to readers of this book is an invitation to join me and other entrepreneurs, product managers, marketers, founders, and successful disruptive innovators in a LinkedIn group set up specifically to offer guidance and discussion about issues in this book, problems you'd like help solving, and to share your war stories and explain how you applied these processes and methods to become disruptive.

To maintain the quality of discussion and assistance at the highest level, this group is private and strictly moderated. Please go to https://www.linkedin .com/groups/Disruption-Design-4384497/about and click the Join button to submit your request for membership. I look forward to seeing you there.

I

Index

Get the eBook for only $10!

Now you can take the weightless companion with you anywhere, anytime. Your purchase of this book entitles you to 3 electronic versions for only $10.

This Apress title will prove so indispensible that you'll want to carry it with you everywhere, which is why we are offering the eBook in 3 formats for only $10 if you have already purchased the print book.

Convenient and fully searchable, the PDF version enables you to easily find and copy code—or perform examples by quickly toggling between instructions and   applications. The MOBI format is ideal for your Kindle, while the ePUB can be utilized on a variety of mobile devices.

Go to www.apress.com/promo/tendollars to purchase your companion eBook.

Other Apress Business Titles You Will Find Useful

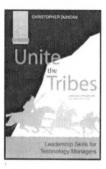